Eroticism and Death
in Theatre and Performance

Eroticism and Death
in Theatre and Performance

Edited by Karoline Gritzner

University of Hertfordshire Press

First published in Great Britain in 2010 by
University of Hertfordshire Press
College Lane
Hatfield
Hertfordshire
AL10 9AB

British Library Cataloguing in Publication Data
A catalogue record for this book is available from the British Library

ISBN 978-1-902806-92-1

Design by Alma Books Ltd
Printed in Great Britain by Hobbs the Printers Ltd

Contents

List of Figures   vii
Acknowledgements   viii
Contributors   ix

Introduction   1
Karoline Gritzner

1. Some *Erōs–Thanatos* interfaces in Attic Tragedy   12
David Rudkin

2. Dying for love: the tragicomedy of Shakespeare's Cleopatra   28
Robert Wilcher

3. Desire and destruction in the drama of Georg Büchner   46
Karoline Gritzner

4. Labyrinths of the taboo: theatrical journeys of eroticism   64
and death in Parisian culture
Richard J. Hand

5. The kiss of love and death: *Eros* and *Thanatos* in the opera   80
Dieter Borchmeyer

6. Eros/sex, death/murder: sensuality, homicide and culture   95
in Musil, Brecht and the *Neue Sachlichkeit*
George Hunka

7. The living corpse: a metaphysic for theatre   109
Dic Edwards

8. Flirting with disaster   123
David Ian Rabey

9. Howard Barker's 'monstrous assaults': eroticism, death   144
and the antique text
Graham Saunders

10. 'Welcome to the house of fun': *Eros*, *Thanatos*   160
and the uncanny in grand illusions
Michael Mangan

11. Visions of Xs: experiencing La Fura dels Baus's *XXX* and   178
Ron Athey's *Solar Anus*
Roberta Mock

12. *La petite mort*: erotic encounters in One to One performance   202
Rachel Zerihan

13. Saint Nick: a parallax view of Nick Cave   224
David Pattie

14. Afterword: The corpse and its sexuality   242
Howard Barker

Bibliography   246
Index   261

Figures

4.1 Gennaro murders his mother Lucretia in the 2007
International Victor Hugo Festival production of
Lucretia Borgia (1833) 71

4.2. Henri demanding one last 'kiss' from Jeanne in the
University of Glamorgan's 2009 production of
The Final Kiss (1912) 74

4.3 Joubert's severed hand in the University of Glamorgan's
2009 production of *The Kiss of Blood* (1929) 75

4.4 Hélène licks her husband's severed hand in the
University of Glamorgan's 2009 production of *The Kiss
of Blood* (1929) 75

11.1 Ron Athey in *Solar Anus* 186

11.2 Sonia Segura and Teresa Vallejo in La Fura dels Baus's
production of *XXX* 189

11.3 Ron Athey in *Solar Anus* 194

12.1 Davis Freeman, *Reflection* 210

12.2 Adrian Howells, *Foot Washing for the Sole* 213

12.3 Angela Bartram, *Tonguing* 217

12.4 Jiva Parthipan, *LICK* 219

Acknowledgements

I would like to thank the Department of Theatre, Film and Television Studies at Aberystwyth University for granting me a period of research leave to edit this collection of essays. Thanks also for the institutional support for the symposium 'Theatrical Aesthetics of Eroticism and Death' (1 May 2004), from which this book springs. Special thanks go to David Ian Rabey for offering me invaluable advice, encouragement and guidance, and to Jane Housham and Sarah Elvins at the University of Hertfordshire Press for their support.

Contributors

Howard Barker is an international dramatist, poet and painter whose best-known plays include *Victory*, *Scenes from an Execution*, *The Castle* and *Gertrude – The Cry*. He has also written plays for marionettes and librettos for operas. He is the Artistic Director of The Wrestling School, a company established to disseminate his works and develop his theory of production. He is also a theorist of theatre and the author of *Arguments for a theatre* (Manchester, 3rd edn, 1993), *Death, The One and the Art of Theatre* (London, 2005), and *A Style and Its Origins* (London, 2007).

Dieter Borchmeyer is Professor Emeritus of Modern German Literature and Theatre Studies at the University of Heidelberg. He is President of the Bavarian Academy of Fine Arts and his principal fields of research are German literature from the eighteenth to the twentieth century and music theatre. He has published on Goethe, Schiller, Mozart and Richard Wagner. His publications include *Mozart oder die Entdeckung der Liebe* (*Mozart or the Discovery of Love*) (Frankfurt, 2005); *Drama and the World of Richard Wagner*, translated by Daphne Ellis (Princeton, NJ, 2003); and *Richard Wagner: Theory and Theatre*, translated by Stewart Spencer (Oxford, 1991).

Dic Edwards was born in Cardiff and has been Director of Creative Writing at Lampeter University since 1994. In 2007 he was awarded a doctorate on the subject of his published plays. He has been writing plays since 1982, when his first play *At the End of the Bay* was produced. Since that time he has had more than twenty productions in Britain and abroad, the latest a production of his play *Casanova Undone* in Copenhagen – previously produced at the Citizens Theatre in Glasgow and The White Bear, London. His plays have also been produced at NIDA (Sydney, Australia) and a public performance reading of his play *The Pimp* took place in New York in 2007. More than fifteen of his plays have been published by Oberon Books (London and New York) and Seren Books (Bridgend). He is also a published poet – his collection *Walt Whitman and Other Poems* appeared in 2008 (London).

Karoline Gritzner is Lecturer in Drama and Theatre Studies at Aberystwyth University. She is the co-editor (with David Ian Rabey) of *Theatre of Catastrophe: New Essays on Howard Barker* (London, 2006). She has written articles on modern and contemporary British drama and theatre (the work of Samuel Beckett, Sarah Kane, David Rudkin, Howard Barker, Forced Entertainment) and on the interrelationship between philosophy and theatre. She is currently completing a monograph on British theatre in the context of Theodor W. Adorno's aesthetic theory (*Drama of the Damaged Self: Adorno and Theatre*).

Richard J. Hand is Professor of Theatre and Media Drama at the University of Glamorgan, Wales. He is the author of *Terror on the Air! Horror Radio in America* (Jefferson, NC, and London, 2006), *The Theatre of Joseph Conrad* (Basingstoke, 2005) and (with Michael Wilson) *Grand-Guignol: The French Theatre of Horror* (Exeter, 2002) and *London's Grand-Guignol and the Theatre of Horror* (Exeter, 2007). He is one of the team of translators for *Victor Hugo: Plays* (London, 2004) and the author of numerous academic articles and book chapters on subjects including radio drama, Japanese theatre and film, and the cross-generic adaptation of fiction into performance media.

George Hunka graduated from Bard College in 1983 with a BA in Languages and Literature. His writings on theatre have appeared in a number of general and specialised publications, including *The New York Times*, *Time Out New York*, *Yale Theater*, *PAJ: A Journal of Performance and Art* and *Contemporary Theatre Review*. In 2008 he founded his own theatre company, theatre minima, which produced his play *In Public*, and in autumn 2010 he will direct the premiere of his play *What She Knew* for the company. He lives and works in New York City. He was recently awarded an Albee Foundation Fellowship and writes a theatre blog at www.georgehunka.com/blog.

Michael Mangan has held Chairs at the University of Wales, Aberystwyth, and at De Montfort University, Leicester, and he is currently Chair of Drama at Exeter University. He has published books, articles and papers on a broad range of subjects, including theatre and gender, theatre and social justice, Shakespeare and Renaissance theatre, the cultural history of popular performance and contemporary British theatre. He has also worked as a playwright, a director, a literary manager, a dramaturg and an actor. His books include *Christopher Marlowe's Doctor Faustus: A Critical Study* (Harmondsworth, 1987), *A Preface to Shakespeare's Tragedies* (London, 1991) and *A Preface to Shakespeare's Comedies* (London, 1996). His monograph *Staging Masculinities: Gender, History, Performance* (Basingstoke, 2002) explores ways in which masculinities have been represented and negotiated on stage. His most recent book is about stage conjuring: *Performing Dark Arts: A Cultural History of Conjuring* was published by Intellect Books (Bristol, 2007).

Roberta Mock is Reader in Performance at the University of Plymouth, where she manages postgraduate research in the Humanities and Performing Arts and leads the MRes Theatre and Performance programme. She is author of *Jewish Women on Stage, Film and Television* (Basingstoke, 2007); editor of *Performing Processes: Creating Live Performance* (Bristol and Portland, OR, 2000), *Walking, Writing and Performance: Autobiographical Texts by Deirdre Heddon, Carl Lavery and Phil Smith* (Bristol, 2009) and Intellect's Playtext series. She is co-editor with Colin Counsell of *Performance, Embodiment and Cultural Memory* (Newcastle, 2009). She has published essays and articles on the theatre of queer Canadian playwright Brad Fraser, and on live artists such as Marisa Carnesky, Oreet Ashery, Annie Sprinkle and Rachel Rosenthal. From 1996 to 2006 she directed and performed with Lusty Juventus physical theatre, a company she co-founded. She is currently preparing a solo performance, attempting to perform herself through food, plagiarism and re-enactment.

David Pattie is Professor of Drama at the University of Chester. He is the author of *The Complete Critical Guide to Samuel Beckett* (London,

2001) and *Rock Music in Performance* (London, 2007), and has published widely on a number of topics: Scottish theatre, contemporary writing for the stage, popular music, and performance in popular culture. He is currently co-editing a collection of essays on Kraftwerk and writing a book on 1950s British theatre.

David Ian Rabey is Professor of Drama and Theatre Studies at Aberystwyth University. He is the author of numerous critical studies including *Howard Barker: Ecstasy and Death* (Basingstoke, 2009), *English Drama Since 1940* (London, 2003), *David Rudkin: Sacred Disobedience* (Amsterdam, 1997) and *Howard Barker: Politics and Desire* (Basingstoke, 1989 and 2009), and co-editor with Karoline Gritzner of *Theatre of Catastrophe* (London, 2006). He is also Artistic Director of Lurking Truth Theatre Company/ Cwmni Gwir sy'n Llechu, for which he has written and published two volumes of plays, *Lovefuries* (Bristol, 2008) and *The Wye Plays* (Bristol, 2004).

David Rudkin is a dramatist, screenwriter, librettist and translator. Born in 1936 to mixed English–Irish parentage of Protestant culture, after an old-fashioned traditional education in Classical studies leading to an Oxford MA, and two years' compulsory service in the army, he taught Latin and music in a secondary school in rural Worcestershire. He has worked for nearly fifty years in theatre, cinema, radio, television and music theatre, and in a wide range of genres: naturalistic, science fiction, Gothic, intimate domestic, epic, always rooted in mythical and archetypal themes. In general, his output has been characterised by mainstream critics as 'uncompromising', 'individualistic' and 'difficult'. He is certainly unfashionable, and his work remains largely unpublished and almost totally unknown. His website at www.davidrudkin.com gives a comprehensive overview.

Graham Saunders lectures in Theatre Studies at the University of Reading. He is author of *Love Me or Kill Me: Sarah Kane and the Theatre of Extremes* (Manchester, 2002), *Patrick Marber's Closer* (Continuum, 2008), and *About Kane: The Playwright and the Work* (London, 2009). He is co-editor of *Cool Britannia: British Political Drama in the 1990s*

(Basingstoke, 2008). He is also a series editor for Continuum's Modern Theatre Guides. He has contributed articles on contemporary British and Irish drama to journals including *Modern Drama*, *Journal of Beckett Studies*, *Contemporary Theatre Review*, *Theatre Research International*, *New Theatre Quarterly* and *Studies in Theatre and Performance*.

Robert Wilcher worked as Assistant Lecturer in English at Fourah Bay College, Freetown, Sierra Leone 1963–65; as Lecturer at Trinity and All Saints' Colleges 1968–72; and as Lecturer, Senior Lecturer, and Reader in Early Modern Studies in the English Department at the University of Birmingham 1972–2007. He is currently Honorary Fellow of the Shakespeare Institute. He has taught all periods, but specialised in Early Modern Literature and Modern Drama. Publications include *Andrew Marvell* (Cambridge, 1985), *Understanding Arnold Wesker* (Columbia, SC, 1991), *The Writing of Royalism 1628–1660* (Cambridge, 2001), *The Discontented Cavalier: The Work of Sir John Suckling in its Social, Religious, Political, and Literary Contexts* (Newark, DE, 2007), and chapters and articles in various books and journals on Shakespeare, Milton, Marvell, Vaughan, Quarles, Beckett, Wesker, Rudkin, Stoppard and Brenton.

Rachel Zerihan was recently awarded a PhD for her thesis on 'Catharsis in Works of Contemporary Female Performance' (Roehampton University). She has published in *Theatre Research International*, *Dance Theatre Journal*, *Esse: Culture and Opinions*, *Body*, *Space Technology Journal* and *Contemporary Theatre Review*. Recent projects include preparing a Study Room Guide on 'One to One Performance' for The Live Art Development Agency and co-editing *Interfaces of Performance* (Farnham, 2009). In 2007, she co-directed a three-day live and digital art programme entitled *Intimacy: Across Visceral and Digital Performance*. Rachel is presently an Associate Lecturer at Queen Mary, University of London.

Introduction

Karoline Gritzner

'A space must be maintained or desire ends.' (Anne Carson)[1]

In his novel *The Golden Ass*, the second-century Latin writer Lucius Apuleius recounts the Greek love story of Eros and Psyche. Aphrodite (Venus to the Romans), the goddess of beauty, love and sexuality, is jealous of the beautiful maiden Psyche, and commands her son Eros (Cupid), the god of love, to strike Psyche with his arrow of desire and make her fall in love with the ugliest man on earth. Eros, however, becomes enamoured with Psyche himself. Aphrodite is enraged by this and curses Psyche never to find a suitable husband. Eros keeps visiting her in the darkness of the night and makes love to her, but leaves before sunrise so that she cannot see him. One night a drop of oil from the lamp falls on Eros's shoulder and wakes him. Psyche recognises him but Eros flies away, leaving her behind, abandoned and sick at heart. Psyche begins a long and painful search for her lover; enslaved by Aphrodite, she is forced to perform impossible tasks. Aphrodite wishes her to die but Psyche's desire for Eros, despite causing her pain and suffering, keeps her alive. Eventually she is reunited with Eros and becomes immortal. They have a daughter called Hedone (Voluptas) – the goddess of 'sensual pleasures'. According to the myth, Psyche experiences desire, love and sexuality in a context of conflict and danger. Greek mythology and art depict her with butterfly wings because in ancient Greek the word 'psyche' (soul) also meant butterfly. These details become significant when we remember that the Greek god Thanatos (death) is the son of Nyx (night) and Erebus (darkness) and a twin of Hypnos (sleep). He is often depicted as a winged god (like Eros) with a sword in his belt; or as a slumbering youth with a torch held upside down and carrying a wreath of poppies, or a butterfly.

1

Mythology tells us that love, sexual desire and death co-exist as conflicting yet complementary forces in the human psyche. Theatre and theory, from the ancient world to the present day, have explored the embodiments and conceptual constellations of sexuality, desire and death in a multitude of ways. Sigmund Freud, for example, was fascinated by the personifications and dramatisations of (unconscious) mental processes in Greek myths. In his groundbreaking psychoanalytic explorations of the human mind, formulated in studies such as *Beyond the Pleasure Principle* (1920) and 'The Ego and the Id' (1923), he distinguishes two classes of instincts which exist in an opposing yet complementary relationship: the life instincts (Eros) and the death drive (Thanatos). This is a refinement of his previous theory that the individual's instinctual needs are dominated by the pleasure principle, which rules our unconscious, the id, and aims for immediate wish-fulfilment. The pleasure principle is held in check by the reality principle, the ego's way of accounting for reality by means of repressing the id. But such a theory could not explain the origins of the destructive tendencies of the mind, such as the repetition of painful, traumatic experiences, which is not in the interests of the ego or the libidinal id. This led Freud to the discovery of the death drive. Eros is self-preserving and life-creating desire, and is often used as an umbrella term for sexual instincts (which create an energy known as libido). The sexual instincts are counterbalanced by the death drive, whose aim is destruction: to 'lead organic life back into the inanimate state'.[2]

Despite the dualistic presentation of both kinds of drive, Freud emphasised that they exist in a relationship of interdependence and fusion. 'We perceive that for purposes of discharge the instinct of destruction is habitually brought into the service of Eros'[3] – for example, in forms of aggressive sexuality such as sadism. But in his work after the First World War and in the face of personal loss (the death of his daughter), Freud no longer perceives the aggressive instincts merely as 'derivatives of Eros' but addresses the dominance of the death drive in modern society and culture. In his famous study *Civilisation and its Discontents* (1930) he draws our attention to the paradox that civilisation, in order to fulfil its aim to establish safe and peaceful conditions of human co-existence, has to repress and control individual instincts and desires. As a result of the pressures of evolution, the aggressive instincts have become externalised into the world

2

where they appear as forms of social and political violence such as war. The sexual impulses, too, are subject to control and repression by civilisation, which prevents happiness but, on the other hand, seems necessary for the maintenance of stability. For Freud, the conflict between civilisation and the human instinctual life is open-ended, but what cannot be denied is the marked tendency towards aggression in society – a manifestation of the death drive on a wider social and cultural level.

Cultural theorists after Freud have argued along similar lines. The Frankfurt School philosopher Herbert Marcuse, for example, argued that capitalist society was a system of repression and domination that produced pseudo-individuals with artificial needs and reified consciousness. He saw a revolutionary potential in the struggle between the pleasure principle and the reality principle (which he termed 'performance principle') if individuals consciously devote their lives to the pursuit of pleasure and the gratification of their sexual desires. Emancipated sexuality (the liberation of Eros) represented for him a radical critique of the 'surplus repression' resulting from capitalist discipline, control and manipulation of individual needs.[4]

According to the postmodernist philosopher Jean Baudrillard, the capitalist order is no longer structured on the basis of contradictory forces of production (pleasure versus reality) but has become an overwhelming sphere of consumption: 'Today the whole system is swamped by indeterminacy, and every reality is absorbed by the hyperreality of the code and simulation.'[5] Furthermore, so-called 'liberated' sexuality has itself become a sign of reification and, like the other forces of production, economic growth and general rationalisation, it appears (or is socially 'staged') as an inverted manifestation of the death drive. Our system 'undertakes to abolish death and, for this very purpose, erects death above death and is haunted by it as its own end'.[6] Martin Heidegger, too, spoke of the necessity to arrive at an authentic relationship with death, and to recognise that death is finitude and nothingness and always already part of our existence. We can experience individual freedom only if we consider our existence as a Being-towards-death.

It seems that in modern society the Freudian 'repressed' returns in the form of repression itself – as the subjugation of individual life and experience under the 'monstrosity of absolute production'[7] and arrested consumption. In this globalised context of growing social and natural 'damage' (Adorno), any attempt to redirect the focus of attention to the sphere of individual instinctual life may seem obsolete and ineffective, unpolitical even. Not so, however, if we acknowledge the labour of the *imagination* which is involved in our conceptualisations of and aesthetic responses to the drives and compulsions of the human body and psyche. In our attempts to 'make sense' of Eros and death we rely on the powers of our imagination; enter the worlds of drama, theatre and performance.

The embodiment of elemental and psychological forces in the mythological world of ancient Greece was carried over into Greek theatre where, especially in the aesthetic form of tragedy, the conflict between life/ love and death is dramatised as an *agōn* ('struggle', 'battle') between the mortal hero or heroine and the gods. The transgression of boundaries is a key principle of tragedy, its primary motivating force, and recognisable in acts such as Oedipus (unknowingly) killing his father and marrying his mother, Antigone's defiance of the laws of the *polis*, or Electra and Orestes's murder of their own mother. What fascinated Nietzsche about ancient Greek tragedy was precisely its dramatisation of instinctual desires and urges in which pleasure and pain are intertwined. In an adaptation of Schopenhauer's dualism of 'will' and 'representation', Nietzsche proposes a vision of Greek culture as a battle between the gods Dionysus and Apollo – a conflict between the spirit of ecstasy, intoxication, irrationality and self-oblivion, and the principle of order, reason, creativity and beauty. It is significant that the Dionysian in Nietzsche's theory contains both life-affirming and destructive elements – Dionysian frenzy is excessive and boundary-breaking and can lead to death. Hence Nietzsche's qualification of the Dionysian as the primary instinctual force which combines Eros and Thanatos. The Dionysian is the irrational, transformational energy (the libidinal force of existence) which became restrained in later developments of Greek tragedy (according to Nietzsche, in the work of Euripides, which emphasised rationalism and the Apollonian *principium individuationis*). The aesthetic genre of tragedy reveals the powerful effects of desire, sexuality and death on the individual. Notwithstanding Plato's caution against the unmoral effects of theatre on the *polis* and Aristotle's attempts to 'defend' theatre by harnessing its 'dangerous emotions' in the process of *catharsis*: the form of tragedy has always attracted us precisely because it offers a glimpse of the unknowable and ultimately unrepresentable world of human desire, passion, love, sex, violence, pain and death.

The associations of theatre with death are longstanding in the Western tradition. Moving into the context of modernity and beginning with Shakespeare, we notice that death in Shakespeare's theatre can be a genre-breaking element; it is dramatised in comic as well as tragic terms. Comedy may try to perceive death as part of the natural order (the death of Antigonus in *A Winter's Tale* is contextualised by the shepherd's observation: 'Thou met'st with things dying, I with things reborn'), whereas death in tragedy is often the result of a perversion of the natural order or a transgression of moral and sexual codes (as in *Macbeth*, *King Lear* and *Hamlet*, for example). The art of theatre in general, but Shakespeare's theatre above all, places all its bets on the power of the imagination: without it, nothing is possible; with it, everything is. Eroticism, too, is triggered and sustained by the imagination. Qualitatively different from the sexual act which aims for reproduction, eroticism is 'sexuality transfigured by human imagination'[8] – the erotic is a poetic elaboration and, hence, an end in itself.

Tadeusz Kantor describes his aesthetic practice as a 'theatre of death', a theatre of impossible presence in which space and time are haunted by ghosts and memories, and the human figure – often modelled on but never entirely replaced by mannequins or wax figures – is suspended between life and death. In his manifesto 'The Theatre of Death' (1975) he articulates his 'ever-deepening conviction that it is possible to express *life* in art only through the *absence of life*, through an appeal to DEATH, through APPEARANCES, through EMPTINESS and the lack of a MESSAGE'.[9] Theatre is the space in which actors and spectators perform their 'ritual of TRANSFORMATION ... AS IF THEY WERE TO EMBARK ON A / DANGEROUS EXPEDITION'.[10] For Heiner Müller, too, 'the essential thing about theatre is transformation, and the last transformation is death, dying. ... And what's specific to the theatre is not the presence of the living actor or of the living spectator, but rather the presence of the person who has the potential to die.'[11]

The art of theatre then is an invitation (or challenge?) to imagine the 'final transformation' of life in every present moment of appearance. As Howard Barker maintains: '*The art of theatre* is a rehearsal for death but more, a confession of ignorance, of the limits of knowledge. ...'[12] Death remains unpronounceable, a secret, in response to which the art of theatre (the tragic form) is a 'step/not beyond' (Blanchot's *pas au-delà*). 'Death is the secret of secrets, the origin of the idea of the secret, of which desire is the highest manifestation *in life* ...'[13] The limits of knowledge with which both death and sex confront us (for we cannot positively *know* anything about the erotic sexual moment either – that form of sexual expression which is *other and more* than reproduction. Words fail us, again and always), this conceptual limitation, generates an endless circulation of desire.

According to Jonathan Dollimore Western culture has always been fascinated by the connections between erotic desire and death. In his book *Death, Desire and Loss in Western Culture* he identifies desire as a 'restless movement' which 'comes to seem destructively insatiable, a permanent lack whose attempted fulfilment is at once the destiny of the self and what destroys it'.[14] There is a tradition of thinking about desire as emerging from an experience of lack and incompleteness, as is epitomised in Plato's retelling of a myth (by Aristophanes) according to which all humans were originally androgynous beings of circular shape who, as a punishment by the gods, were cut in half. This was the origin of (idealist) love and erotic desire – our longing to find the 'other half' who will make us complete. But, as Jan Kott says, 'the paradox and sadness of eroticism consists in the fact that its absolute fulfilment is not possible'.[15] This is what makes Eros 'bittersweet' (Anne Carson) – a contradictory movement of desire, pleasurable and painful at the same time. '[E]rotic imagination never creates a fully developed situation, or a complete person. The erotic partner of imagination and desire is created or given only in fragments.'[16] The fragmented erotic other, because he is incomplete (a secret?), positions himself at the boundary between creation (life) and dissolution (death). Accordingly, the status of eroticism and death as 'limit experiences' (Blanchot) suggests that the promise of fulfilment or ecstatic *jouissance* which is contained in the image of the other, the object of desire, is connected to the pleasure and pain of transgression. This was the view of Bataille who, like Sade, associated sex with death, arguing that the fully expressed sexual and erotic desire causes a dissolution or loss of self, a 'breaking down of established patterns' and a disturbance of 'regulated social order'.[17]

Bataille argues that eroticism signifies a break from the social order of work, reason and calculation; it is an aspect of human sexuality that is divorced from the reproductive drive and through which the individual experiences the shifting grounds of existence. Eroticism is associated with transgression and approaches the condition of death, for its aim is dissolution of self and continuity of experience. The erotic state can be a heightened form of consciousness in which the furthest possibilities and intensities of selfhood are explored. Eroticism is an unknown territory, a mental and emotional *terrain vague*, and in this it resembles death also. The spiritual, sacred dimension to the experience of eroticism is captured by Bataille's use of the term 'sovereign' to describe erotic desire's movement of transgression and effect of transfiguration.

Alphonso Lingis, too, juxtaposes erotic life to normal life (the order of reason and work) and shows that our socially constructed sense of stable identity and integrity can be radically undermined as the result of our sensuous erotic encounter with the body of another. 'And what else is erotic craving but a craving to be violated?'[18] The 'dangerous emotions' of eroticism can create a sense of empowerment or vulnerability, pleasure and pain experienced simultaneously, an 'exultation of risking oneself, of plunging into the danger zone, of expending our forces at a loss'.[19] We enter the intimate erotic relation, or are driven to it, with a sense of fear and at the risk of losing our sense of stability, identity, security; we are seduced by Eros at the risk of danger, violation, dissolution, in other words: death.

There is an inherent theatricality involved in erotic activity, which is suggested, for example, in the process of seduction as a form of self-performance for an other. The erotic (performance) can be an empowering experience especially for women, as Baudrillard suggests in his book *Seduction*, where the feminine is constructed as a principle of reversibility. A similar, but politicised, perspective on female eroticism is presented by the Caribbean-American poet Audre Lorde: 'When I speak of the erotic, then, I speak of it as an assertion of the life-force of women; of that creative energy empowered, the knowledge and use of which we are now reclaiming in our language, our history, our dancing, our loving, our work, our lives.'[20]

The temporality of eroticism and death is peculiar: rooted in experiences of mutability, transformation and crisis, they are both confrontations with the unknowable and make us sensitive to the value and passing of time. It is perhaps no surprise that the intersections between eroticism and death find some of their most poignant expressions in the ephemeral arts of theatre and performance where our encounters with bodies, words, sounds and images are subject to a dynamic of mutability and a heightened experience of time. The theatricality of eroticism and death points beyond representation; its gesture is anti-mimetic, sublime even, for it binds together contradictory impulses and energies which disrupt the logical order of understanding and representation. Theatre is the space in which real and imagined encounters, relations and contacts are enabled or deferred, made actual or possible (the erotic itself creates a space in which every movement, gesture, word, is heightened, made different). The theatre can be an invitation to imagine ourselves and the world and people around us differently; it can alter the parameters of our psychic worlds and affect us viscerally; it can be a dialogue, an address, a challenge, a risk, a seduction.

Viewed from the perspective of subject–object dynamics, the theatre is a relation of desire: a space permeated with possible ways of looking, moving, speaking and being which structure the subject's relation to the other. This dialectical understanding of theatre in terms of desire is informed by Lacan's famous theory of the mirror stage, which is crucial to the formation of ego-identity. The infant identifies with the reflected image of his/her body as an 'ideal-I', a perfect *imago* of autonomy and wholeness. This narcissistic fiction of identity at the same time creates an awareness of separation and alienation, structuring the subject's mental development in terms of a desire for the imaginary 'ideal-I' which is contrasted with the reality of the socially determined and imperfect 'ego-ideal'. Lacan emphasises that the identification with an idealised and objectified self-image during the mirror phase is a process of misrecognition (*méconnaissance*), a form of imaginary (self-)knowledge. The theatrical stage set-up and performance condition may be understood as an imaginary order in which *méconnaissance* operates by structuring the self's relation to the other in terms of a dialectic of absence and presence. The desire for the lost and unobtainable object of desire (Lacan's *objet petit a*) contains a dramatic and theatrical dimension which emerges when desire compels us to reach beyond the boundaries of the pleasure principle itself, to a point of impossible and deadly *jouissance*.

Some of the most striking explorations of desire can be found in Surrealist art, which draws attention to the inherently dramatic nature of the Freudian model of the unconscious where the forces and compulsions of the human mind exist in relationships of crisis and tension. In Surrealism the unconscious expresses itself in symbols, images, forms and words that can have an unsettling and disturbing effect on our sense of (objective and empirical) reality. In many of their art works, manifestos, exhibitions and performances the Surrealists explored eroticism and the death drive as essential forces of transgression and excess. The theme of the 1959 international Surrealist exhibition EROS (Exposition international du surréalisme), for example, was Sade's notion of transgressive desire and liberty. This theme was ritualistically explored in a performance by the Canadian Surrealist Jean Benoît, entitled *The Execution of the Testament of the Marquis de Sade*, which involved the artist removing his tribal costume piece by piece while Sade's testament was read out. The performance ended with Benoît burning the word 'Sade' onto his naked chest with a hot branding iron. In the exhibition catalogue, André Breton talked about eroticism as a 'privileged place, a theatre of provocations and prohibitions in which life's most profound urges confront one another'.[21] The Surrealists' aim was to restructure reality by confronting us with the 'unbound desires' of the unconscious and, as Breton says in *Mad Love*, to search for images of 'convulsive beauty' in erotic love, passion and desire.

The revolutionary politics of the Surrealists, expressed in their manifestoes, exhibition installations and performances, were concerned with harnessing the liberating powers of Eros.[22] Feminist critiques of male Surrealist practices have focused on their representations of women and female erotic sexuality and argued that they were objectifying and essentialising. This is not to overlook the important contributions made by female artists to the Surrealist movement, to which the exhibition 'Angels of Anarchy: Women Artists and Surrealism' at Manchester Art Gallery (26 Sept 2009–10 Jan 2010) has recently drawn attention. Much of Surrealist art can be accused of being phallic and male-centred (foregrounding male desire in performative terms and representing women as passive erotic objects), but female Surrealist artists challenged this notion in early attempts at subverting the male gaze and challenging gender boundaries with their provocative art. The female body was presented as constantly changing and out of reach of the fixing (male) gaze. Such strategies were later explored by explicit body performers and avant-garde live artists who developed new strategies of (self-)presentation and experimentation with the body as a means of questioning and challenging the aesthetics and politics of gender and sexuality.[23]

The essays collected in this volume explore many (and more) of the above-mentioned manifestations and representations of Eros and death in theatrical, musical and cultural texts and performances, both historical and contemporary. One of the central concerns of this book is to propose or work out what may be intrinsically theatrical or performative about the encounter between eroticism and death. The essays explore the ways in which various forms of theatre and performance embody the dynamics of desire and death by, for example, identifying Eros and Thanatos as transgressive, liberating or healing but also aggressive and destructive forces. Many of the essays locate their discussions of eroticism and death in specific cultural–historical contexts and thus provide a sense of how drama and theatre reflect changing attitudes to sexual desire and death. As well as offering particular historical perspectives, the collection contains essays that engage with contemporary dramatic writing and theatre/performance practice.

Our encounter with eroticism and death in theatre and performance is real and imaginary at the same time. The transient movement of bodies in the space and time of the here and now can be seductive and yield a visceral affect; but our encounter with the unknown and invisible will ultimately depend on the work of our imagination, which alone has the power to turn the theatre into a *space of desire*.

Notes

1. Anne Carson, *Eros the Bittersweet* (Champaign, IL, 1998), p. 26.
2. Sigmund Freud, 'The Ego and the Id', in *The Standard Edition of the Complete Psychological Works of Sigmund Freud*, vol. 19, trans. and ed. James Strachey (London, 2001), p. 40.
3. *Ibid.*, p. 41.
4. See Herbert Marcuse, *Eros and Civilization: A Philosophical Inquiry into Freud* (Boston, MA, 1966).
5. Jean Baudrillard, *Symbolic Exchange and Death*, trans. Iain Hamilton Grant (London, 1993), p. 2.
6. *Ibid.*, p. 152.
7. Theodor W. Adorno, *Minima Moralia: Reflections from Damaged Life*, trans. E.F.N. Jephcott (London, 1978), p. 15.
8. Octavio Paz, *The Double Flame: Love and Eroticism*, trans. Helen Lane (London, 1995), p. 20.
9. Tadeusz Kantor, 'The Theatre of Death', in *A Journey through other Spaces: Essays and Manifestos, 1944–1990*, trans. Michal Kobialka (Berkeley, CA, 1993), p. 112.
10. Tadeusz Kantor, 'The Second *Insegnamento*', in *A Journey through other Spaces*, p. 237.
11. Heiner Müller in an interview with Alexander Kluge in autumn 1995. See video and transcript at http://muller-kluge.library.cornell.edu/en/.
12. Howard Barker, *Death, The One and the Art of Theatre* (London, 2005), p. 31.
13. *Ibid.*, p. 35.
14. Jonathan Dollimore, *Death, Desire and Loss in Western Culture* (New York, 2001), p. xvii.
15. Jan Kott, 'A Short Treatise on Eroticism', in Jan Kott, *The Memory of the Body: Essays on Theater and Death*, trans. Boleslaw Taborski (Evanston, IL, 1992), p. 74.
16. *Ibid.*, p. 71.
17. George Bataille, *Erotism: Death and Sensuality*, trans. Mary Dalwood (San Francisco, 1986), p. 18.
18. Alphonso Lingis, *Dangerous Emotions* (Berkeley, CA, 2000), p. 91.
19. *Ibid.*
20. Audre Lorde, 'The Uses of the Erotic: The Erotic as Power', in Audre Lorde, *Sister Outsider: Essays and Speeches* (Freedom, CA, 1984), pp. 53–9, p. 55.
21. André Breton, preface to the EROS exhibition catalogue (1959) quoted in Alyce Mahon, 'Staging Desire', in Jennifer Mundy (ed.) *Surrealism: Desire Unbound* (London, 2001), p. 286.
22. See Alyce Mahon, *Surrealism and the Politics of Eros, 1938–1968* (London, 2005).
23. See Rebecca Schneider, *The Explicit Body in Performance* (London, 1997).

1

Some Erōs–Thanatos *interfaces in Attic Tragedy*

David Rudkin

First, some definition: *Erōs* and *Thanatos*, not in Freudian metaphorical sense but in Greek immediate sense – 'ἔρως as the sexual drive, θάνατος as death itself. And if I speak of 'Attic' rather than 'Greek' Tragedy, it is because the more traditional term, while perfectly respectable, yet suggests a background of a single 'Greek' cultural unity, which there was not at this time. Our entire surviving corpus of Tragedy 'in Greek' was written from within a context of one regional dialect – that of Attica – and produced for the civic/religious festivals of its city Athens during her near-century of political and naval dominance. Where extant Tragedy is concerned, we are talking of a short time-span: from 472 BCE to 406 or soon thereafter; from the heady aftermath of the Athens-led victory over Xerxes of Persia to the years of her fall and the dismantling of her democracy.

I shall discuss four characters from what little we possess of Attic Tragedy: the princess Iphigenia, offered as a human sacrifice; an orphan daughter of King Oedipus, Antigone, who, rather than betray a 'higher law', submits to the sentence of death; a young queen married into a foreign land, Phaedra, afflicted with transgressive *Erōs*; and the object of her desire, her stepson Hippolytus, who repudiates *Erōs* altogether. With each of these characters, we shall find *Erōs* or an *Erōs* schema coming to logical consummation in unnatural death.

For our first figure, Iphigenia, it all begins, as it shall end, at Aulis – the deep narrows of a natural harbour on the Aegean coast of Greece. Here, two Bronze Age warlords, Agamemnon of Mycene and his brother, the king of Sparta, have assembled a mighty force to embark for a punitive war against the Asian city of Troy. Punitive because, while a Trojan prince was recently a guest in Sparta, he had seduced and taken back home with him the Spartan queen. The Greek forces – with their legendary 'thousand ships' – are to deliver retribution on the Trojans, and, at whatever human cost to the Trojans and to themselves, recover Queen Helen and their own insulted pride. But their thousand ships cannot sail, because day after day north-easterlies are blowing, pinning them in the sound. This is the situation as given in our oldest Tragic source for it, the opening play in the trilogy conventionally known now as the *Oresteia*. The Aeschylus text vividly suggests the atmosphere at Aulis caused by the prolonged delay: the impending disaffection, desertion, mutiny. The military priest and prophet Calchas attributes the adverse winds to the wrath of the goddess Artemis. If she is to be prevailed upon to still these winds, and release the ships, she will exact a high price. Precisely what, is not spelled out; but the inference is soon clear. For Agamemnon to have his war, he must offer Artemis in sacrifice his own eldest child.

Why should Artemis require this? If we are to understand her wrath at our distance of 2,500 years, we need to try to understand something of Artemis herself. So far as concerns the events at Aulis, and to start from the traditional simplicities, Artemis is, among other aspects, 'goddess "of" virginity'. This 'goddess-of-*x*' formula is a very crude equation, particularly with Artemis. We do better to think of the virgin estate – in girl or boy – as her *domain*. The virgin girl or boy is a sacred property of that domain; thus to harm one would arouse her wrath. There is an obverse to this: to sacrifice to her a virgin child, duly consecrated, would be to make a very high order of offering. But to the *Oresteia* audience, human sacrifice is not a historical memory. It might at times, as here, intrude into their mythology, but it is a barbarity to them. So what sort of 'presence' is this Artemis in their lives, that in this story, in this play, she could plausibly demand the ritual slaughter of an innocent child? How is that consistent with the Artemis they know?

The more we consider Artemis, the more aspects to her do we find. Her 'virgin' domain extends naturally enough to all the untouched wilderness and untamed creatures there, hence her identification with the hunt: it takes place on her territory, and needs to be conducted with due deference to her. What to us seems contradictory at first is that this 'huntress virgin' ordains also the domain of pregnancy and childbirth. In Greek common parlance of those times, the pains of labour were 'the arrows of Artemis'. This apparent contradiction retires somewhat once we envision Artemis as her archetype, a Moon-goddess. She is Apollo's sister, and, unlike her brother-god the consistent Sun with his vitalising light and warmth, the Moon is a cold presence, separate-seeming from us, aloof, shifting shape, keeping her dark side ever hidden from us – metaphorically virgin indeed, yet, in that very rhythm of her phases, visibly ordaining a woman's body-cycle of menstruation and birth. She is, as Moon, herself inviolable, causing us necessary pain of life – and as Artemis, physically 'out there' somewhere beyond our city wall in her untamed wild, where it could be all too easy to cross her and offend her. Something such had happened on the road to Aulis.

Aeschylus does not stage the scene at Aulis. It has all happened ten years before the play begins. As the senators of Agamemnon's royal city make their ceremonial first entrance onto the space, they give us an exposition, on a massive scale, of the issues and perplexities that will drive the whole trilogy: is there a moral function to human suffering? Is there an ultimate rightness at work in the universe? In the greater pattern of things, what is the role of individual human will? This is not philosophical abstraction: there are motifs at work, phrases, words, that will recur, mutate and evolve quite symphonically throughout the onward organic process of the trilogy. All this exposition is orchestrated in song and dance, deploying a range of highly formalised metrical schemes and (we presume) musical modes. The language is difficult, its syntax often condensed and elliptical, its vocabulary double-edged, at times chimerical. How much of this in performance would an Athenian audience have distinctly heard, let alone understood, we are at liberty to doubt. But what the reverend seigneurs of Mycene are telling us – they say they were witness to most of this – is that at Aulis the two commanders are warned that Artemis is enraged, not so much by their intended war as by their moral evasion of the meaning and consequences of that war. As they had set out with their forces on the march to Aulis, there appeared a hideous portent by their road: two eagles tearing at a pregnant hare in the very moment that her young are being born. The eagles, one a golden, the other a white-tail, are identified by these attributes as Agamemnon and his lesser brother. Eagle-like, they will fall on Troy; Zeus has sent them – that is, their cause is just. But their prey, a helpless creature of the wild, giving birth, and her ravaged new-born young, are emphatically in the domain of Artemis. Likewise, the helpless mothers and children of Troy: they too are in the domain of Artemis.

Immediately a question presents itself. If – as the prophet Calchas insists – Artemis is 'revolted by the eagles' feast',[1] why does she require in propitiation an even more revolting act? More revolting, because while what the eagles are doing is true to their created nature – the Elders call them the 'winged hounds of Zeus'[2] – is it equally true to Agamemnon's *human* nature to sacrifice his own daughter?

I think at Aulis we come near to a liminal moment in the world story-pattern of human sacrifice. Early in the Old Testament, when the Lord bids Abraham go into the land of Moriah, and on a mountain there sacrifice Isaac, his own son,[3] that father will learn instead that Yahweh is no longer pleased with human sacrifice, and will be content with the ram from the thicket. It is a moment of change that will distinguish the Children of Israel from all the other peoples around them, still passing their children through the fires to Moloch and the rest. Is Agamemnon at such a moment? To put it in our own anachronistic existentialist way: is Artemis offering Agamemnon a chance to think again? Surely Agamemnon *could* do otherwise. He could refuse to pay the price that Artemis demands. He could publicly put human sacrifice behind him, into the cultural past, as Abraham does; and his culture would take a major evolutionary step forward. He must then, to be logical, repudiate his war – or at least his part in it. The cost to him would be terminal; to his authority, his pride, perhaps even his life. And he has of course no way of knowing, if he refuses Artemis her sacrifice, how catastrophic her response might be. By comparison, Yahweh made it simple for Abraham. For Agamemnon, much more is unknown; as he sees it, he has only a choice of evils: to 'murder his own child, the glory of his house',[4] or to be a *lipónaus*, a deserter, and betray his allies. In practice, he sees that he has no choice: he takes on, in a famous Aeschylean phrase, the *anánkēs lépadnon* – the 'yoke of what he must'[5] – and agrees to the sacrifice. So Iphigenia comes to Aulis.

The Elders, in their elliptical, allusive Aeschylean mode, give us mind's-eye glimpses of the scene, almost like a montage of film stills. The overall informing image is of the victim held high, horizontal above the altar, face down; one man grips her by her ankles, another holds her around the waist, a third by her shoulders; her throat is exposed to the sacrificial knife; the officiant holds a bowl to catch the spurt of blood from the severed carotid artery. The Elders tell us of Iphigenia held just so, 'like a goat-kid',[6] face down above the altar, her mouth stopped with a gag to staunch any curse from her that might bring ill upon her family. Her girdle is 'violently' undone, her saffron-dyed garment spills to the ground. Yet even in her nakedness, she is *prépousa*, 'seemly', the Elders say, 'as in a painting'.[7] She casts on those about to slaughter her a piteous look; she struggles to speak, but the voice that, by her father's table in the men's quarters at home once sang to him in 'virgin' song, is gagged.

Prépousa: we note the Elders' cautionary emphasis on her 'seemliness'. Iphigenia herself, so physically constrained, can do nothing to shield her nakedness. It is more as though the Elders (i.e. the poet) were doing that for us. It suggests a cultural anxiety to cancel the sexuality of the victim, to preclude inappropriate thoughts. A later poet will be more specific: when, some thirty years on, Euripides comes to describe a similar scene, the sacrifice of a Trojan princess, he will have her taking care to fall 'with propriety, and hide what should be hidden from men's eyes'.[8] But this very caution inevitably touches a sexual note.

And here with Iphigenia that note sounds on. Silenced, the Elders say, is the voice that once sang in 'virgin' song. An objective observation, and poignant – but Aeschylus's word-choice for 'virgin' here is rustic and dark: *ataúrōtos* – 'unbulled'.[9] Likewise with the natural reference to that voice singing in 'the men's quarters': boundaries demarking masculine and feminine territories, socially and at home, are strict; yet even this objective social allusion serves further to remind us of Iphigenia's sexual vulnerability. And in the very image of her brought among the army at Aulis, masculine territory, the primary cultural resonance is of a young girl leaving her maiden estate. To the Athenian audience, and many an audience since, Iphigenia is her father's *property*. Against such background, her father would normally be ritually handing her over to be the property of a husband. The marriage-resonance is further enhanced by two little words: *krókou baphàs* – her garments are 'saffron-dyed'.[10] In Aeschylus's compacted verse, there is no space for irrelevant detail. Saffron is for festal wear. Traditionally, in saffron, Iphigenia would be coming as a bride. Intimations of a wedding, then, contextually exist: the socialisation of *Erōs*. But here is a marriage where the bride is brought to die.

* * *

Fifty years later, the Aulis story will be given a play of its own, and here the wedding scenario is explicit. *Iphigenia at Aulis* is Euripides's last play, left unfinished, completed we are told by his son, and our text now showing signs of further interference by a later hand. For Euripides – for simplicity we'll call its author that – it is specifically to be married that Iphigenia comes to Aulis. At least, that is what she has been led to believe. The wretched Agamemnon, torn between his human nature as man and father and his public identity as commander-in-chief of the coalition, is threatened with mutiny and intrigue against him, and with shame if he fails; after much havering, he miserably consents to the sacrifice that Artemis demands. He sends his wife a deceitful letter: he has found the girl a husband. And so poor Iphigenia comes – with mother, sister, baby brother, servants and all, and a cartload of dowry. Deceived also is the fictive husband, the Greek hero Achilles, who does not even know his name has been taken in vain.

Here or there in Euripides's text we find echoes of the *Oresteia* – notably of its famous image of Agamemnon consenting to take on himself the *anánkēs lépadnon* – the 'yoke of what he must'. But this is no *hommage*. This echo is to point a contrast: with Euripides we have an Agamemnon made of poorer stuff. Alas, he cries, into what *anánkēs zeúgmata*, 'harness of compulsion', *empeptōkamen*, are we 'fallen'.[11] The later poet is under no obligation slavishly to follow the *Oresteia*, but Aeschylus is a dominating presence and, when Euripides defies or deviates, as here, it is to a purpose. We've already noted his foregrounding of the wedding scenario, which is, I think, not intended merely to pile on the pathos. I sense that, if the pretext of a wedding was already in the tradition for Aeschylus to use, he did not use it because at that juncture of the *Oresteia* there was no moral focus to spare for it. (Although perhaps it does indeed inform those allusions we have noted.) Euripides diverges from the *Oresteia* here, I think, for a dramaturgical reason. Given that he is crafting a whole play around the events at Aulis, it is difficult to see how he can mobilise the drama other than by means of the wedding-device. There is a further divergence. At his Aulis, the fleet is not stormbound. So far from raising north-easterlies to pin the ships in the sound, his Artemis has stilled this place in an unnatural calm: '... voice of neither birds nor sea ... and silence of the winds ...'.[12]

17

The effect is of time suspended, all nature holding her breath, waiting for Agamemnon to make his decision.

The play's very first words – those, that is, that are judged authentic – strike up a theme of femininity and sex: a genealogy of a mother; to her, three daughters born; in the fullness of time their suitors coming. The play's first choral ode introduces a more overtly sexual theme: maidens of Aulis, as it were an Iphigenia multiplied, enter singing of Artemis the virgin goddess and the grove here sacred to her. But they sing in excitement, too, of the sands of Aulis nearby, thronged now with the wondrous sight of soldiery and panoply of war. Oh brave new world, that hath such manhood in it. They've caught sight even of Achilles himself, legendary heroic icon, running swift as the wind. A disquieting motif: the virginal domain of Artemis and the aggressive domain of soldiery, adjoining … We sense the boundary in peril. Last, almost a throwaway, the girls' hymn touches an ominous note. That grove of Artemis, they innocently sing, is, in one Greek word, *polythýtos*: it has seen 'many a sacrifice'.[13]

Theirs is not the only innocence soon to be violated. Achilles has been cruelly compromised. The soldiers, too, will be given a corrupting lesson in *Realpolitik*. But that is to come. For now, they hurry to catch a glimpse of the newly arrived Iphigenia and speculate who the lucky husband is to be. Today, they say, shall be *makárion* for her, a 'day of bliss'.[14] But the word *makárion* can denote also the 'bliss' of the immortals. Indeed, it can be used as euphemism for the dead, as the Germans and Scandinavians use *seelig*. That she'll be, before this same day is done. And Iphigenia's husband, the one to whom unknowing she is truly consigned, is indeed an immortal: Hades, Lord of Eternal Night.

Iphigenia runs in joy to greet her father. He cannot look her in the eye. The dialogue darkens with *doubles entendres*: 'Oh father, I wish I could come with you to Troy.' 'You too [child] have a journey to go; you'll soon forget me there.'[15] And in the cruel scene with the child's mother, replying to her question what day shall the wedding be: 'At the right time of moon.'[16] A sinister ambiguity, for what else is that moon but Artemis? Her sacrificial knife was traditionally a crescent-shapen silver blade. Our inner eye glimpses here the flash of that blade.

And Iphigenia herself, when she discovers the truth? Rather as might a Schiller heroine, faced with the reality of the fate that she cannot avoid,

Iphigenia works out a strategy of *choosing* it. If only by her sacrifice can the winds be released, and Greece set sail for her just war, so be it. In fierce proud lines to her mother, 'I am daughter of all Greece, not yours alone. ... *This* is my marriage, these my children': her body given to Greece, to spare her slavery.[17] And *Erōs* arises in one last irony. The husband-who-never-was-to-be, Achilles, now morally moved at the sight of her ideal heroism, is sexually moved too: 'Now more even than before do I desire your bed.'[18] Iphigenia, in ceremonial wreath, not as a bride but as sacrificial victim, bids her farewell to the light, and goes to her true husband, *Thanatos*.

* * *

Between Aeschylus and Euripides, in time, meanwhile, mid-century, has come the dramatist who seems of the three the most remote in morality and temper. With only seven of his tragedies surviving from a lifetime's output, each a single play from a distinct stage in his development, it is rash to make generalising statements about the phenomenon we call Sophocles. Perhaps it is safe to say this much: the few protagonists of his that we possess exist each in an assertive self-exile from the conventional world, bestrangered by a human emotion or compulsion that they embody to extremes. The archetypal transgressor Oedipus, Electra in her disproportionate grieving, the proud suicidal Ajax, the towering unfaithful demi-god Heracles, the soldier Philoctetes with his stinking wound yet without whose bow the war can not be won – these giant figures live, suffer, rage and die before us in an obdurate solitude – and are hardly citizen material. I add this point because we must never lose sight of Attic Tragedy as a *civic* manifestation, the material of a drama contest officially presented before a militarised citizen audience celebrating their communal identity. And for much of the time of which I speak, Athens is at war. To us, inheritors of a more individualist tradition, and who look to theatre almost by definition for a subversive voice, this civic aspect of Attic Tragedy is quite alien.

To the Sophocles audience, then, his Antigone will be a character more problematic, I think, than to us, who have somewhat adopted her as an icon of civil disobedience, of Resistance indeed. Daughter of the disgraced, exiled, now dead king Oedipus, she lives on in her city, now under the autocratic rule of her uncle Creon. A brother of hers has led an attempted coup against Creon and lost his life. Creon has issued an edict that this rebel's body is to be left unburied as carrion, to rot. Antigone refuses to obey. Twice she goes out and with her own hands does her best to bury her brother's corpse. The second time she is arrested; in bitter dispute with Creon she refuses ever to submit. She is obeying a higher law than any ruler's edict. Creon condemns her to death.

Insofar as Antigone insists on a proper burial of the dead, rebel or not, the Athenian audience will find her sympathetic. To leave the dead exposed is repulsive to Athenian sensibility; it also suggests the ethos of a barbarous regime. Even in battle, Greek armies granted each other 'time out of war' to bury their fallen. Yet for that audience it is not so simple. To them, the *pólis* – the city-state and its laws – are the one stronghold they know against barbarism or tyranny. Thus the dramatist's opening gesture – his Antigone *outside* the *pólis* gates, whispering in conspiracy in the darkness of night – will immediately disquiet them. And where later in the play her appeal to a 'higher law'[19] might induce a post-Judaeo-Christian empathy in us, perhaps we should pause and problematise ourselves a little: for Antigone's 'higher law', read the radicalised Muslim's *jihad*. In fact, Antigone and Creon each have a case. Their collision formalises a debate that any democracy must have with itself about the primacy of law but also about the necessity of rightful disobedience. The play could equally be known as *Antigone and Creon*. His name is more emblem than name: it means simply 'the man in power'. After Antigone's final exit, there is a good third of the play still to run – for *his* learning process. And where his learning begins is in one of the grimmest locations in world drama – Antigone's bridal chamber. Sophocles as good as calls it that. Antigone was to have married Creon's son; instead, by Creon's sentence she is to be entombed alive, in a cell dug out in the rock. A hideous rightness here – no mere sick joke, but a moral chiasmus: one dead unburied, one buried alive. And where Aeschylus might have been metaphorical and allusive, Sophocles is grimly explicit: the rock chamber is 'bridal' for it shall witness the consummation, or *a* consummation, of the marriage of Antigone.

For, after hearing that dreadful sentence, and her obdurate acceptance of it, what first word is it that the Chorus cry? These Senators of Thebes, in honour of what do they strike up and sing? Conscience? Courage? The laws of the gods? Or would that be for the Chorus to take sides? No. *Erōs*!

they cry. *Erōs* the unconquerable. *Erōs*, that falls on beast and man and gods alike. Their song darkens. They weep to see this marriage-bed that Antigone has chosen, the *pankoítan thálamon*, 'bed where all are brought at last to lie'.[20] Antigone takes up the song in harrowing lament: 'I go my last road, I look my last on the light of the sun. Death, who brings us all to bed, leads me while I yet live … to wed the waters of Acheron.'[21] Her metaphorical marriage to Death will become more physical, for her young husband-to-be, Creon's son, will die there too. Breaking and scrambling his way in to find she has hanged herself, he falls on his own sword. Hers the traditional woman's way of suicide, his the man's; and the archetypal sexual emblematism too – the constricting noose, the phallic sword. As the young man's body falls onto hers, in close-shot as it were his dying gasps *ekbállei*, literally 'ejaculate', an *oxeían rhoēn* – 'sharp spurt' – of deep red blood onto her white cheek; then, as though the camera pulls back, we see his body fall entwined about hers *nekrós perí nekrói* – 'corpse about corpse' – in *telē numphikà* – 'consummation of marriage' – *ein Haídou dòmois* – 'in the House of Death'.[22]

* * *

As with Antigone, but from different causes, Queen Phaedra comes to us in a perspective somewhat altered by our Romantic inheritance. We owe our more familiar, corseted Phaedra to the Jansenist French Classical court dramatist Racine; he inherits (and remodels) her from the lurid Phaedra of the Roman *côterie* dramatist Seneca: ancestral to both is the Phaedra of two plays by Euripides, one now lost to us, although there are signs that Seneca had access to it. So it may be as well to summarise her story as told in the surviving Greek original. A young foreign bride brought home by a conquering civilising king, she falls in love with his young son by a former marriage. In the fever of her desire, she becomes ill, delirious, is in danger of wasting away. To save her, her Nurse propositions the young man. He vehemently refuses. Phaedra, in terror that her transgressive desire will now be revealed, hangs herself – leaving a letter for her husband the king, accusing his son of attempting to rape her. In a terrible relapse into magic and barbarity, the king conjures a monster from the sea to destroy his son.

It can come as something of a shock to go back to this prime source. The Greek Phaedra may be obscurely recognisable, an ancestral ghost. The chief surprise will surely be that the central character of the Euripides play is not she at all, but the young stepson. The play has from the beginning been conventionally known by his name. So too had the lost earlier play been a *Hippolytus*. In that working, we are told, Phaedra herself made the sexual advance to him, on stage, and he retreated, covering his face in shame. This scandalised the audience; and Euripides later returned to the theme, to make good the improprieties of his earlier play in a second working, the version that we have.[23] For Euripides, then, the issue does seem to have been Hippolytus. And certainly, at least in the surviving play, his issue with Hippolytus is that, while Phaedra's natural desire for him may take a pathological turn, his natural rejection of her is yet pathological at source. Where Phaedra suffers from inappropriate *Erōs* and in excess, the young man rejects *Erōs* altogether. And here we meet Artemis again. It is Artemis to whom he has vowed himself, he devotes himself exclusively to activities in her domain: an obsessive solitary horsemanship to and fro down along the edge of the sea; the hunt in her untamed wild; and a fanatical virginity.

Yet is it true that he rejects *Erōs*? Euripides shows all this young man's *Erōs* going to Artemis. The Artemis we met at Aulis was of quite limited aspect. She has other faces, other names, other manifestations – eastward across the Aegean, for instance, in Asia Minor, she is not virgin so much as 'Great Mother', her icon hung with breasts. Her temple in Ephesus was one of the seven wonders of the world. And we glimpse her here in the New Testament, where Paul's preachings about Jesus cause the silversmiths of Ephesus, who make images of her, to fear for their livelihood. They foment an uproar in the city; a multitude crowd into the amphitheatre to deny Paul entry and cry against him with one voice for some two hours, *Megálē hē Ártemis Ephesíōn*, 'great is Diana of the Ephesians!'[24] (In our English Bible she is given her Roman name.) We've met what in myth she demanded at Aulis; historically, in Asia Minor, she can be demanding in a different way: notoriously, certain of her priests castrate themselves and consecrate to her their severed genitals. Figuratively, this Hippolytus is such a self-castrating devotee. But, unbalanced a character though he is, and calamitous though his life-choice may be, his dramatist invests him with a passionate integrity; no 'negative criticism' here. We first meet him talking to Artemis – praying is too solemn a word; he speaks to her in wonder and love. He has brought her a crown he has wreathed of wild flowers from a mysterious meadow on the mountainside. It is a meadow, he says, where scythe of man has never cut 'nor iron ever came',[25] a place so charged with the immanence of Artemis that only the truly chaste may enter there. In this haunted declaration of love, we recognise a young man's *Erōs* all invested in a Feminine who can never be humanly real. He savagely repudiates Real Woman. His word for her is *kíbdēlos*, 'false coin',[26] in Existentialist terms 'inauthentic'. There are seeds of a fascist pathology here; and, indeed, at one alarming moment, he prays aloud for a world where women are housed separately from human society, maintained only for breeding purposes.[27] Critics shy from this as a Euripidean extravagance – but where else does the logic of this character lead? No doubt to a modern sensibility this Hippolytus is 'difficult'. I suspect that he began to become difficult a very long time ago – probably well before even Seneca, who for perhaps this very reason switched the focus to Phaedra, and thus refracted our perception of the story forever.

And who is it who begins this play about this difficult young man? Not his goddess, but her opposite, Aphrodite, who tells us directly who she is, and that she is resolved to punish Hippolytus for his abnegation of her; that she shall use Phaedra as her mechanism, Phaedra whom she has inflamed with a sexual desire as unbearable as it is transgressive; and this shall be the catalyst to bring Hippolytus down – this very day. Watch it happen. The play will enact the young man's *hubris* as a mortal who, in his overweening, thinks he can overlook a major goddess and spurn the gift she brings; it will enact too, in his exclusive devotion to a counter-goddess in her domain of the solitary and the asocial, his *hamartía* – literally, 'getting it wrong': two famous academic 'tragic faults' mediated by the dramatist with living urgency. Phaedra is the hapless human instrument of a divine wrath visited on a central figure whose capital offence and whose tragedy it is. The play is an organism of marvellous formal symmetry: its very dramaturgy balances and opposes the two conflicting feminine principles at work – like a massive gateway to the play, at its opening, the one herself on the space, countered by a human celebration of her opposite; at its close an equal reciprocation in reverse. The symmetry is itself a dialectic, the form a meaning.

And, within this dialectical frame, the image-system is alive with elements ambiguously charged with *Erōs* and with *Thanatos*. The steeds that, down along the shore, the young man obsessively trains – emblems of his own potency, and at the same time his sublimation – will ultimately prove his death. A second, deeper irony is that, although all his psychic space might be devoted to Artemis as virgin, yet Artemis herself *requires* her opposite; she also brings childbirth: his very *Artemis* is incomplete. Ironic also will prove Phaedra's anxiety about the beam above her marriage-bed: if Hippolytus came to her there, that beam would see the *Erōs* that they do. Then it will cry out to the husband what it has seen. Some dismiss this as another Euripidean 'oddity'; but it is humanly recognisable. In the event, it is from that beam that she will hang herself. And crowning all ironies is the inhibiting impulse that the Greeks called *aidōs*. A problematic concept to us, it is particularly ambivalent here, at work in one way on the desiring and in quite another on the desired. *Aidōs* is the force, says Hippolytus, that preserves for Artemis that virgin meadow on the mountainside. For 'base' individuals (he implies, I think, 'debased' by sex), it is a precinct not to be entered with sickle and scythe: *Aidōs* is gardener there.[28] That is, in perfect chastity, the bee and the stream do all the husbanding that the meadow needs. It is a beautiful sentiment, but a rather Victorian notion of the bee. And not good agriculture. Likewise one-sided is Phaedra's *aidōs*: for her, it is a sense of guilty shame. In a problematic line she lists it emphatically as one of her besetting pleasurable weaknesses.[29] When she hangs herself, she is burdened *katá*, downward, with it – *aidōs* has physically bowed her head.[30]

In their great central lyric of the play, while Phaedra's suicide is happening off-stage, the Chorus intimate it to our inner eye. At first they seem to be focused on something quite fanciful and inappropriate. Young women of the city, who empathise with Phaedra yet have no claim on our interest in similar burdens of their own, sing of their wish to escape from reality into a utopia of release, joy, beauty and harmony. In fact, they wish for wings. This, too, has been dismissed as a Euripidean absurdity. As dramatic poetry it is cruelly accurate. For suddenly, in the second strophe, we are on this real earth. We see, in the verse itself, white 'wings' indeed – the sails that speed Phaedra here from her native Crete. In onomatopoeia we hear the shock of sea-water against the ship's timbers; we hear the groan of the mooring-rope cast ashore for our new queen to set foot upon her new homeland. We see that step in close-shot.[31] Then, in the lyric's bleak coda, these elements that tell a journey of marriage now mutate to elements of death: now Phaedra's feet are off the ground, the rope that groaned is now about her neck, it is the timber above the marriage bed that carries her now – the dreaded beam cries out indeed.

It is Aphrodite – sex in person – who has' come upon the space before us to achieve this. And the compulsively virgin boy who rejects her, now unjustly accused of the filthiest sexual transgression in his universe, cannot make his father believe him. All his values go for nothing, are caricatured and mockingly flung back in his face. Suddenly an extraordinary change takes place in him. Salt water all but springs to his eyes, a cry is torn from him, calling on the memory of a woman, no less: his own mother, and her agonies when she bore him,[32] her 'arrows of Artemis'. Childbirth: in this startling moment suddenly his Artemis is complete. But Aphrodite's punishment of him is not. In the beginning, myth has it, from the foam of the sea – *aphrós* – came *Aphro-ditē* rising. As Hippolytus rides into exile, drawn by those horses of his along that strand, out at sea the enormity of a wave begins to rise, closing from sight the landmarks of the earth. Towering to the sky, swelling, swirling with *aphrós* (the word itself is there[33]), it comes rolling toward the shore and, breaking there, gives birth to the monster that shall craze his horses and destroy him – the bull from the deep. From there could have come for him the obliterating exaltation of Aphrodite and all *Erōs*; instead has come the exterminating agony of *Thanatos*.

In a remorseless final scene, he is brought to lie before us, human wreckage broken and bleeding on the space. Now only, in his last living moments, does his beloved Artemis appear to him. 'Lady,' he cries to her, does she see him in his agony? 'I see it,' she says; but 'weeping is for humankind'.[34] What else should she say? Artemis, remote, unreachable, and very much to the moral point. But all his life has been a celebration of her: how can she simply let him pass into the dark? 'I must,' she says: 'your celebration's ended. Now you die.' Hippolytus cannot understand: he has been her living image in the earth; how can she not intervene to save him? She has a devastating answer: 'I demanded all your love. Yours was the responsibility to share it better ...' There it is. In our world of vacuous bleatings about 'faith', and of regressive fanaticisms, she comes as a healthy shock of cold pure water, this ancient extinct goddess on the space, and her clear-eyed injunction to us to be *adult*. Our myths are not an answer; they pose the problem. Her parting words are comfortless: 'It has its rightness, this is how you die …' One last sad protest is torn from him: 'I walked with you so long; you go from me so easy.' But the light of her presence is already faded. The space is left for human closure to the play: 'form as meaning' indeed, for it is we mortals who must do the living, and the dying.

In that last yearning protest of his, an achingly beautiful line in the Greek,[35] there is a word-choice that should give us pause. Where I have rendered in old-fashioned Puritan phrase 'I walked with you...', we have the one word *homilía*, from which derive our homily, homiletic, and whose verb in Greek today means simply 'speak', as in 'speak a language'. The Classical noun broadly means 'converse'; more broadly, 'interaction'. A literal translation of the line could legitimately even be 'From our long intercourse you take easy leave' – yes, because in Euripides' time *homilía* is also a polite Greek word for sexual activity. The dying Hippolytus is surely innocent of that *entendre*. But our dramatist must certainly intend, and his audience hear, the thematic irony.

To conclude. In this 'difficult' figure of Hippolytus one may hardly speak of an *Erōs–Thanatos* 'interface' as such. Where with Iphigenia an *Erōs* scenario led instead to *Thanatos*, where with Antigone *Erōs* preempted is perverted in an act of *Thanatos*, where with Phaedra her *Erōs* brings about her *Thanatos*, in Hippolytus his *Erōs* is his *Thanatos*: they are embraced.

Notes

1. Aeschylus, *Agamemnon*, 138. (All translations from the Greek are my own.)
2. *Ibid.*, 136.
3. Genesis xxii.1–14.
4. Aeschylus, *Agamemnon*, 208.
5. *Ibid.*, 218.
6. *Ibid.*, 232.
7. *Ibid.*, 242.
8. Euripides, *Hecuba*, 570.
9. Aeschylus, *Agamemnon*, 245.
10. *Ibid.*, 239.
11. Eurupides, *Iphigenia at Aulis*, 443.
12. *Ibid.*, 9–10.
13. *Ibid.*, 185.
14. *Ibid.*, 439.
15. *Ibid.*, 666.
16. *Ibid.*, 717.
17. *Ibid.*, 1386ff.
18. *Ibid.*, 1410f.
19. The basis of her first reply to Creon: Sophocles, *Antigone*, 450–5.
20. *Ibid.*, 804.
21. *Ibid.*, 807ff.
22. *Ibid.*, 1238f.
23. In this 'later' working, the 'unseemly and reprehensible' [of the earlier working] are 'corrected'. So tells us, in his synopsis of the play, the great Alexandrian scholar and editor Aristophanes 'of Byzantium', admittedly writing a good 600 years later, but who manifestly had access to sources we no longer have.
24. Acts xix.
25. Euripides, *Hippolytus*, 76. Phrases in quotes are from my translation (published Heinemann: London, 1980) for the Royal Shakespeare Company.
26. *Ibid.*, 616.
27. *Ibid.*, 645f.
28. *Ibid.*, 78f.
29. *Ibid.*, 385. The jury will be out for ever as to what exactly Euripides means Phaedra to be saying here. One possible reading is that she is using *aidōs* as a euphemism for sex itself, to her a guilty or shameful activity or desire. The common Classical Greek word for sexual organs is formed from the same mysterious noun.
30. *Ibid.*, 771–2: *kat-aid-estheîsa*, 'brought down by *aidōs*'.
31. *Ibid.*, 752ff.: the ship is *leukópteros*, 'white-winged'; the swell of the sea 'striking [the ship] with its salt' is (a noisy word) *halí-ktypon*. The moorings, as they are cast to bind the ship to her new homeland's shore, are heard in thick-clustered sounds, *ekdēsanto plektàs peismátōn arkhás*; and last of all (Greek word-order) 'onto the mainland earth she sets foot'.
32. *Ibid.*, 1082: lit. 'Oh unhappy mother, oh bitter pangs of giving birth'.
33. *Ibid.*, 1210 *périx aphròn kakhlázōn*: 'swirling foam around'.
34. *Ibid.*, from 1395ff.
35. *Makràn dè leípeis rhaidíōs homilían: ibid.*, 1441.

2

Dying for love: the tragicomedy of Shakespeare's Cleopatra

Robert Wilcher

I

In his study of religion, ideology and power in the drama of Shakespeare and his contemporaries, Jonathan Dollimore rejects 'the Romantic reading' of *Antony and Cleopatra* represented by the work of George Wilson Knight in favour of a cultural materialist perspective upon the play which denies the validity or independent existence of any transcendental value-system that might be taken as an alternative to the political ideology embodied and endorsed by Octavius Caesar and his followers.[1] Wilson Knight's chapter on the 'transcendental humanism' of *Antony and Cleopatra* had argued that the heroic lovers were crowned by the 'potency of love's vision transfiguring mortality' and that their double suicide embodied 'the high metaphysic of love which melts life and death into a final oneness'.[2] While acknowledging that 'the play's captivating poetry' can on occasions be 'rapturously expressive of desire', Dollimore insists that 'the language of desire, far from transcending the power relations which structure this society, is wholly in-formed by them'.[3] It is true that the drama of Antony is illuminated by much of what Dollimore has to say about the 'emerging disjunction' between 'heroic *virtus*' – glossed as an 'idea of self-sufficiency' that 'suggests a transcendent autonomy' – and 'the dominant material forces and relations of power' in the 'new age of imperialist consolidation' that dawns with the victory of Caesar.[4] But it is a distortion of the play to focus exclusively on the predicament of the hero. Without embracing either the Romantic or the cultural materialist analysis unreservedly, I want to suggest that there is not only more than one drama in this radically experimental work of art, but also more than one *kind* of drama, each with its own protagonist, and, furthermore, that these dramas bring into deliberate and creative conflict ways of processing human experience that will always stand in contradiction to each other.[5] In particular, I want to make a case for regarding Cleopatra, who is not given much attention in Dollimore's account of the play, as Shakespeare's most powerful exemplar and champion of a system of values that is neither dependent upon nor subservient to the belief that meaning can only be conferred by the 'material forces and relations of power' operating in the historical continuum over which the Emperor Augustus is the latest figure to assume temporary control.[6] And I shall approach this task by concentrating on Shakespeare's engagement with the theatrical aesthetics of eroticism and death, which comes appropriately to a climax in *Antony and Cleopatra*.

II

The close association between eroticism and death was, of course, inherent in Elizabethan literary usage, which frequently exploited the metaphorical figure that likened orgasm to dying, as in John Donne's 'The Canonization':

> Call us what you will, we are made such by love;
> Call her one, me another fly,
> We are tapers too, and at our own cost die.[7]

Donne was drawing here upon a piece of Aristotelian lore spelt out in another of his poems, 'Farewell to Love': 'since each such act, they say, / Diminisheth the length of life a day.'[8] Each sexual 'dying' hastens the approach of that final climactic moment when 'gluttonous death' will 'instantly unjoint' body and soul.[9]

The conjunction of sexual dying and ultimate death is a prominent feature of Shakespeare's ongoing exploration of human sexuality across the spectrum of his plays. A few examples will have to suffice as prologue to a discussion of its significance in *Antony and Cleopatra*. In the fevered imagination of a young man anticipating his first sexual encounter, the very faculties on which he depends for his experience of being alive are

29

threatened with an overload that can only result in short circuit and extinction:

> I am giddy. Expectation whirls me round.
> Th'imaginary relish is so sweet
> That it enchants my sense. What will it be
> When that the wat'ry palates taste indeed
> Love's thrice-repurèd nectar? Death, I fear me,
> Swooning destruction, or some joy too fine,
> Too subtle-potent, tuned too sharp in sweetness
> For the capacity of my ruder powers.
> (*Troilus and Cressida*, 3.2.16–23)[10]

For another young man, meditating on the benefits of ceasing to be – 'To die, to sleep – / No more, and by a sleep to say we end / The heartache and the thousand natural shocks / That flesh is heir to' – the prospect of death is momentarily as enticing as the prospect of sexual orgasm is for Troilus: ''tis a consummation / Devoutly to be wished' (*Hamlet*, 3.1.62– 6). Killing rather than dying is the only way of freeing himself from the agony of sexual jealousy for the baffled soldier who, in Valerie Traub's powerful reading of *Othello*, idealises and eroticises the corpse of the wife whose active sexuality has so overwhelmed his sense of separate selfhood in the act of consummation that he can 'safely sexualize Desdemona only posthumously, after she is permanently immobilized and sacramentally elevated'.[11] Kissing her sleeping lips, he is almost diverted from the course of justice by her 'balmy breath':

> One more, one more.
> Be thus when thou art dead, and I will kill thee
> And love thee after. One more, and that's the last.
>   *He kisses her*
> So sweet was ne'er so fatal.
> (*Othello*, 5.2.17–20)

But perhaps most productive in relation to Shakespeare's aesthetic practice is the enactment of death as the only possible consummation of a youthful passion that would not be able to retain its purity and intensity in a world riven by family conflict and subject to the processes of time. Romeo closes his life with a gesture of love: 'O true apothecary, / Thy drugs are quick! Thus with a kiss I die' (*Romeo and Juliet*, 5.3.119–20). Juliet, too, consummates love and life with the word which elides death and orgasm, but reinforces it with a gesture that gives the symbolic identification of the two physical events a more powerful charge of eroticism than Romeo's kiss:

> Yea, noise? Then I'll be brief.
>   *She takes Romeo's dagger*
> O happy dagger,
> This is thy sheath! There rust, and let me die. (5.3.168–9)

There is nothing transcendent about these deaths, however, since the two young lovers confirm the supreme worth of the 'passion' that 'lends them power' only by escaping from the inimical environment that threatened its continuance in this life. Their sacrifice of life for love measures the tawdry values of those they leave behind, but it contains no hint of anything beyond death. It is simply better not to be than to drag out existence on a lower plane than that experienced in the brief blaze of their passionate commitment to each other. They survive only as names that can be invoked and as an example that can be relayed to future generations: 'For never was a story of more woe / Than this of Juliet and her Romeo' (5.3.308–9).

John Donne, however, opens up the possibility of transcending a society and a literary discourse in which erotic love is confined to the material sphere of existence or consigned to memory. Later in 'The Canonization', after airing the commonplace that lovers 'die' at their own 'cost' like tapers burning down, he permits his imagination to reach beyond the witty conceit of 'the phoenix riddle' – 'we two being one are it' – to encompass a vision of the erotic relationship that transforms him and his mistress into saints, who will be invoked (not merely remembered) by future generations and petitioned to 'beg from above / A pattern of your love!'[12] The poem turns on a second occurrence of the familiar pun, which takes the lovers to the other side of literal death by means of an erection that is also a resurrection in a linguistic move that ascends the aesthetic and epistemological scales from 'riddle' to 'mystery':

So to one neutral thing both sexes fit
We die and rise the same, and prove
Mysterious by this love.

In returning now to *Antony and Cleopatra*, I want to suggest that Egypt's queen becomes the vehicle for a similar move into transcendence which depends upon a daring and complex management of theatrical genres.

III

The first thing to notice is the unusual structure of this play. It differs from the common Shakespearean pattern by having two distinct and widely separated climaxes, with the death of Antony at the end of Act 4 and the death of Cleopatra delayed until the end of Act 5. In the only other instances of two characters sharing equally the focus of tragic attention, both deaths are concentrated into a flurry of activity towards the close of the final act. Romeo and Juliet, as we have seen, die within moments of each other and the two Roman heroes, Brutus and Cassius, whose deaths constitute the tragic climax of *Julius Caesar*, both commit suicide at the end of the battle against Octavius and Antony. The structure of *Antony and Cleopatra* is, of course, partly determined by its source in Plutarch's *Lives*, but the fact that this *is* a history play as well as a tragedy affects the way in which the double climax is handled in theatrical terms.

Antony, you might say, belongs to two different dramatic plots, both of which terminate at the end of Act 4. In one of them, which might be called *The History of Antony and Caesar*, he is the antagonist of Octavius and his suicide in defeat seals the triumphant rise to supreme power of 'the young Roman boy'. In the other plot, which might be called *The Tragedy of Antony*, he is the lover of Cleopatra and he kills himself when the news of her death makes continued life unbearable:

So it must be, for now
All length is torture. Since the torch is out,
Lie down, and stray no farther. (4.15.45–7)

In the same way, Cleopatra is also involved in two plots – or her story can be viewed from the two different perspectives of history play and tragedy:

32

in the one, she figures as the ruler of Egypt and her fate is bound up with the political plans of Octavius, which leads her to take refuge in her monument after the battle; in the other, she is the heroine of a tragedy of love, for whom 'All's but naught' when her lover is dead. 'Look, / Our lamp is spent, it's out,' she exclaims to Charmian and Iras, echoing Antony's earlier image for the fading of purpose from the world. Like Antony, this Cleopatra cannot contemplate survival without her lover:

> Shall I abide
> In this dull world, which in thy absence is
> No better than a sty? (4.16.62–4)

In his dying moments, Antony projects two different generic images of himself, as if he is aware of reaching the climax of two different kinds of play. As he comes into the presence of Cleopatra for the last time, mortally wounded but not dispatched by his own hand, he raises the situation to tragic grandeur with a piece of magnificent rhetoric that is typical of Antony, the heroic lover:

> I am dying, Egypt, dying. Only
> I here importune death awhile until
> Of many thousand kisses the poor last
> I lay upon thy lips. (4.16.19–22)

Magnificent, but not transcendent: he is like a grizzled Romeo, dying to this world upon a kiss. And Cleopatra, too, is concentrating on the experience of their last moments together in 'poetry of great tenderness', which is yet 'quite clear-eyed' in its acknowledgement of both the 'life-enhancing value of their love' and its imminent end.[13] When he has been drawn up to her place of refuge in the monument, she greets him with words that insist upon one final surge of life before death parts them:

> O come, come, come!
> *They heave Antony aloft to Cleopatra.*
> And welcome, welcome! Die when thou hast lived,
> Quicken with kissing. Had my lips that power,
> Thus would I wear them out. (4.16.38–41)[14]

As death approaches ever nearer, Antony is preoccupied with Cleopatra's safety in an Egypt now under the control of his rival – 'Gentle, hear me. / None about Caesar trust but Proculeius' (4.16.49–50) – and with the image he will leave behind him as a man who was once 'the greatest prince o'th' world, / The noblest':

> and do now not basely die,
> Not cowardly put off my helmet to
> My countryman; a Roman by a Roman
> Valiantly vanquished. (4.16.57–60)

Both versions of Antony – the tragic lover and the heroic warrior – have spoken their last, and Cleopatra delivers over his body the combination of lament and praise that conventionally accompanies the passing of one of the great spirits of the earth at the end of a Shakespearean tragedy:

> O, withered is the garland of the war.
> The soldier's pole is fall'n. Young boys and girls
> Are level now with men. The odds is gone,
> And there is nothing left remarkable
> Beneath the visiting moon. (4.16.66–70)

The last words of Act 4 lead us to expect that the play's action will be rapidly concluded, with the surviving protagonist of the tragic story committing herself to death like Juliet:

> We'll bury him, and then what's brave, what's noble,
> Let's do it after the high Roman fashion,
> And make death proud to take us. Come, away.
> This case of that huge spirit now is cold.
> Ah, women, women! Come. We have no friend
> But resolution, and the briefest end. (4.16.88–93)

Instead of being 'brief' like Juliet, however, Cleopatra makes the audience wait the entire length of another act before fulfilling the project she has just conceived – of doing it 'after the high Roman fashion'.

The next scene begins *not* with the completion or even the continuation of the tragedy of Antony and Cleopatra, but with the concluding ceremonies of the military and political drama in which Caesar regards himself and Antony as the primary characters, and casts Cleopatra as a mere distraction. Caesar is still dealing with the aftermath of victory when Decretas brings him news of Antony's suicide, and his first reaction is to register the significance of this event for a world dominated by Dollimore's 'material forces and relations of power': 'The death of Antony / Is not a single doom; in the name lay / A moiety of the world' (5.1.17–19). He then launches into a generous tribute to his 'brother', 'competitor' and 'mate in empire' in just the kind of speech that might bring a history play to a formal close:

> I must perforce
> Have shown to thee such a declining day,
> Or look on thine. We could not stall together
> In the whole world. ... – that our stars,
> Unreconciliable, should divide
> Our equalness to this. (5.1.37–47)

But this movement towards closure is interrupted by a messenger, who brings news that Cleopatra has locked herself in the monument, and Caesar turns from the final act of his military contest with Antony to the ongoing concerns of politics and his plan to make the Egyptian queen the central exhibit in his victory procession when he returns to Rome. As he sends Proculeius to her a new dramatic plot is set in motion, in which Cleopatra's determination to 'make death proud to take us' – another pun that eroticises the moment of death – will come into direct conflict with Caesar's determination to capture her alive:

> Go, and say
> We purpose her no shame. Give her what comforts
> The quality of her passion shall require,
> Lest in her greatness, by some mortal stroke,
> She do defeat us; for her life in Rome
> Would be eternal in our triumph. (5.1.61–6)

The rest of Act 5 will pursue this new drama to its conclusion in which the Queen of Egypt *does* defeat the Emperor of Rome by a 'mortal stroke' and contrives to achieve her *own* eternal triumph. This final phase of *Antony and Cleopatra* – which modern editions designate Act 5, Scene 2 – is modelled on the structure of a tragedy in the classical manner, and is in stark contrast to the extravagant geographical and temporal sweep of the history play in the first four acts, which embraces the inset tragedy of Enobarbus and culminates in the tragedy of Antony. The prologue to the formally concentrated *Tragedy of Cleopatra* occurs in the first scene of Act 5, when, as we have just seen, Caesar lays down the terms of his ensuing contest with Cleopatra. From then on there is a single action, confined to the single location of the monument, performed continuously, with each episode devoted to an encounter between the protagonist (who never leaves the stage) and one of a series of visitors. It is a perfect example of the Aristotelian tragic machine, which has at its centre the crucial confrontation upon which the resolution of the dramatic action will depend.

IV

Before we look at the use to which Shakespeare puts this remarkable imitation of classical art, however, we need to consider another aesthetic element which disrupts and undermines the genres of history play and tragedy that have so far dominated the discussion – the element of carnival comedy in which Cleopatra is most at home. As defined by Mikhail Bakhtin, the 'festive laughter' of this kind of comedy 'is gay, triumphant, and at the same time mocking, deriding'.[15] J.L. Simmons makes the most pertinent Shakespearean comparison: 'In Egypt, as in Falstaff's tavern, the sanctions and restrictions of society have been overturned into one endless holiday spirit.'[16] Much of Cleopatra's 'infinite variety' stems from her Falstaffian love of play-acting and the unpredictability that makes her such an enchanting companion – as Antony readily admits in the opening scene:

> Fie, wrangling queen,
> Whom everything becomes – to chide, to laugh,
> To weep; how every passion fully strives
> To make itself, in thee, fair and admired! (1.1.50–3)

One early example of this subversive playfulness offers an insight into the system of values that governs Cleopatra's carnival world. Her teasing prompts Antony into an eloquent expression of his commitment to the 'sport' of love rather than the 'business' of power:

> Let Rome in Tiber melt, and the wide arch
> Of the ranged empire fall. Here is my space.
> Kingdoms are clay. Our dungy earth alike
> Feeds beast as man. The nobleness of life
> Is to do thus; when such a mutual pair
> And such a twain can do't – in which I bind
> On pain of punishment the world to weet –
> We stand up peerless. (1.1.35–42)

The ringing grandeur of this is capped by Cleoptra's mocking reply – 'Excellent falsehood!' – which deflates his rhetoric and leads her into a witty proof that they are both little better than fools – an illustration of Bakhtin's insight that the laughter of carnival is 'directed at all and everyone, including the carnival's participants'.[17] In this exchange, Shakespeare's verbal art draws us into responding to both Antony's poetry of love's magnificent excess and Cleopatra's joyful debunking of that excess. But behind the teasing is a vital affirmation. At the heart of Cleopatra's comic world is the conviction that *falsehood* can be *excellent* in its imaginative daring, even though the creative lies of poetry may be vulnerable to the sour judgement of those Roman observers who can see Antony only as a 'strumpet's fool' upon whom 'dotage' has taken such a hold that it 'o'erflows the measure'.[18]

Antony's declaration of the 'peerless' nature of the love of 'such a mutual pair' belongs not to carnival but to another kind of comedy, defined by Northrop Frye in the third essay of his *Anatomy of Criticism* as the 'fourth phase of comedy', which begins to move 'out of the world of experience into the ideal world of innocence and romance'. Frye describes this ideal realm of romance as a 'green world' and relates it specifically to the world of desires that is brought into being by the imagination:

> The green world has analogies, not only to the fertile world of ritual, but to the dream world that we create out of our own desires. This dream

world collides with the stumbling and blinded follies of the world of experience, of Theseus' Athens with its idiotic marriage law, of Duke Frederick and his melancholy tyranny, of Leontes and his mad jealousy, of the Court Party with their plots and intrigues, and yet proves strong enough to impose the form of desire on it. Thus Shakespearean comedy illustrates, as clearly as any *mythos* we have, the archetypal function of literature in visualizing the world of desire, not as an escape from 'reality,' but as the genuine form of the world that human life tries to imitate.[19]

When his imagination is dominated by the green world of Cleopatra's Egypt, Antony's poetic utterances create what one might call an heroic version of this *mythos*.

That Cleopatra's way of evaluating human experience partakes of both carnival and green world comic values is demonstrated most clearly in Act 1, Scene 3.[20] She has been playfully taunting Antony in the role of jealous mistress to a married man in order to distract him from the 'Roman thought' that is tempting him back towards Caesar's world of 'business', when she is stopped momentarily in her tracks by the news that his wife, Fulvia, is dead. She quickly recovers, however, and uses his lack of sorrow to berate him on her own account: 'Now I see, I see, / In Fulvia's death how mine received shall be' (1.3.64–5). Antony protests that his love for *her* is 'true' and will stand 'an honourable trial'. Her reply encapsulates one of the principles upon which her comic vision of the world is founded:

> So Fulvia told me.
> I prithee turn aside and weep for her,
> Then bid adieu to me, and say the tears
> Belong to Egypt. Good now, play one scene
> Of excellent dissembling, and let it look
> Like perfect honour. (1.3.75–80)

Those lines are fundamental to the challenge that Cleopatra will eventually make to Caesar's world of 'business', in which 'the strong necessity of time' overrides all other values. If the dissembling is excellent enough, how can the simulated emotion be distinguished from the real thing? Indeed, is the notion of such a distinction tenable or even necessary? In Cleopatra's creative vision, performance is all, and a part played with sufficient commitment and exuberance may establish its own validity: an imaginative order may be called into existence which transcends the mundane realm in which wives have prior claims over mistresses. In such an order, conjured into being by words and gestures, the radiance of eternity may outshine the dull processes of time.

After the final battle is lost, Antony is convinced that he has been betrayed by 'this false soul of Egypt' and vows that 'the witch shall die'. But as soon as he learns that Cleopatra has taken her own life (a lie carefully rehearsed by the queen so that it will have maximum impact on her angry lover), he not only discards his identity as heroic soldier – 'Unarm, Eros. The long day's task is done, / And we must sleep' (4.15.35–6) – but he also embraces Cleopatra's imaginative world in which the death that is the proper end of tragedy (after which the only kind of survival is a story told to future generations) is countermanded by the perfected relationship that is the proper end of comedy:

> Eros! – I come, my queen. – Eros! – Stay for me.
> Where souls do couch on flowers, we'll hand in hand,
> And with our sprightly port make the ghosts gaze.
> Dido and her Aeneas shall want troops,
> And all the haunt be ours. Come, Eros, Eros! (4.15.50–4)

Coppélia Kahn has pointed out that the repeated invocation of Eros turns Antony's comrade-in-arms into 'a displaced allegorical representation' of sexual desire and that 'the panting cadences' of the *double entendre* 'would then suggest that Antony envisions suicide as the very consummation of his passion for Cleopatra'.[21] As he falls on his sword, the catastrophe of a tragedy is transformed by a feat of imagination into the union of two lovers that marks the ritual conclusion of a romantic comedy:

> But I will be
> A bridegroom in my death, and run into't
> As to a lover's bed. (4.15.99–101)

Antony does not maintain this transcendent vision up to the point of death, being drawn back into the orbit of the history play and expending his final thoughts upon Cleopatra's safety in the new world ruled by Caesar and his own personal heroic status as 'a Roman by a Roman / Valiantly vanquished'. But Cleopatra herself is another matter.

V

Cleopatra opens her own tragedy by clearly identifying the values that are at stake in her contest with Caesar:

> 'Tis paltry to be Caesar.
> Not being Fortune, he's but Fortune's knave,
> A minister of her will. And it is great
> To do that thing that ends all other deeds,
> Which shackles accidents, and bolts up change. (5.2.2–6)

She will prove her greatness by deliberately embracing the death that will put her beyond the reach of accident and change, the powers that govern the world over which Caesar can now call himself lord and which render his ambitions 'paltry'. But in the episodes with Proculeius and Dolabella, there are hints that she is not yet fully committed to doing 'that thing that ends all other deeds', in spite of her earlier vow to 'do it after the high Roman fashion'. Why has she kept a portion of her treasure, if she is resolved to make 'the briefest end'? Why does she try to persuade Caesar that 'majesty, to keep decorum, must / No less beg than a kingdom' (5.2.17–18)? Why is she so anxious to know whether Caesar intends to lead her captive through the streets of Rome? Why, above all, does she send Proculeius back to him with a submissive message?

> I hourly learn
> A doctrine of obedience, and would gladly
> Look him i'th' face. (5.2.30–32)

She may be merely mocking Caesar's apparent power over her – knowing that it is 'paltry' compared with the greatness of the act she is preparing to perform. She may be playing for time, lulling him into a false sense of security until she can seize her opportunity to 'make death proud' to 'take' her. She may be entertaining the possibility that she might yet come to some accommodation with this latest Roman conqueror of Egypt. After all, she joked earlier about *her* conquest of '[b]road-fronted Caesar' and 'great Pompey' (1.5.29–34) and may be nursing a secret hope that this new warrior will also be susceptible to her charms.

In the confrontation which forms the fulcrum of the condensed dramatic action of Act 5, she plays the part of an abject victim, kneeling meekly and refusing Caesar's request that she rise:

> Sir, the gods
> Will have it thus. My master and my lord
> I must obey. (5.2.111–13)

Martha Tuck Rozett interprets this scene as a piece of 'elaborate play-acting' by both characters, in which 'Cleopatra enacts the humble and self-belittling captive and Caesar the gracious captor.'[22] Just as plausible is the view that Egypt's queen is trying to work her magic upon the Roman general, as she has already worked it on Dolabella. Indeed, her comment on the interview may be taken to indicate that she was seriously tempted to betray her honourable purpose until she saw through Caesar's game: 'He words me, girls, he words me, that I should not / Be noble to myself' (5.2.187–8). Perhaps she would have been content to live, if she had been able to make any impression on this cold politician.[23] The point, however, is not that we should seek to convict her or acquit her of vacillation and unworthy motives, but that we are not given enough evidence to be sure either way. Shakespeare brings us up sharply against the impossibility of telling the difference between 'excellent dissembling' and 'perfect honour'.

In the world of the history play, the mistress of 'excellent falsehood' may be dismissed as a 'triple-turned whore'. But in the final episode of her tragedy the distinctions between dissembling and honour cease to matter and the creative imagination that makes her the queen of comedy becomes the means of transcending the 'dungy earth' over which Caesar reigns as emperor.[24] Convinced that she will be 'shown / In Rome', she gives orders for the construction of one final, unforgettable image:

> Show me, my women, like a queen. Go fetch
> My best attires. I am again for Cydnus
> To meet Mark Antony. (5.2.223–5)

Of all her roles, she chooses the one celebrated by Enobarbus in his famous 'barge' speech as the ultimate expression of her self; and as she imagines it, with the full intensity of that creative energy which will always be felt to 'o'erflow the measure' by those who are confined by the expedient and the practical, so she looks beyond death to a continuation of a relationship that she now claims as the greatest reality she has known:

> Give me my robe. Put on my crown. I have
> Immortal longings in me. ... – methinks I hear
> Antony call. I see him rouse himself
> To praise my noble act. (5.2.275–80)

Like Antony as he prepared to end his life, she transforms the tragic ceremony of death into the comic ceremony of marriage, triumphantly imposing what Frye termed 'the form of desire' upon 'the world of experience': 'Husband I come. / Now to that name my courage prove my title' (5.2.282–3). In this exalted state of mind her eternal marriage to Antony translates death itself into an aspect of sexual play – 'The stroke of death is as a lover's pinch, / Which hurts, and is desired' (5.2.290–1) – and almost her last words call up yet another image, more simple but no less sublime, of the natural consequences of the sexual desire that is consummated as she is 'taken' by death:

> Peace, peace.
> Dost thou not see my baby at my breast,
> That sucks the nurse asleep? (5.2.303–5)

Charmian gives her verdict on this last, great performance by a woman whom 'everything becomes': 'It is well done, and fitting for a princess / Descended of so many royal kings' (5.2.321–2). Duncan Harris argues that the effect of this brilliantly contrived spectacle on a theatre audience goes beyond the confirmation of her ultimate loyalty to love and to Antony:

Cleopatra's death scene finally shows us what we have been asked to envision, but it does more than show us the Cleopatra of Enobarbus' famous lines. Not only the meeting on the River Cydnus but also the special qualities of the lovers embodied in their distinctive language, the image of Antony created in Cleopatra's eulogies, and the lovers' death-haunted dreams of each other are finally and convincingly substantiated on the stage.[25]

If it was 'well done', like a perfect work of art, it scarcely matters that doubts can still be cast on Cleopatra's moral character – that Caesar can report that 'her physician tells me / She hath pursued conclusions infinite / Of easy ways to die' (5.2.348–50).

At the end, Caesar returns us to the rational and material world of history and politics, in which causes of death are inquired into and the appropriate public gestures are made: 'Our army shall / In solemn show attend this funeral, / And then to Rome' (5.2.357–9). But if that supplies the 'fitting' conclusion for a *history* play, the exhilarating climax of the *tragicomedy* of Cleopatra has provided its audiences with an experience of transcending the world that is dominated by power relations and subject to accident and change – an experience engineered by a different kind of power, that of the human faculty that can devise an aesthetic consummation in which experiences of death and love unite in a single erotic fantasy.

Notes

1. Jonathan Dollimore, *Radical Tragedy: Religion, Ideology and Power in the Drama of Shakespeare and his Contemporaries* (Brighton, 1984), pp. 206–7.
2. George Wilson Knight, *The Imperial Theme: Further Interpretations of Shakespeare's Tragedies including the Roman Plays*, 3rd edn (London, 1951), pp. 249, 262.
3. Dollimore, *Radical Tragedy*, p. 207.
4. *Ibid.*, pp. 206, 209.
5. See Barbara Vincent's discussion of 'the contest of genres' in this play, which has generated a 'conflict of interpretations' among the critics (p. 60), in 'Shakespeare's *Antony and Cleopatra* and the Rise of Comedy', *English Literary Renaissance*, 12 (1982), pp. 53–86. See also Robert Wilcher, '*Antony and Cleopatra* and Genre Criticism', in Nigel Wood (ed.), *Antony and Cleopatra*, Theory in Practice Series (Buckingham, 1996), pp. 92–125.
6. Leonard Tennenhouse, another cultural materialist critic, dismisses the kind of interpretation in which 'sexuality – at least from a modern perspective – appears to transcend politics in the play' (p. 142). He devotes more space than Dollimore to Cleopatra, regarding her as 'the ultimate subject and object of illicit desire', who 'threatens to pollute the aristocratic community' (p. 144) and whose death is a 'ritual purification' that delivers 'the world over to patriarchy' (p. 146). Leonard Tennenhouse, *Power on Display: The Politics of Shakespeare's Genres* (New York and London, 1986).
7. John Donne, *The Complete English Poems*, ed. A.J. Smith (Harmondsworth, 1971), p. 47.
8. *Ibid.*, pp. 56–7.
9. 'Holy Sonnet 6', *ibid.*, p. 311.
10. All quotations from the plays of Shakespeare are from *The Complete Works*, ed. Stanley Wells and Gary Taylor (Oxford, 1988). Act, scene and line numbers are given in brackets in the text.
11. Valerie Traub, *Desire and Anxiety: Circulations of Sexuality in Shakespearean Drama* (London and New York, 1992), pp. 40–41.
12. Donne, *Complete English Poems*, pp. 47–8.
13. Derick R.C. Marsh, *Passion Lends Them Power: A Study of Shakespeare's Love Tragedies* (Manchester, 1976), p. 191.
14. Pope emended 'when' to 'where' in this passage and was followed by many subsequent editors, but the Folio reading makes perfectly good sense: 'live once more before you die'.
15. Mikhail Bakhtin, *Rabelais and His World*, trans. Hélène Iswolsky (Bloomington, IN, 1984), p. 8.
16. J.L. Simmons, 'The Comic Pattern and Vision in *Antony and Cleopatra*', *English Literary History*, 36 (1969), pp. 494–5.
17. Bakhtin, *Rabelais and His World*, p. 8.
18. Bakhtin describes the self-validation of carnival values for those who commit themselves to its festive spirit: 'While carnival lasts, there is no other life outside it. During carnival time life is subject only to its laws, that is, the laws of its own freedom' (*Rabelais and His World*, p. 7).
19. Northrop Frye, *Anatomy of Criticism: Four Essays* (New York, 1965), pp. 181–4.
20. Vincent sees Cleopatra as 'a particularly compelling embodiment of the conventions of romance' and interprets Egypt as 'an eternal realm, which transfixes Romans in the endlessly recurrent and fertilizing experience of love' ('*Antony and Cleopatra* and the Rise of Comedy', pp. 56–7).

44

21. Coppélia Kahn, *Roman Shakespeare: Warriors, Wounds, and Women* (London and New York, 1997), p. 131.
22. Martha Tuck Rozett, 'The Comic Structures of Tragic Endings: The Suicide Scenes in *Romeo and Juliet* and *Antony and Cleopatra*', *Shakespeare Quarterly*, 36 (1985), p. 161.
23. In *Elizabethan Love Tragedy 1587–1625* (London, 1972), Leonora Leet Brodwin reads Cleopatra's behaviour in this way: 'Having tried those means prescribed by the decorum of nobility whereby she might preserve her life with honor, and failing in these, she can now meet death, not as a mad dog, but a sovereign queen' (p. 250).
24. Rozett comments that 'Shakespeare's Cleopatra embarks upon preparations for her final act with a contagious liveliness that makes the characters seem as if they are participating in a comic resolution – which, in a sense, they are' ('Comic Structures of Tragic Endings', p. 161).
25. Duncan S. Harris, '"Again for Cydnus": The Dramaturgical Resolution of *Antony and Cleopatra*', *Studies in English Literature*, 17 (1977), p. 228.

3

Desire and destruction in the drama of Georg Büchner

Karoline Gritzner

Georg Büchner was about to embark on a university career in natural sciences when he died from typhus fever in 1837, at the age of twenty-three. His brief activities as a political revolutionary resulted in persecution and exile, and his literary work remained obscure during his lifetime – only *Danton's Death* saw publication (in a bowdlerised form), none of his plays were staged until many decades after his death, and his *Woyzeck* remained an incomplete manuscript. Büchner's untimely death continues to draw our attention to the radically unfinished nature of his achievements, which eventually began to receive scholarly and public attention in the late nineteenth and early twentieth century. Today he is generally acknowledged as a forerunner of modern literature and theatre, as an innovator of dramatic form and precursor of practically all major modernist movements (from naturalism to expressionism, absurdism and docudrama). When Heiner Müller speaks of Büchner the 'wound',[1] he reminds us of the political significance of Büchner's fractured aesthetic project in which we discover and rediscover an immediate, urgent, agonising expression of human desire and human frailty staged against the backdrop of a damaged world, *our* world.

Materialist readings of Büchner's work, such as those offered by Lukács and Glebke, argue that Büchner fiercely rejected all manifestations of idealism (philosophical, aesthetic, moral) in favour of a deterministic worldview; and that his revolutionary attitude was the result of his deep concern with the 'economic liberation of the masses'.[2] According to this view, the literary practice of Büchner the materialist and socialist was primarily concerned with exploring the human being's objectified existence under conditions of social and material exploitation. For example, prostitution in *Danton's Death* is understood as a form of sexual and class oppression in a patriarchal system; and more than any other character it is Woyzeck who represents the ultimate victim of economic poverty and ruthless social oppression. Even Büchner's numerous references to uncontrollable human 'nature' in expressions such as the prostitute Marion's 'It's simply my nature – can anyone escape it?',[3] or Woyzeck's 'But, Doctor, when it's a call of nature!'[4] are explained as 'merely the necessary reaction to circumstances' (*'nur die notwendige Reaktion auf die Umstände'*).[5] A forceful example of Büchner's anti-idealist determinism is found in this letter to his parents:

> I feel contempt for no one, least of all because of their intellect or education, since no one can prevent himself becoming a fool or a criminal; since we would presumably all be equal if our circumstances were equal; and since circumstances lie beyond our control.[6]

There is little doubt that in Büchner's work sexuality is significant as a socio-political issue, but in my view it cannot be reduced to an empirical or historical question alone. The tendency to understand his deterministic worldview and presumed rejection of free will as a mere reaction to economics is unsatisfactory and reductive when one tries to make sense of the status of eroticism and death – a thematic relationship which is typically *resistant* to deterministic explanations – in Büchner's work. I would argue that the encounter with eroticism and death in his drama brings to the surface a tragic worldview in which fatalism combines with a residual (post-Romantic) idealism, which suspends our ability to draw clear distinctions between necessity and possibility, the real and the imaginary.

Attitudes to idealism and romanticism

Büchner's attitude to the established conventions of idealism in philosophy and the arts in the early nineteenth century was ambivalent and contradictory. The dominant Hegelianism of the time put forward a unifying philosophy of spirit and a totalising conception of history as the progress of reason. Having lost the energetic, youthfully erratic and decidedly anti-philosophical spirit of the German *Sturm und Drang* ('storm and stress') movement of the 1770s (which inaugurated a 'literary' revolution before the political French Revolution), the subsequent period of so-called Jena Romanticism (1800–1810) was characterised by a preoccupation with subjectivity, the nature of the Absolute, and theoretical system-building. German romanticism and Hegelian idealism still provided the cultural and ideological context of Büchner's formative years in the 1820s and 1830s, a time during which his oppositional artistic and political sensibility began to take shape. As Maurice Benn has argued, Büchner's 'metaphysical revolt' was primarily directed against Christianity and the conception of spiritual freedom as celebrated in philosophical as well as literary idealism (Kant and Schiller).[7] His work contains a critique of poverty and social injustice combined with an empirical, materialist and scientific outlook on society, history and nature. But Büchner the socialist writer, founder of the revolutionary 'Society for Human Rights' and co-editor of an illegal political pamphlet, also, at the same time, held the opinion that the human being was merely 'froth on the waves' and that history was pervaded by a 'hideous fatalism'.[8] This tension between his political awareness of a need for social change and his expressions of fatalism and futility continues to preoccupy Büchner studies, with scholars such as Reddick arguing that the statements on fatalism and determinism are capricious and ultimately insignificant expressions of a thinker who 'was wholly, extravagantly positive and harmonistic in his fundamental assumptions'.[9] His interest in the spirit of the French Revolution, ambiguously captured in *Danton's Death*, and his astute awareness of social inequality, poverty, the exploitation and suffering of the working classes not only in his region but in Germany as a whole indicate that, in short, his political awareness and activities seem to require an optimistic outlook, a belief in the possibility of social and political change resulting from the breakdown of old structures.

Others maintain that the consciousness of suffering which gives rise to revolutionary praxis can itself be mapped onto a tragic, fatalistic worldview according to which humanity equals suffering which equals the desire to end suffering by means of a revolution. The most convincing supporter of this cyclical view was the Marxist literary critic Raymond Williams, who stated that all revolutions are 'born in pity and terror' and therefore are 'inescapably tragic'.[10] As Williams has shown, tragedy might well prove a useful concept for Marxism, and, more recently, Eagleton has argued along similar lines. Eagleton tries to reclaim tragedy for the left ('the left should not airily ditch the notion as antiquated and elitist'[11]) by arguing that the concept of the tragic makes us aware of our finitude, constraints and frailty, and that today such awareness carries political and ethical value in any attempt to transform the status quo. Perhaps Büchner was the first socialist with a tragic sensibility who showed us in historical dramas such as *Danton's Death* that '[t]he tragic contradiction is clear: the practice of revolution may itself give the lie to the very humanity in whose name it is conducted.'[12]

It is in Büchner's openness to the ultimately unanswerable questions surrounding human desire, passion, love, sexuality and death that important aspects of his tragic sensibility and romantic disposition become apparent. This is a sensibility grounded in the principles of 'storm and stress' which share an interest in the irrational aspects of human nature, the powers of intuition and instinct which urge (*drängen*) us on and on, causing unpredictable transgressive action or death-like ennui. Danton, afflicted by the excesses of the Revolution, in which sex and death collide, moves variably between states of sexual intimacy and existential loneliness. And the torn soul of Woyzeck is a sharp blade racing through the world with a desperate passion so fixed on the erotic object that he loses all direction and control. Hot fever, the desire that undoes the mind, transmutes into the cold grip of death.

Büchner writes to his beloved Minna (we hear the voice of the tormented Romantic Lenz, of whom more later):

My silence torments you, and me too, but I just couldn't help myself. Dear, dear heart, do you forgive me? I have just come in from outside. A single resonant tone from a thousand larks bursts through the brooding summer air, a heavy bank of cloud wanders over the earth, the booming wind rings out like its melodious tread. The spring air freed me from my frozen, rigid state. I was horrified at myself. A sense of being dead continually pervaded me. Everyone's face was the face of death, with glassy eyes and waxen cheeks, and then, when the whole machinery began to grind away with jerking limbs and grating voice … oh, poor screaming musicians that we are …[13]

Büchner's critical attitude to the idealism of the Romantic movement is expressed in some of his personal letters as well as his literary work. The novella *Lenz* (written in 1835/6 and left in near-completed draft form) is based on the troubled life of the *Sturm und Drang* poet Jakob Michael Reinhold Lenz (1751–1792). Büchner presents a complex picture of a gifted individual who is afflicted by psychological, moral and spiritual uncertainty. In addition, the novella rejects idealisation in classical literature and puts forward a new anti-Aristotelian theory of drama that emphasises theatre's need to respond to the needs and preoccupations of the common people. Büchner's Lenz admires Shakespeare for having put individuals on stage rather than generic, lifeless puppets, an attitude that echoes the historical Lenz's 1771 study on theatre, '*Anmerkungen über das Theater*' ('Notes on the Theatre'). In this text Lenz engages with Shakespearean drama and argues that Aristotle's claims, according to which fate and the gods determine human behaviour and constitute tragic action, are no longer valid for the Christian world of the eighteenth century. The actions of the Greeks were determined by an 'iron fate' (*eisernes Schicksal*) which remained unexplainable and mysterious, but the modern, enlightened attitude is quite different. 'We hate actions whose origins cannot be explained, and we take no part in them.' ('*Wir aber hassen solche Handlungen, von denen wir die Ursachen nicht einsehen, und nehmen keinen Teil dran.*')[14] The modern age is sensitive to the particularity of individual human nature and this is reflected in a new theatrical aesthetic. Thus, the modern drama will present 'characters who create their circumstances' ('*Charakteren, die sich ihre Begebenheiten erschaffen*') and who are able to 'turn the entire great machinery independently and steadily' ('*die selbstständig und unveränderlich die ganze große Maschine selbst drehen*').[15] Consequently, the godheads in the clouds are reduced to spectators – no longer of lifeless images or static marionettes, but of real, complex human beings. Lenz's faith in the possibilities of self-determining humanity was, of course, a reflection of Enlightenment ideas; but the revolutionary fervour with which he expressed his ideas tended to blur the boundaries between rational explanation and passionate experience, leading to his own mental breakdown.

Büchner's story of Lenz, too, emphasises the importance of representing individual action and emotion on the stage rather than abstract images or lifeless puppets, as is articulated in the text's famous discourse on art (the *Kunstgespräch*), which contains a decidedly romantic sensibility: 'The writers and artists I like above all are those that most strongly convey the reality of nature, with the result that their work engages my feelings.'[16] ('*Der Dichter … ist mir der Liebste, der mir die Natur am Wirklichsten gibt, so dass ich ueber seinem Gebild fuehle.*')

However, Büchner's narrative treatment of Lenz's personal life and opinions on art reveals important contradictory perspectives on aesthetics and human nature alike. There exists an interesting tension, not only in this short story but in Büchner's whole literary *oeuvre*, between the claims of self-directed individuality on the one hand and the forces of a supra-individual determinism and fatefulness on the other, realised not least in humanity's subordination to the 'great machinery' of history (the French Revolution and subsequent rebellions in continental Europe during Büchner's time). Especially his dramatic work expresses multiple perspectives on the individual's responses to inner and outer determinism, showing the self in conflict between the supra-individual forces of political/historical necessity and the drives of inner nature. However, despite Büchner's aesthetic rejection of the determinism or 'iron fate' of the mythical ancient world as represented in classical tragedy, his project cannot be neatly summed up in terms of a post-Enlightenment materialist philosophy either, one which argues that all aspects of human pain and suffering are the direct, unequivocal effects of economic and social exploitation. To reduce Büchner to a spokesperson of a new anti-idealist, economic–empirical determinism that 'explains' (and thereby reduces) individual human pain and suffering as a direct result of systemic violence, social injustice and material poverty, is to put forward a homogeneous, static, one-dimensional picture of humanity which would contradict Büchner's intentions of showing the contradictory nature and 'flesh and blood' of the human being.

To some, Büchner's critique of abstract idealisation in representational art is not, however, a rejection of concepts such as beauty, harmony or even wholeness. As Reddick suggests, one could interpret Büchner's presentation of fractured, suffering and alienated human experiences as the negative expression of an underlying yearning for unity and harmony (see his book *The Shattered Whole*). According to this view, the artist's preferred paratactic and elliptical style and his effective employment of textual fragments and (at his time still uncommon) use of dramatic prose and 'ordinary', unheroic language do not detract from an underlying comprehensive social, political and philosophical vision. For a short but significant period of his young life Büchner was politically active: he was the founder of two protest movements and the co-editor of a political pamphlet, *The Hessian Messenger* (*Der Hessische Landbote*), which called for a revolution among the impoverished peasant and worker communities in the Grand-Duchy of Hesse. The government banned the publication and persecuted the men behind it. Büchner's friend and co-editor, Friedrich Ludwig Weidig, was eventually captured, tortured and killed; Büchner himself abandoned work on the pamphlet, discontinued his political activism and escaped to Switzerland, where he was about to embark on a university career in medical science. In a letter to his fiancé Minna Jaeglé in 1834 he writes:

> I've been studying the history of the French Revolution. I felt as though utterly crushed by the hideous fatalism of history. I find in human nature a terrible sameness, in human circumstances an ineluctable violence vouchsafed to all and to none. Individuals but froth on the waves, greatness a mere coincidence, the mastery of geniuses a dance of puppets, a ridiculous struggle against an iron law that can at best be recognised, but never mastered.[17]

The contradiction between his political activism and his tragic, nihilistic outlook on life remains of great interest to Büchner scholarship and it offers a key contextual perspective on the treatment of sexuality, love and death in his work.

Büchner's political and aesthetic sensibilities cannot be divorced from one another; both are shaped by his outlook on human and non-human nature. His engagement with 'nature' partly suggests an influence of the work produced by the earlier *Sturm und Drang* movement, of which Goethe was an enthusiastic early member and which he called, in his autobiographic *Poetry and Truth*, a literary revolution.[18] Büchner's work displays general aspects of the Romantic sensibility, such as a critique of Enlightenment rationality and an emphasis on emotion and feelings as the main effect of art. However, by the time he was producing literary work in the 1830s Romantic ideals in Germany had become consolidated in a depoliticised Hegelian-inspired idealism. In other words, Büchner writes in a post-revolutionary context and from a post-Romantic but not anti-Romantic perspective. His aesthetic impulse may be usefully compared to the work of the influential German poet Heinrich Heine (1797–1856), who attempted to renew the German Romantic movement by drawing attention away from an exclusively idealist preoccupation with the medieval and the transcendental towards a social engagement with the here and now. His love of folk songs and folk culture, his occasional satirical tone and his general disillusionment with the advancing materialism and social inequality of his time can also be observed in Büchner, who was equally outraged by the exploitation and suffering of the poor and whose literary work reveals a deep compassion for the social underdog. Furthermore, Heine was an influential figure in the socialist literary grouping called 'Young Germany' in the 1830s and 1840s (as well as Karl Gutzkow, Büchner's main supporter). Büchner himself was associated with the group and endorsed their political activism and critique of Christianity. Young Germany distanced itself from the apolitical idealism of Romanticism and sought to further socialist ideals, but the work of their members was banned by the German authorities. It is worth pointing out, however, that Büchner's relationship to the movement was fraught, as he did not fully endorse all their principles and activities and became increasingly sceptical about the possibilities of an effective political revolution under the then current economic and social circumstances. In a letter to his brother Wilhelm in 1835 he says: 'I have been completely convinced for six months now that nothing can be done, and that anyone who sacrifices himself in *present* circumstances is throwing himself away like an idiot.'[19] And he criticises Gutzkow's plans for reform in a letter in 1836: 'Reform society by means of *ideas* deriving from the educated class? Impossible! Our age is purely *material*; … You will never bridge the gulf between the educated and uneducated classes of society.'[20]

Much of Büchner's work and attitude can be considered as an extension or continuation of the spirit of this radical Romantic outlook on the world. Like Büchner and the earlier *Sturm und Drang* movement, these Romantics were concerned with showing us real 'human beings of flesh and blood whose sorrow and joy [we] can share emotionally and whose deeds and actions fill [us] with revulsion or admiration'.[21] The repeated call for a more realistic presentation of character and the forging of a closer relationship with nature and attention to its mystery and transformational power are key interests in Büchner's work.

Body, sex, and the revolution

> 'For what's the point of a revolution
> Without general copulation?'
> (Peter Weiss, *Marat/Sade*)

Büchner's theatrical aesthetics is decidedly visceral; it would be possible to formulate a discourse of the body based on *Danton's Death* and *Woyzeck*, one which sees something inevitable and uncontrollable in bodily desire. There is a blurring between uncontrolled human and animal sexuality in passages where Danton expresses his rage (cynical or tormented?) at the mob's behaviour: 'Oh what fun they're having! ... Doesn't it make you want to leap in amongst them, tear your trousers from your body, and fuck them from behind like dogs in the street?' (*DD*: p. 32). Later on, with increasing awareness of approaching death (his own and everybody else's), his views on the uncontrollable physical dimension of life become even more nihilistic: 'What does it matter whether we hide our pricks behind garlands of roses, vine or laurel – or leave the filthy thing for dogs to lick and all to see? ... The world is chaos, nothingness its due messiah.' (*DD*: p. 69) Woyzeck's response to seeing Marie dance with the Drum-Major contains the same animal imagery and world-weary tone, but it is more desperate and agonising: 'Why don't God blow out the sun when he sees the whole world writhing in lechery, men and women, man and beast. They're at it in broad daylight, before your very eyes, like dogs in the street. The bitch! The bitch is hot, so hot! Go on, go on!' (*W*: p. 128) On the other hand there are powerful examples of sacrificial love: for example, Julie's and Lucille's unmitigated devotions to their husbands (Danton and Camille, respectively), which leads to madness (Lucille) and acts of suicide. Woyzeck's murder of Marie, too, contains a sacrificial and suicidal dimension where aggressive, jealous love culminates in an eroticised act of murder (repeated stabbing of the female body) leading, eventually, to Woyzeck's own death.[22]

There is a strong suggestion that in their ambivalent attitudes to the sexual body, which combines feelings of ennui with the strong emotions of fatal attraction, the characters are finding ways of distancing themselves from the determinism of politics, history and the totalising destruction of their daily lives. Especially in *Woyzeck* an active self emerges in the central character's desperate acts of resistance, however self-destructive and futile they are. This is not to suggest that Büchner puts forward the acts of sex and death as modes of utopia, or that the sexual encounter, suicide and murder are significant because they promise redemption and reconciliation. The apparent resolution of sexual tension in death, so strongly dramatised in *Woyzeck* and hinted at in Danton's longing for an experience of self-loss in the beloved other ('I love you like the grave' he says to his wife Julie), is precisely that: apparent and momentary, a briefly comforting emotion but actually the effect of shattering experiences.

Danton's Death is Büchner's engagement with the radicalisation of the ideals of the French Revolution, which led to a reign of terror, destruction and disillusionment. This historical drama is unconventional not least because it pitches the private against the public, containing multiple and complex perspectives on love and sexuality in an unstable historical and political context. Befitting the fragmentary, episodic character of the work, no unified model of love is put forward; instead we encounter a variety of perceptions ranging from idealistic, romantic love (Julie's love for Danton which results in her suicide; the love bond between Lucile and Camille; Danton's own repeated expressions of his love for his wife), to erotic, sexual desire (Marion's speech) and observations of uncontrolled, animalistic, 'hungry' sexuality. The significance of sexual activity in this play is twofold: on a sociological level sex is connected to the demonstration and maintenance of male power, its manifestation as prostitution being a signifier of poverty and class oppression. On another level, and more interestingly, the play is fuelled by oppositional attitudes to the political value of sexuality, where Robespierre's puritanical moralism clashes with Danton's 'materialist affirmation of life [and] philosophy of enjoyment'.[23] Danton's liberal, epicurean sensibility seems to be the main cause for his disillusionment and withdrawal from political action.

The ultra-leftist moralist Robespierre sees in uncontrolled sexuality a form of social destruction and an obstacle to the realisation of the Revolution's ideals, without being aware that his radicalisation of the socialist programme implies the annulment of individual freedom. Danton, on the other hand (similar to, but less excessive than, his contemporary Sade) sees a liberating and to some extent utopian possibility in sexual expression, but at the same time he is struck by the sameness (the essential fatalism) of human behaviour. Throughout the play Danton is aware that the revolution demands and devours its victims (himself, his supporters and eventually his enemies too), and this might be a reason for his melancholy appearance and inability (or unwillingness) to perform radical political action in the face of death. On the other hand, he is portrayed as sexually active in the erotic company of his wife and lovers and as commentator on others' sexual activities: 'Oh what fun they're having! It's in the air, I can smell it, as if the heat of the sun were hatching lechery' (DD: p. 32).

The debate about sexual freedom versus political virtue in this historical drama is, however, not presented in dialectical terms (as is the case in Peter Weiss's Marat/Sade, for example) or viewed from a meta-historical perspective. It seems that Büchner was not sufficiently detached from the historical material (the failure of the French Revolution) to resolve historical contradictions in aesthetic terms. After all, his literary efforts began immediately after his own failed attempts at political revolution in Hesse in the years 1834 and 1835. His attitude to history was like his attitude to all things human and scientific – Büchner the medical student and literary genius approached life and art with a 'corporeal immediacy'[24] and sensuality which made him reject the abstract idealism of conventional romantic tragedy and the one-dimensional character portrayals of melodrama. Life, for Büchner, means *experience* above all, not abstract ideas. This is also apparent in his non-literary writings, where he attacks the reifying and totalising principles of rationalist philosophy, revealing Cartesian reason as an abstract, de-individualising dogmatism.[25]

Büchner's engagement with historical subject matter, the French Revolution, in his first drama reveals the author's sceptical attitude to historical idealism (Hegelian historicism) in its treatment of the 'world-spirit' as a violent, dogmatic idea: 'SAINT-JUST: The world-spirit acts through us in the realm of ideas just as, in the physical realm, he acts through floods or volcanoes. What difference does it make whether people die of an epidemic or the revolution?' (*DD*: p. 42). The play is also an important example of eroticism in his writing. *Danton's Death* is full of sexual imagery and metaphors that establish connections between the private and the public, between people's erotic lives and the aims and reality of revolutionary politics. For example, the play begins with a card game in an erotically charged atmosphere: 'the kings and queens tumble on top of each other such disgusting fashion, and the knaves soon follow after.' (*DD*: p. 6) Danton comments on women's duplicity and their powers of seduction: 'You women, you could make a man fall in love with lies.' (*DD*: p. 5) At the same time we see him at the feet of his beloved wife Julie, whom he loves 'like the grave' and who will later sacrifice her own life for him. Flirtatious erotic sexuality is juxtaposed with life-transcending true love on the one hand and animal sexuality on the other. Thrown into the play's rich discourse on love are tendentious statements on the supposedly utopian and transformational potentials of sexual love, voiced here by Danton's closest supporter Camille: 'We want naked gods and priestesses and Olympian athletes and, oh, from melodious lips the sounds of wicked, limb-melting love.'(*DD*: p. 7) The gods of liberated sexual love will be the 'guardians of the Republic'.

The most fascinating erotic figure in the play is the prostitute Marion, whose monologue about her own sexual awakening puts forward eroticism as an experience of boundlessness, continuity, self-transcendence and, notably, religious gratification: 'But I became like an ocean that devours everything and bores its way deeper and deeper. ... I know no pause, no change. I am ever the same. A ceaseless yearning and holding, an ardent fire, a swirling stream. ... It makes no difference in the end what gives people pleasure, whether it's flowers or toys, naked bodies or pictures of Christ, it's all the same feeling, those that enjoy the most are those that pray the most.'[26] The discovery of an intimate connection between self and nature, so often a concern in Büchner's private letters and literary work, is given repeated emphasis in this speech. Marion possesses an overwhelming, indiscriminate sensuality that affirms her own 'continuous' being while leading others to their death (her first lover drowns himself). Marion's experience of personal dissolution through erotic transgression is juxtaposed with idealist conceptions of history expressed by Robespierre and St Just. Employing Hegelian terms, they defend the revolutionary 'reign of terror' in terms of a victory of the objective and transparent *Weltgeist* (the world-spirit or absolute Idea) over and against intimate, private experience.

On the surface, we are confronted with two types of anti-individualism: the one erotic, the other historical. But there are important differences: erotic self-abandonment may be the result of a subjective demand and thus still an expression of individuality (a realisation of the self's innermost nature) even at the point where discontinuous selfhood disappears. Historical self-loss, on the other hand, is politically and ideologically motivated, as was the case in the Hegelian idealism which dominated Büchner's time and which enters *Danton's Death* most directly in the speeches of Robespierre's supporter St Just. St Just's disregard for individual experience and indifference to human suffering in the face of historical developments point towards the perverse resolution of the Revolution in a politics of terror and destruction – all in the name of freedom and equality. If it is the desire of the *Weltgeist* to realise itself as an absolute Idea at the expense of human difference and individuality, what better way of answering the doctrine of the Idea than with the principle of Eros – also an idea, undoubtedly, but one rooted in the material tensions of the body and permeated by what Marion calls a 'ceaseless yearning and holding, an ardent fire, a swirling stream'.

Another juxtaposition that determines the play and is used as a political tool is the contrast between virtue and vice. Part of the Jacobins' pseudo-moralistic and puritanical worldview was a rhetoric of moral cleansing by means of extreme violence, as defended by Robespierre and St Just. Danton represents 'vice' as opposed to Robespierre's 'virtue' – an opposition of moral behaviour that is later repeated in *Woyzeck* – and Danton's sexual promiscuity and easy morals are criticised by his opposition in an increasingly precarious power struggle among the leaders of the Revolution. As in all of his work, Büchner offers us a mixture of insights into existential angst and fraught social/economic conditions; he raises questions about the spiritual and psychological constitution of man and woman. *Danton's Death* also contains critiques of religion and ideological (political) systems, but at no point does the play articulate a coherently formed moral position or social message.

As Matthew S. Buckley has pointed out, there is a striking 'emphasis on the body and its sensations' in Büchner's dramatic work, whose characters display an 'obscenity and intense sexuality' which contribute to the 'modern' quality of his writing.[27] An emphasis on transgressive sexuality is most clearly visible in *Danton's Death*, where prostitution is a key theme. The play addresses the destruction of individuality and personal freedom under the regime of the emerging radical Jacobins,[28] and the private realm of sexuality may be considered as a refuge from the public attacks on the individual. From another perspective, sexual activity is also presented as subject to the general economy of exchange, which determines the relationship between poverty and prostitution: 'WIFE: We work with all the rest of our body, why not with that bit as well?' (*DD*: p. 9)

Death in the Revolution is mass-produced; it is no longer of private concern but becomes a public and political performance, a spectacle. The guillotine instrumentalises death; it is a machine of destruction in an 'increasingly mechanistic, functionalistic world'[29] – a damaged world which Büchner never ceased to criticise. At the same time the guillotine is an erotic symbol of its own: 'LACROIX: Good night, Danton! Mademoiselle's thighs are your guillotine, her mons Veneris your Tarpeian Rock' (*DD*: p. 22).

The body and its sensations is also a key concern in *Woyzeck*, Büchner's last and unfinished play, which is based on documentary sources surrounding a real-life murder case. Lenz's demand in the *Kunstgespräch* that the artist should 'enter completely into the life of the meanest of men ... the most everyday people in the world [whose] pulse of feeling is the same in almost everyone'[30] can be taken as the play's prevailing idea. The fact that the play is a fragment (literally incomplete and existing in the form of three versions on which the writer had worked until shortly before his early death) adds to the overall effect of the play as a portrayal of twitches and shudders. The double emphasis on social determinism/exploitation and existential isolation, together with an unsentimental, unromantic dramatisation of sexuality and violence and a disjointed, 'open' dramatic form, make *Woyzeck* one of the best examples of Büchner's modernist sensibility and an avant-garde achievement. It is also the play in which Büchner's resistance to social injustice and systemic violence is most forcefully expressed in an unsentimental yet affective sketch of a human tragedy. Erotic desire and destruction merge in *Woyzeck*, which is a tragedy of passion as much as one of the first proletarian dramas. The common soldier Woyzeck loves Marie, the erotic centre of the play, but loses her to the more financially successful Drum-Major. Woyzeck stabs her to death in a rage of jealous revenge, an act which destroys both of them. In a remarkable blend of poetic and realistic formal elements Büchner draws our attention firmly to the pain and suffering of this working class anti-hero, who is oppressed by the iron law of an exploitative social system and driven by an inner compulsion (resulting from broken love and his mental confusion) to an act of murder with tragic consequences.

The determining factors (inner and outer, psychological and social) in Büchner's aesthetics of 'flesh and blood' are more complex than is often assumed. *Woyzeck* foregrounds the desires, pain and suffering of the human body and mind, but the articulation of sexual desire is limited: neither Marie nor Woyzeck or the Hauptmann are able to clearly and openly speak their desires; their curt, fragmented expressions are distinctively different from the ways in which Marion speaks of female desire in *Danton's Death* or indeed from Danton's reflections on women, love and his awareness of death. One of the recurring central motifs of the play is human 'nature' and the question of whether it can be controlled or even put to medical, scientific use (as argued by the Officer and the Doctor), or whether it represents an inescapable and mysterious aspect of humanity. In the case of Woyzeck, his 'nature' is also a reflection of his poverty, lack of agency and perceived immorality: 'You see, us common folk, we don't have no virtue, all we got is our nature; but if I was a gent with an 'at and a watch and a nice smart coat and could talk all posh, I'd be virtuous alright. ... But poor, that's what I am' (W: p. 120). Even Marie's sexual transgression, her affair with the Drum-Major, is put down to a problem of 'nature', which is no real excuse for her action as far as Woyzeck is concerned. He is fundamentally shaken by her display of lechery and responds to the traumatic realisation of having lost his one true love, his object of desire, with madness and violence.

As has been mentioned above, Büchner's overriding concern with human pain and passion cannot be explained wholly as a reflection of his materialist–socialist outlook. Büchner's work captures a mesmeric tragic force which reveals itself most strongly when he dramatises the individual's relation to the destabilising forces of sexuality and death in a context of deterministic power structures. In Büchner's drama the human being, in his/her struggle against the 'iron fate' of history and politics, discovers another fateful constellation of inner forces. What the Freudian discourse would later identify as the unconscious, Büchner referred to as instinctual human 'nature': it is the same pool of contradictory impulses, distortions and unexplainable motivations, in which desire exposes the limitations of rational thinking. A child of Romanticism, Büchner understood the (external and internal) world as crisis and challenge. His experimental approach to dramatic form (what Benn calls his 'aesthetic revolt'[31]) was met with a subversive political attitude, both of which remained incomplete, unfinished projects pervaded by the (Romantic) spirit of fragmentation. The 'fragmentary demand' (Jean-Luc Nancy[32]) of Büchner's politics and aesthetics may be understood as the call of a non-transcendent infinite, an 'Other' which inhabits the 'flesh and blood' of the present moment. In Büchner's theatrical renderings of the inverted world the realms of sex and death become modes of subjectivisation in Rancière's and Žižek's sense[33], where the self makes a claim for universality and recognition (sovereignty) through extreme and ultimately non-discursive individual experience. The individual's claim to truth, validity and freedom in this damaged world is emphatically made in a body of work where 'physiology [is] captured by poetry' ('*Physiologie aufgefangen in der Dichtung*')[34] – even though the claim fails to be understood (as is the case in the catastrophic worlds of Danton and Woyzeck) and destruction is the overriding result of human efforts. But Büchner's demand for autonomy does not go unheard: 'everything exists for itself', he exclaims in his final public lecture – this might also be the principal lesson of Eros, and of death.

Notes

1. See Heiner Müller, 'The Wounded Woyzeck', trans. Carl Weber, *Performing Arts Journal*, 10(3) (1987), pp. 73–5. He delivered this speech on occasion of being awarded the Georg Büchner Prize in 1985.
2. See Georg Lukács, 'The Real Georg Büchner and His Fascist Misrepresentation' (1937), in Georg Lukács, *German Realists in the Nineteenth Century*, trans. Jeremy Gaines and Paul Keast (London, 1993), pp. 69–94, p. 73. Michael Glebke in *Die Philosophie Georg Büchners* (Marburg, 1995) argues that Büchner puts forward a Marxist–materialist philosophy which understands the human being as entirely determined by economic and material needs.
3. Georg Büchner, *Danton's Death*, in *Complete Plays, Lenz and Other Writings*, trans. John Reddick (London, 1993), p. 18. Hereafter referred to as *DD* in the text.
4. Büchner, 'Woyzeck', p. 121. Hereafter referred to as *W* in the text.
5. Glebke, *Die Philosophie Georg Büchners*, p. 47.
6. Büchner, letter to his family in 1834. *Complete Plays*, p. 192.
7. See Maurice B. Benn, *The Drama of Revolt: A Critical Study of Georg Büchner* (Cambridge, 1976), p. 41ff.
8. Büchner, letter to Minna in 1834. *Complete Plays*, p. 195.
9. John Reddick, *Georg Büchner: The Shattered Whole* (Oxford, 1994), p. 30.
10. Raymond Williams, *Modern Tragedy* (London, 1966), p. 77.
11. Terry Eagleton, *Sweet Violence: The Idea of the Tragic* (Oxford, 2003), p. 22.
12. *Ibid.*, p. 59.
13. Büchner, *Complete Plays*, p. 194.
14. Jakob M.R. Lenz, 'Anmerkungen übers Theater', in Jakob M.R. Lenz, *Werke und Schriften*, Band 1 (Stuttgart, 1965–6), p. 341.
15. *Ibid.*, p. 343.
16. Georg Büchner, *Lenz*, in *Complete Plays*, p. 150.
17. Büchner, *Complete Plays*, pp. 195–6.
18. See Johann Wolfgang Goethe, *Dichtung und Wahrheit*, ed. Klaus-Detlef Müller (Frankfurt am Main, 2007).
19. Büchner, *Complete Plays*, p. 200.
20. *Ibid.*, p. 204.
21. *Ibid.*, p. 202.
22. Owing to the unfinished nature of the text, it is not clear how Büchner intended the play to end. The real Johann Christian Woyzeck, on whom the play is based, was publicly decapitated for the murder of his lover. Despite obvious signs of mental illness, a series of medical examinations had deemed Woyzeck sane and fully accountable for his actions. Büchner's dramatisation presents a Woyzeck who is determined by inner and outer forces. The three distinct manuscripts of the play contain four different scene sequences, which suggest different emphases and endings. In performance, to emphasise dramatic effect, the play often ends with Woyzeck's suicide, suggested in the scene where he throws the bloody knife into a pool of water and goes further and further out to wash the stains of blood from his own body. But there are other scene fragments which suggest that Woyzeck, drenched in water, returns to his child who rejects him, and that the incident will draw legal and scientific attention, leading to trial and punishment ('POLICEMAN: A good murder, a proper murder, a lovely murder, a lovely a murder as anyone could wish, we've not had a murder like this for years', p. 138). See John Reddick's 'Notes to Woyzeck' for a discussion of possible scene arrangements and endings in Büchner, *Complete Plays*, pp. 247–65.
23. Lukács, 'The Real Georg Büchner', p. 85.

24. Matthew S. Buckley, *Tragedy Walks the Streets: The French Revolution in the Making of Modern Drama* (Baltimore, MD, 2006), p. 124.
25. See, for example, his early philosophical essays and his scientific trial lecture 'On Cranial Nerves' where he criticised the utilitarian, functionalistic approach to natural sciences, which reduces the human being to a machine. See also Reddick's discussion in *Georg Büchner: The Shattered Whole*, p. 33ff.
26. See Büchner's *Danton's Death*, in *Complete Plays*, pp. 18–19. Translation slightly modified.
27. See Buckley, *Tragedy Walks the Streets*, p. 121. Büchner is generally considered a forerunner of twentieth-century avant-garde theatre and was a key influence on the naturalist (Hauptmann) and expressionist movements (Wedekind).
28. In this sense his play is similar to Peter Weiss's *Marat/Sade*, which also juxtaposes two visions of the revolution, both radical but with differing assumptions about the importance of personal freedom. Sade appears as the defender of radical individuality, the pursuit of pleasure and sexuality even at the cost of other people's lives, whereas Marat is the proto-Marxist defender of a non-hierarchical, classless society.
29. Reddick, *Georg Büchner: The Shattered Whole*, p. 40.
30. Büchner, *Lenz*, in *Complete Plays*, p. 149.
31. See Benn, *The Drama of Revolt*.
32. See Ian James, *The Fragmentary Demand: An Introduction to the Philosophy of Jean-Luc Nancy* (Stanford, California, 2006) where James argues that Nancy's philosophy 'unfolds as a decision to respond to the demand imposed by the multiple and fragmentary' (p. 3).
33. See Jacques Rancière, *The Politics of Aesthetics: The Revolution of the Sensible*, trans. Gabriel Rockhill (London, 2004) which includes an afterword by Slavoj Žižek.
34. Durs Grünbein, 'Den Körper zerbrechen (1995)', in Dietmar Goltschnigg, *Georg Büchner und die Moderne: Texte, Analysen, Kommentar*, Band 3, (Berlin, 2004), p. 539.

4

Labyrinths of the taboo: theatrical journeys of eroticism and death in Parisian culture

Richard J. Hand

From the early nineteenth century, gaslight began to illuminate the public thoroughfares of Paris at night. From the 1850s through to the 1870s, Baron Haussmann's reconstruction of Paris created wide, airy boulevards and avenues which permitted daylight to stream into the city. These two events combined to create the myth of *La Ville-Lumière*: 'The City of Light'. The lighting – and enlightening – of the city encouraged exploration and experience. Parisian culture invented a suitable term to describe the pedestrian's unravelling of the metropolitan experience: *flânerie*, the art of urban wandering. The concept of the *flâneur* acquires acute significance in the work of Charles Baudelaire who, in 'The Painter of Modern Life' (1863) and other writings, suggests, in Keith Tester's words, that 'the *flâneur* is basically the hero of modernity'.[1] This modern hero may well navigate 'The City of Light' but it is a journey that frequently leads the *flâneur* into 'dark' labyrinths: after all, what defines the radiance of a metropolis other than its complementary darkness? Paris is not only a city of light but a city of arcades, tunnels and holes.

This aspect of Paris has found its most powerful evocation in Walter Benjamin, whose *Das Passagen-Werk/The Arcades Project* is monumental in significance and in size: although tragically unfinished, its incompleteness is appropriate – the fragmentary text is like a labyrinth without end. Benjamin's schema, notes and observations encompass all aspects of the history and features of Paris. In doing this, Benjamin creates a form of textual *flânerie*: an eclectic text which resembles the modern urban experience. This essay looks not at Parisian arcades but Parisian theatre: another realm closed off from the crystal clarity of daylight but equally important as a journey and an exploration of fantasy. In particular, we will look at case studies of drama by Victor Hugo and also the Théâtre du Grand-Guignol: both examples lead their audience into a taboo world of death and eroticism. But before we enter the theatre, we will take a wander through the diverse – and no less dramatic – labyrinths of subterranean Paris.

L'Ossuaire Municipal – the vast Catacombs of Paris – is a mazelike network which ingeniously re-used nearly 200 miles of quarry tunnels to house the mortal remains of millions of erstwhile Parisians. In *Crowds and Power*, Elias Canetti suggests that the pleasure of being in a cemetery becomes a fixation with text and with time: reading the headstones the visitor begins to calculate the age of the buried both in terms of who died young and who died old but also in terms of 'how long it is that some of the buried have lain there'.[2] In the Catacombs there is no comfort of text and time: one is confronted by a tidal wave of death with anonymous and uncountable skulls and bones in stacks, piles and patterns. *L'Ossuaire Municipal* was evocatively documented by Félix Nadar in his pioneering photographic project of 1861 and the Catacombs has a history of use during the 1871 French Commune and by the French Resistance in the Second World War. Despite being an empire of death, along certain pathways the Catacombs even seem to parody the world of the living. For example, Christopher Prendergast convincingly interprets one of Nadar's photographs in these terms: 'The tiered rows and heaps of skeletal remains … resemble nothing so much as a ghoulish replica of faces seen during a night at the opera or the theatre.'[3] In the realm of fiction the Catacombs are an evocative point of reference or location: Edgar Allan Poe refers to 'the great catacombs of Paris' in 'The Cask of Amontillado';[4] the pop star Pink made her acting debut in the Paris-set horror movie *Catacombs* (2007); and urban legends of lost tourists abound. In short, the Catacombs continue to exude a major cultural resonance. They are arcane: antithetically modern and yet similarly dark and labyrinthine is the technological wonder of the *Paris Métropolitain*: the Métro.

The Métro followed the examples of underground transit systems pioneered by London, New York City and Budapest in the nineteenth century, and opened in 1900. The system expanded rapidly until its lines totalled well over 100 miles in length, and swiftly became part of Parisian life, culture and identity. If we look for myths of the Métro, we might consider that masterpiece of Art Deco erotic illustration, the narrative cycle *Idylle Printanière* (1933) by Fédor Rojankowski ('Rojan') – originally entitled *De Montparnasse à Pigalle* – which portrays (without words) a chance sexual encounter between two apparent strangers initiated on the *Paris Métropolitain*.[5] We are the undetected voyeur to this explicit performance although, in one startling drawing, we are 'caught' and Rojan has the woman stare out at us, her eyes wide in shock. Rojan's use of the Métro as a catalyst for theatrical eroticism is not unique. The Métro in Paris, epitome of the modern urban environment, was increasingly to become, in Christopher Prendergast's words, a 'disreputable location'[6] as the twentieth century proceeded: a place of violence, crime or sexual amorality. Prendergast gives the example of Marcel Proust, who successfully conjoins the Métro with the Catacombs – sex with death – in *A la recherche du temps perdu* (1913–27), when he imagines the Métro as a location of sexual abandon while being used as a bomb shelter during the First World War: 'while apocalypse rages above ground, furtive orgy takes place below "dans les couloirs du Métro, noirs comme des catacombs"'.[7]

The linking of *l'amour* and *la mort* in French has become something of a cliché, but nonetheless in Parisian culture there is a constant interplay and exchange between the erotic and death. Some of Walter Benjamin's notes in *The Arcades Project* demonstrate this. According to Benjamin, in the fifteenth century the Cemetery of the Innocents – the graveyard for children – was, in 'spite of the incessant burials and exhumations going on there ... a public lounge and a rendezvous (where) prostitutes strolled under the cloisters'.[8] Benjamin also unearths examples of the argot of nineteenth-century pornography with women talking about sexual intercourse in funereal terms: 'in the anus the forefinger as sexton, on the clitoris two fingers as deacons' while in 'the temple [is] the sacrificer'.[9] The language is religious/sacrilegious to capture the ritual and, in every sense, the *performance* of coition which, although action is evidently being taken to heighten the woman's stimulation and pleasure, is characterised by a sense of ruin, sacrifice and death.

This sex-and-death amalgamation can sometimes take truly disturbing forms. The nineteenth-century *Journal of Psychological Medicine and Mental Pathology* recounts an extraordinary and dramatic case entitled 'Impulsive insanity – the French vampire' in which a Parisian doctor, G. Sigmoud, describes an 1849 crime wave which had an 'erotic manifestation'.[10] A recently buried young girl and woman were disinterred and found partially disembowelled with evidence that the 'putrifying remains exhibited that there had been an attempt to perpetrate crime, and to gratify an unnatural appetite'.[11] Public outcry followed these gruesome acts of necrophilia and the guards of 'the catacombs and cemeteries of the dead' were trebled and all kinds of traps and watchdogs were put in place until the villain – nicknamed the 'vampire' – was finally apprehended in the Cemetery of Montparnasse.

In addition to the Catacombs and the Métro, the *Égouts de Paris*, the sewers, have achieved a powerful metaphorical status keying into popular fascinations and fears. Victor Hugo proclaims '[a] sewer is a mistake', denouncing it for literally flushing away the ordure that should be recycled to enrich the land, emphasising that 'Paris manure is the richest of all'.[12] This is from *Les Misérables*, a novel which makes powerful use of the concept of sewer life and wastage in its analysis of the proletarian mass, the 'lowlife' of Paris, trapped in despair but also the crucible of once and future revolution. The sewers have also proved a powerful metaphor in relation to issues of sexuality. Christopher Prendergast explains how the issue of civic control extended to the question of policing prostitution, which was yet another facet of society 'figured by the analogy of the sewer' (such as 'women of the gutter'). It also served as an allusion 'to the heavily tabooed area of the anal-erotic'.[13]

As well as in Hugo's sweeping historical realism and issues of social legislation, the Paris sewers are all-important in the Gothic fantasy of works such as Gaston Leroux's *Le Fantôme de l'Opéra/Phantom of the Opera* (1911) in which Eric, the eponymous anti-hero, haunts that acme of performance culture, and probably the most important landmark of the Haussmann reconstruction, the *Palais Garnier*: the Paris Opéra. Yet the Phantom always withdraws to reside in the equally famous – and equally theatrical – sewers. The potency of the Paris sewers extends beyond French culture: 'It Happened' (11 May 1938), a classic episode of the US horror radio show *Lights Out*, features a surprisingly brutal tale of an American schoolgirl abused in the Paris sewers by a maniac who makes jewellery from the bones of people lost or drowned in the *Égouts*. The currency of the *Égouts* extends into popular music: Tom Waits, in the grotesque song 'Singapore' (*Rain Dogs*, 1985) – described by Jay S. Jacobs as 'a deranged sea shanty road tune'[14] – sings of having '[w]alked the sewers of Paris ...' in the opening verse.

We have seen how the Catacombs, the Métro and the sewers have taken on a potent significance and signification beyond their actual and essential function beneath 'The City of Light'. Part of this is an erotic resonance. Paris in the nineteenth century, and for much of the twentieth, was the capital of the world's sex industry and Montmartre, especially around Place Pigalle, was its Vatican. Montmartre was home to the risqué titillations offered by the Moulin Rouge and other performance venues. But it also went further in catering for every sexual persuasion or predilection, from the services of its street prostitutes through to the legendary *maisons de tolérance* – legalised brothels – which are evocatively captured in Robert Brassai's 1930s photographs. Brassai's documentation of the 'Suzy'[15] – unusually, not in Montmartre but in the Quartier Latin – depicts a bordello lit up like a chapel for midnight mass. The austere madam greets the customer; whereas some brothels were open salons in a mass performance of customers and courtesans, Suzy's was evidently a somewhat macabre place that resembled a crypt and guaranteed anonymity, with a labyrinth of trapdoors and curtains and sliding doors that meant that no male customer need see another.

Montmartre was also the centre of industry for the subtlest of erotica to the most explicit pornography, with a monopoly on literature, photographs, drawings and, ultimately, short films. Many examples of this material consciously emphasise their identity as 'Parisian' through textual emphasis or visual iconography. In terms of fiction, literary constructions of erotic Paris can be found in the cheapest of chapbooks through to the works of the modernist period such as Henry Miller's *Tropic of Cancer* (1934) and the short stories of Anaïs Nin. Arguably, the establishment of specific location and 'backdrop' in such examples enhances their theatricality. Paris is also a capital of theatrical sex, not just in the aforementioned erotic venues and brothels but in metaphor: Walter Benjamin quotes the memoirs of Horace de Viel-Castel (1883), who argues that the virtue of Parisian women 'strongly resembles the curtains in theatres, for their petticoats rise each evening three times rather than once'.[16]

In stark contrast to the subterranean Paris we have explored, the greatest landmark of Paris is the *Tour Eiffel*: the great *erection* of Paris. The Eiffel Tower was an icon even in pornographic imagery. One *belle époque* photograph in the Rotenberg Collection of erotica shows a woman arching her legs as she lowers herself onto a model of the Eiffel Tower so that it begins to penetrate her vagina.[17] In another image, a caricature sketch entitled 'Mine d'Or/Gold Mine', a woman sits astride an engorged phallus which ejaculates coins into her open purse. In this image, the Eiffel Tower is merely a grey silhouette dwarfed by the *real* erection of Paris: the penis exploited by the sex industry.[18] In both images, the women are completely controlling and dominant: if this is a struggle, the Eiffel Tower will be the loser, subsumed and engulfed by the feminine opening, the triumphal arch, an *Arc de Triomphe*. This allusion to the other great Parisian landmark is apposite and one is reminded that, in contrast to the indelible memorial to France's war heroes that is the *Arc de Triomphe*, the Eiffel Tower was described from its opening as being merely a temporary feature for the 1889 *Exposition Universelle*, an erection that would not last long. Its longevity across three centuries would astonish all those who first saw it rise.

We have seen how the fabric of Paris has been used to interweave the taboos of eroticism and death in an often theatrical way. The performance or ritualistic language of sexuality and the use of theatrical metaphor notwithstanding, around the same time we find Henry James constantly using Paris as the zenith of theatre to London's nadir. In his dramatic criticism, James persistently celebrates the French theatre, which he implies excels London theatre both socially and aesthetically. The theatres hidden in the gloomy back streets of London's dingy theatreland are a startling contrast to Paris, where 'the various temples of the drama are scattered along the clean, bright Boulevard'.[19] In 'The London Theatres' (1877) James describes the process of going to the theatre as a somewhat uncomfortable and Dickensian experience which serves as a 'reminder that the arts of the stage are not really in the temperament and the manners of the people'.[20]

In contrast to the intellectual and demanding French spectator, James sees the English audience member as vulgar and easily pleased (a condescending bias towards the English audience which will inevitably thwart his own numerous attempts to be a successful playwright). Most profoundly, James argues that in England the theatre 'is a social luxury and not an artistic necessity'[21] and he is dismayed with the nature of the drama performed, which he sees as inauthentic and unrepresentative: 'The English stage of to-day … certainly holds the mirror as little as possible up to nature – to any nature, at least, usually recognized in the British Islands.'[22]

James would seem to be demanding theatrical realism, but it is important to emphasise that it is a certain kind of realism. By his own admission, James describes himself as 'very much like a Francisque Sarcey',[23] the influential French theatre critic who extolled the importance of technical perfection and would acclaim the dramatists of the 'well-made play' Eugène Scribe and Victorien Sardou as standing amongst the very greatest of playwrights. The concept of 'holding a mirror up to nature' would soon begin to take on a different revolutionary form with the establishment in 1887 of the Théâtre Libre by André Antoine. The type of plays James adored and the theatres that presented them would not be appropriate for the new realism and naturalism which would aim to show the taboos of reality in all their brutality. But even Henry James's hygienic temples of drama had presented the taboo. Ten years before James was born, Victor Hugo's *Lucrèce Borgia* (1833) was a huge success when it premiered at Paris's Théâtre de la Porte Saint-Martin, even if its use of 'common' prose rather than verse drama was a provocation to many at the time. The play presents Lucretia Borgia, history's ultimate *femme fatale*, and Hugo exploits two aspects of the Borgia myth: a central theme in the play is incest and the key action is poisoning. Hugo mixes precise historical detail with free poetic licence, exploiting the abiding, if embellished, legend of the ruthless, passionate and 'impetuous Borgia blood'[24] to create a work that is remarkable for its constant interplay of passion and poison, sex and death.

The central plot concerns a group of young Venetian men including Gennaro, a dashing young blade of unknown parentage. He is, in fact, the illegitimate and incestuous son of Lucretia Borgia but has never been told. Lucretia is the only person who knows who he is, and in their first encounter 'love' is misconstrued: she is besotted at seeing her son while Gennaro is sexually aroused at being approached by an attractive older woman and he chases her offstage. This sequence is, when considered, an irony as morally unsettling as it is profoundly dramatic. When they return from whatever happens offstage, Gennaro's comrades recognise Lucretia and publicly surround and humiliate her, driving her to the ground and spitting her name at her.

In the third and final act of the play we see Lucretia's revenge against these violators. She believes that Gennaro has been persuaded to leave Ferrara. Gennaro and his comrades drink the night away in what they directly call a 'veritable orgy',[25] carousing with the alluring Princess Negroni and her group of young women with dialogue that is surprisingly hard: 'On the lips of a lady, "no" ... means "yes".'[26] Suddenly the women exit and the men are left alone, literally and metaphorically sword-less. They hear monks outside solemnly chanting, signifying a funeral. The monks come into the chamber and beneath the cowls the young men expect to see the concubines returned. But on pulling up one hood they see the livid face of an old monk: an emblem of *Thanatos* where *Eros* was expected. Then Lucretia appears dressed in black, literally dressed to kill, and she reveals to the men five coffins with their names on them: the wine they have been drinking has been poisoned. It is to be a hideous orgy of death. To her horror, Gennaro steps forward: 'we need six coffins, madam.'[27] The young men begin to weaken and they are led away for their last rites by the monks, leaving Lucretia and Gennaro. She is still unable to tell him the truth, and as he begins to falter he thrusts a dagger into her. It is only as she is dying alongside him that she finally declares: 'Gennaro! I am your mother!'[28]

Figure 4.1. Death of the ultimate *femme fatale*: Gennaro (Oliver Jones) murders his mother Lucretia (Ruth Majeed) in the 2007 International Victor Hugo Festival production of *Lucretia Borgia* (1833) at the Gatehouse Theatre, London, directed by Richard J. Hand. (Photo: Mike Davies, Media Resources, University of Glamorgan)

Lucrèce Borgia is, in many ways, an opera without music and it is little surprise that Gaetano Donizetti almost immediately adapted Hugo's play into his opera *Lucrezia Borgia* (1833). Although it is easy to dismiss Hugo's play as melodrama, its sustained fusion of the erotic and the deathly and its exploitation of the taboo make it a remarkable work. When she so ruthlessly eliminates all the young men in a strange and macabre 'gang bang' of death, it is genuinely startling, as is the final scene, with Gennaro penetrating his own mother. Lucretia is a character as attractive and irresistible as she is deadly. She is described as being 'like a terrible phantom haunting the whole of Italy, like a spectre looming over everyone'.[29] She is very much a Gothic anti-heroine, perhaps even a female precursor to Dracula, not least because she is finally vanquished by being stabbed: an act of penetration.

The play is Hugo's strange and exciting theatrical journey into eroticism and death, but it was not merely an aesthetic voyage. It is a key moment in Hugo's biography. The role of Princess Negroni was played by an actress called Juliette Drouet, the legendary mistress of Hugo. Hugo's own grandson Léon Daudet, in his *belle lettristic* biography *The Tragic Life of Victor Hugo* (1939), describes the first encounter of Hugo and Juliette Drouet at the *Lucrèce Borgia* rehearsals as love at first sight, but it is in powerful terms. He sees Hugo as a man at this stage of his life abused professionally and domestically, and in Juliette a woman dejected by her affairs and the father of her daughter, a man we are told who had 'unnatural practices' and liked 'lesbians'.[30] We are also told that Hugo could 'mentally undress a woman with the rapidity of lightning'[31] and when he beheld Juliette 'a hundred varying and localised sexual indulgences came into his mind, along with numberless poetic conceptions'.[32] As André Maurois says in his biography of Hugo, once temptation had reared its head the 'idea shocked him, the poet of the hearth and of the family'.[33]

Just as the play he was producing rips apart the values of family and morality, so Hugo beheld the death of himself as the family man. Biographical approaches are, of course, always questionable and yet in this case we have a fascinating yarn full of passion, adultery and devastating choices curiously akin to the eroticism and death of *Lucrèce Borgia*. Hugo's own journey is as theatrical as the journeys taken by Gennaro and his mother and it seems that this is curiously apt for the Parisian theatrical context. The sex and horrific death in *Lucrèce Borgia* – a disruptive and destructive force on many levels it would seem – makes Hugo's play a clear precursor to the excesses displayed in the Théâtre du Grand Guignol, the most important theatre of death and eroticism in the history of Paris.

The Théâtre du Grand-Guignol opened in 1897 on the wave of Théâtre Libre-inspired realism and naturalism. On its opening night they performed Oscar Méténier's *Lui!*, a play about a prostitute trapped in a Montmartrean brothel bedroom with a murderer. The success was such that the theatre swiftly moved from the naturalistic 'slice of life' to specialise in the 'slice of death' and became a popular theatre for Parisians and tourists alike. The journey to the Grand-Guignol, located in Montmartre, is one of the greatest in theatre history: the venue was located down a cul de sac in the heart of Pigalle and was the only theatre in an area of brothels and sex shows. For tourists and the bourgeois audience the performance started as soon as they left the Métro and weaved their way through the labyrinthine side streets of the heart of the world's sex industry. The Grand-Guignol was formerly a small chapel and always retained its religious murals and two giant angels in the rafters, enhancing the morally dubious but quasi-religious experience (rather like the aforementioned Suzy brothel snapped by Brassaï or the sexual argot of women noted by Benjamin). It would seem that the audience was a mixture: the Grand-Guignol became famous on the tourist trail and yet it retained a loyal clientele. The theatre also became a favourite haunt for adulterous couples, who could hire a grilled box at the back which would allow them to see but not be seen. The ultra-realism on display also had an erotic appeal to those with a sadomasochistic taste. Agnès Pierron reveals that 'cleaning ladies would find traces of sexual pleasure from the audience'[34] on the seats.

The term Grand-Guignol is now synonymous with heightened horror, but it was never Transylvanian: its horrors were always the actual or the possible. It is a theatre that made its reputation through its explicit and realistic stage effects and, so the legend goes, its ability to drive people to unconsciousness or nausea: as a gimmick they even had a resident doctor and, it is claimed, the first bar within a theatre for those who needed a stiff drink. Some favourite stage effects included throat-slitting, beheading, amputation and acid attacks as well as the unmistakably Freudian eye-gouging. There are countless examples of blinding, including in one of the very last plays the Grand-Guignol would stage: the denouement of Eddy Ghilain's *Les Blousons sanglants/The Bloody Jackets* (1961) is set in the Catacombs and features a razor and spoon being used to remove a woman's eyes. The Grand-Guignol also strove to be innovative in its horrors, such as in Ghilain's *Le Cercueil flottant/The Floating Coffin* (1960) wherein a woman has her nipples cut off with scissors before being burned alive.[35]

The Grand-Guignol always displayed a repertoire of short drama, interspersing horror plays with sex comedies which nonetheless shared the same themes, such as adultery and revenge, sadism and humiliation, betrayal and destruction. Often the short plays adhere to a structure familiar in pornography, with an inexorable build-up to a violent and blood-letting climax as, perhaps, a kind of 'cumshot'. As Hand and Wilson explain:

> [There is a] similarity between the structure of pornographic literature and performance and many a Grand-Guignol play. The plays are short and the narrative is often very simple with an uncomplicated and unambiguous exposition heading towards a clearly signposted ending.[36]

A clear example of this can be found in Maurice Level's *Le Baiser dans la nuit/The Final Kiss* (1912). The play presents Henri, hideously disfigured in a vitriol attack, who is visited by Jeanne, the woman who attacked him in a fit of jealous rage. The ensuing encounter is a classic game of cat and mouse which exploits a careful manipulation of suspense. Eventually, Henri, who seems to have forgiven her, pointedly asks her for one last 'kiss'.[37]

Figure 4.2. Henri (Colin Butcher) demanding one last 'kiss' from Jeanne (Sarah Murray), in the University of Glamorgan's 2009 Grand-Guignol Laboratory production of Maurice Level's *The Final Kiss* (1912), directed by Richard J. Hand. (Photo: Mike Davies, Media Resources, University of Glamorgan)

Grabbing Jeanne, he pours acid on her face in an act of revenge and the play ends with her writhing in agony as, ideally in a set piece of Grand-Guignol stage-effects virtuosity, her face melts away. The play's exploitation of trepidation and suggestion, culminating in explicit violence, is distinctly parallel to an erotic narrative of persuasion, foreplay and climax.

In Jean Aragny and Francis Neilson's *Le Baiser de sang/The Kiss of Blood* (1929), a gentleman called Joubert visits hospital complaining of a painful finger. After a meticulously crafted sequence in which the surgeon can find nothing wrong with it, a distraught Joubert hacks through his own finger with a scalpel. This violent set piece is merely an appetiser for the denouement of the play. It transpires that Joubert's condition is psychosomatic and he is tortured with guilt, believing he has murdered his wife, Hélène. In fact, she survived and stalks Joubert like a vengeful ghost: she kissed the finger which pulled the trigger of the gun and caused him 'unbearable'[38] agony. At the end of the play, Hélène returns with her deadly embrace – the potent bloody 'kiss' of the title – and kisses Joubert's hand. Partly to abate the agony and partly to appease his demoniacally insatiable wife ('my memory will haunt you every night. I will appear the moment you try to forget. I will never leave you!'),[39] Joubert cleaves off his own hand with an axe and presents it, in suppliant desperation, to an ecstatic Hélène, before collapsing dead.[40]

Figure 4.3. Joubert (Paul Owens) brandishes his severed hand in an attempt to satisfy his wife in the University of Glamorgan's 2009 Grand-Guignol Laboratory production of Jean Aragny and Francis Neilson's *The Kiss of Blood* (1929), directed by Richard J. Hand. (Photo: Mike Davies, Media Resources, University of Glamorgan)

Figure 4.4. Hélène (Sabrina Dickens) licks her husband's severed hand in ecstasy in the University of Glamorgan's 2009 Grand-Guignol Laboratory production of Jean Aragny and Francis Neilson's *The Kiss of Blood* (1929), directed by Richard J. Hand. (Photo: Mike Davies, Media Resources, University of Glamorgan)

Another example is to be found in Pierre Chaine and André de Lorde's *Le Jardin des supplices*/*The Torture Garden* (1922), an adaptation of Octave Mirbeau's 1899 masterpiece of Decadent erotica. In some respects, the Grand-Guignol dramatisation makes the original work more complex. Mirbeau's novel focuses on the disturbing practices of a group of sadomasochistic Europeans who exploit colonial China. In Chaine and de Lorde's play, a level of political intrigue is added, with some of the characters being involved in espionage against the underground nationalist movement the 'Scarlet Dragon'. However, despite the development of the 'spy story', the play's finale is once again an example of the Grand-Guignol's quasi-erotic denouement. The central female character in the play is Clara Watson, an Englishwoman with particularly sadistic tastes. Towards the end of the play she falls into an orgasmic seizure as she watches a prostitute skinned alive in the 'Torture of the Ribbon of Flesh'.[41] But members of the 'Scarlet Dragon' entrap Clara and exact their revenge:

> Ti-Mao (*to Ti-Bah*): First of all, the eyes ... let us begin with the eyes ... those eyes which loved to feast on suffering and death. (*Ti-Bah goes towards Clara and grabs her head with her left hand, a red-hot needle in her right hand*)
> Clara: No! Not that! Help!
> Ti-Mao (*to Ti-Bah who is beginning to push the needle into Clara's eye*): Slowly, Ti-Bah! Don't press it in too fast ... don't push it in ...
> Clara: Ah! Ah! Ah!
> Ti-Mao: Not so fast ... Twist the needle under her eyelid ... Don't push it in too quickly ...
> Clara: Ah! Ah! Ah! Ah!
> Ti-Mao: Not so fast ...
> (*The curtain descends slowly over the cries of Clara.*)[42]

In this and other plays, when the curtain descends it is a moment that often leaves the narrative open even if, experientially, the passion has just been 'spent'. This sexualised violence or violent sexuality was not exclusive to the Grand-Guignol, however. To return to pornographic photographs from the Rotenberg Collection, we find a sequence of images from the same period in which two men have sex with one young and one much older woman.[43] They explore a variety of sexual positions and possibilities but there is also an image of horror: the old woman stretches out the penis of one of the men on a table and the other man wields an axe. The visual narrative is arguably a precursor to the violent finale of Nagisa Ôshima's *Ai no corrida/In the Realm of the Senses* (1976), but is unquestionably parallel to the contemporaneous Grand-Guignol.

The Théâtre du Grand-Guignol, the greatest 'labyrinth' in theatrical history, was a catacomb or sewer of art: a *trou* located at the end of a cul de sac or, as another great erotic writer Colette would describe it, in loaded terms, a 'pleasant theatre, secret and remote from the street'.[44] Although a fan of the Grand-Guignol, Colette regrets that in the Grand-Guignol 'there are many more ways to die than there are to make love'.[45] However, perhaps this essay of textual *flânerie* has demonstrated that, in aspects of Parisian culture, violence and death is eroticism and eroticism is violence and death. Certainly, Victor Hugo, the Grand-Guignol and numerous other creators, whether celebrated or anonymous, demonstrate that the most taboo and repellent idea can be, in every sense, the most stimulating.

Notes

1. Keith Tester, *The Flâneur* (London, 1994), p. 6.
2. Elias Canetti, *Crowds and Power* (Harmondsworth, 1973), p. 322.
3. Christopher Prendergast, *Paris and the Nineteenth Century* (Oxford, 1992), p. 81.
4. Edgar Allen Poe, *Tales of Mystery and Imagination* (London, 2003), p. 336.
5. See Gilles Néret (ed.), *Erotica Universalis* Volume II (Cologne, 2000), pp. 326–55.
6. Prendergast, *Paris and the Nineteenth Century*, p. 100.
7. *Ibid.*, p. 101.
8. Walter Benjamin, *The Arcades Project* (Cambridge, MA, 1999), p. 514.
9. *Ibid.*, p. 504
10. G. Sigmoud, 'Impulsive Insanity – the French Vampire', *Journal of Psychological Medicine and Mental Pathology*, 2 (1849), p. 579.
11. Sigmoud, 'Impulsive Insanity', p. 579.
12. Victor Hugo, *Les Misérables* (Harmondsworth, 1982), p. 1062.
13. Prendergast, *Paris and the Nineteenth Century*, p. 100.
14. Jay S. Jacobs, *Wild Years: The Music and Myth of Tom Waits* (Toronto, Canada, 2000), p. 161.
15. Robert Brassai, *The Secret Paris of the 30s* (London, 1976), non-paginated.
16. Benjamin, *The Arcades Project*, p. 491.
17. Mark Rotenberg, *Forbidden Erotica: The Rotenberg Collection* (Cologne, 2000), p. 99.
18. Rotenberg, *Forbidden Erotica*, p. 101.
19. Henry James, *The Scenic Art* (London, 1949), p. xvii.
20. *Ibid.*, p. 100.
21. *Ibid.*, p. 100.
22. *Ibid.*, p. 93.
23. *Ibid.*, p. 96.
24. Maria Bellonci, *Lucrezia Borgia* (London, 2000), p. 34.
25. Victor Hugo, *Four Plays* (London, 2004), p. 271.
26. *Ibid.*
27. *Ibid.*, p. 280.
28. *Ibid.*, p. 286.
29. *Ibid.*, p. 239.
30. Léon Daudet, *The Tragic Life of Victor Hugo* (London, 1939), p. 37.
31. *Ibid.*, p. 38.
32. *Ibid.*
33. André Maurois, *Victor Hugo and His World* (London, 1966), p. 54.
34. Quoted in Stephen Jones, *Clive Barker's A–Z of Horror* (London, 1997), p. 112.
35. Graphically displayed in a production still reproduced in Agnès Pierron, *Les Nuits-Blanches du Grand Guignol* (Paris, 2002), p. 148.s
36. Richard J. Hand and Michael Wilson, *Grand-Guignol: The French Theatre of Horror* (Exeter, 2002), p. 74.
37. *Ibid.*, p. 192.
38. *Ibid.*, p. 252.
39. *Ibid.*, p. 262.
40. The stage directions at the final moments of the script of *Le Baiser de sang/The Kiss of Blood* merely state that Joubert 'hacks his hand off at the wrist' (Hand and Wilson, *Grand-Guignol*, p. 264). In the University of Glamorgan's 2009 Grand-Guignol Laboratory stage production of the play, the rehearsal process developed the scene into an example of the grotesquely erotic: an example of extreme violence being in parallel

with, and allusive to, an erotic, perhaps even pornographic, narrative. The climax of the play in performance compelled the actor playing Joubert – kneeling down and sweating – to brandish his hand to Hélène and press himself against her body while blood continued to drip from the stump at the end of his arm. Similarly, in rehearsal the actor playing Hélène located an ecstatic response to her husband's self-inflicted amputation and demise: this gradually evolved into the actor triumphantly licking the oozing blood and inserting the stump into her mouth. The sequence in the 2009 production blatantly linked *l'amour* and *la mort*, locating the sensual, the erotic and the ecstatic within the plot's closing moment of self-mutilation and death.

41. Hand and Wilson, *Grand-Guignol*, p. 227.
42. *Ibid.*, p. 230.
43. Rotenberg, *Forbidden Erotica*, pp. 368–77.
44. In Agnès Pierron, *Le Grand Guignol: le théâtre des peurs de la belle époque* (Paris, 1995), p. 1379.
45. Quoted in Hand and Wilson, *Grand-Guignol*, p. 230.

5

The kiss of love and death:
Eros *and* Thanatos *in the opera*

Dieter Borchmeyer

'Un bacio ... ancora un bacio'
Giuseppe Verdi, *Otello*
'Der Liebeskuß ist die erste Empfindung des Todes'
Richard Wagner to Cosima, 15 August 1869

'For love is as strong as death, jealousy is as severe as Sheol' says the Bible's *Song of Solomon* (8:6). Death and love, Eros and Hades (in the bible: Sheol) are equally powerful adversaries. They fight each other – just as Mozart's Don Giovanni resists the Commendatore returning from the other world and the hell that threatens to devour him: a tremendous *agon* between *Eros* and *Thanatos* in the last moments of the *dissoluto punito*. On the other hand, love and death may be joined in mystical sympathy, as they are for Tristan and Isolde – as delimitation experiences they are secretly one and the same. Thus, in Hofmannsthal's early short drama *Der Tor und der Tod* (*The Fool and Death*), death explains to Claudio, who is loath to die, that he is a heathen death, not a Christian one: not a 'skeleton', as he appears in Hofmannsthal's later adaptation of the medieval morality play *Jedermann* (*Everyman*), but 'kin of Dionysus and Venus', a 'great god of the soul'[1] who lets the ego become one with the world in the delimitation experience of death and love.

At least in the theatre, love often does not end in death but, especially in moments of dying, triumphs over earthly existence – as a metaphysical power which points towards the next world or the essence of all things.

As Schopenhauer says, death may be unable to touch the 'indestructibility of our essential being'; death cannot remove love as a guarantor of the indestructible. Death may shatter the lovers' earthly existence, but it cannot destroy their love as such because it defines itself precisely in relation to death and often only shows itself in its purest form through death. In Schiller's *Kabale und Liebe*, as in Verdi's opera *Luisa Miller*, it is only the certainty of death by means of poison which enables the lovers to confess their wholehearted love. They remove all doubt about themselves and each other's love. And Wagner's Tristan and Isolde, too, experience their eternal mutual love only in the moment when they believe to be drinking the death potion. Then they are prepared to give themselves to this love without consideration for society or other people. They are prepared to die because eternal love for them is possible only in death. Death is here the catharsis, the purifying power of love. And how often is this the case in other examples of opera.

Lessing wrote an archaeological study entitled *Wie die Alten den Tod gebildet* (*How the Ancients Shaped Death*), the main thesis of which is that during Antiquity death was not depicted as a fearsome skeleton, as it was in the Christian tradition, but rather as a spirit with an overturned torch, as the brother of sleep. 'What can depict the end of life more clearly than an extinguished, overturned torch?'[2] And in his naenia 'Die Götter Griechenlands' ('The Gods of Greece') Schiller writes 'Then, no ugly skeleton / approached the dying man's bed' – this is the same image Death itself rejects in Hofmannsthal's drama – but rather: 'Quietly and sadly, a spirit / lowers his torch.'[3] The torch of death: in Wagner's *Tristan and Isolde*, the image of the dying torch becomes the ultimate emphatic expression of the lovers' death wish.

Love does not fear death – at least not in myths, in poetry and music, as demonstrated by the innumerable martyrs for love, ready to expire and never afraid of any kind of torture, who populate especially the operatic stage. In fact, it is more likely that death shuns love, as the founding myth of all love tragedies shows: through his singing and playing the lyre, Orpheus is able to convince the powers of the netherworld to return his beloved to him, to allow a dead person to return to life just once. Nevertheless, the power of the netherworld turns out to be stronger than the power of love, and it pulls Eurydice back into the realm of shadows.

The Orpheus myth is the founding myth of music. The first complete opera (by Rinuccini and Peri) that has come down to us is entitled *Euridice* (1600), and with *Favola d'Orfeo* Monteverdi began his career in musical drama 400 years ago. Even where it did not make a stage appearance outright, this myth makes itself heard throughout the entire history of opera, for example in Mozart's *Zauberflöte* (*Magic Flute*). Tamino soothes and appeases nature, be it animals or the elements, with his music – no longer with song accompanied by a string instrument, as in Antiquity, but with the 'absolute' music of modernity: the playing of the flute, which makes singing impossible.[4] And like Orpheus, he has to brave the challenges of death and the underworld in his mystery trials, culminating in the trial by fire and water.

Resounding love vanquishes the power of death. 'Death, where is thy sting?' (first letter to the Corinthians) asks the modern redeeming power of love and music united in triumph. In Tamino, however, the Orpheus myth is almost reversed at one crucial point of the opera. As Orpheus may not turn around to look at Eurydice until he returns to earth, so Tamino must turn away from Pamina until the end of the rite of initiation which he has consented to. Going even further than the antique myth, he must be able to appear as if he does not love her anymore, to torment her soul, if he wants to win her. Even the deepest sorrow of his beloved, the announcement that she will die – a consequence of her unbending love, if it cannot be fulfilled on earth – cannot move him to break the vow of silence he has sworn to the priests. Pamina does not understand this commandment. Abjuration is foreign to her, love is the only law she knows. And when it appears to her that her unconditional love has been betrayed by Tamino, she can only think of giving herself over to another unconditional power: death, which will now be her 'bridegroom' in the shape of the dagger: *Thanatos* as *Eros*.[5]

As enemies, but also in their secret sympathy, death and love are almost dialectically related to one another. This is evident in the Bible, evident in the myths of Antiquity. The French language has a special ability to express the eternal relation between love and death through the proximity of its terms: *l'amour – la mort*. Romain Rolland turned this similarity of sound and meaning into the title of his 1925 drama *Le jeu de l'amour et de la mort* (*The Play of Love and Death*). Every great love drama is such a play of love and death. Every great love carries death in its heart. Love can even be a 'deadly illness', as in Goethe's *Sorrows of Young Werther* or his *Elective Affinities*.

Why, however, is the affinity between love and death so often the topic of opera – so often that one can even call it one of the favourite subjects of this genre? It is futile to argue about a ranking of the arts, but in one aspect music reigns supreme over the other arts: only in music – only in opera – do the two most powerful forces of life, *Eros* and *Thanatos*, find their supreme expression. This is because of its singular structure, its ability to turn successive and transitory moments of drama into simultaneous events. Events that must happen successively in drama can take place in opera next to each other, together, within each other, as a *nunc stans*.[6]

Only music is able to bring the moment of love's bliss and the moment of death to a 'standstill', to perpetuate it.[7] These are the scenic moments which those ignorant of opera often declare to be ridiculous: that characters who have been shot – as Gustav III in *Ballo in maschera* or Posa in Verdi's *Don Carlo*, or even Gilda, delivered to her father Rigoletto as a corpse in a sack – still find the breath to sing long dying arias. This contradicts 'dramatic' probability; accordingly, the love duet hardly has a counterpart in spoken drama. There, lovers' dialogues are usually motivated by some kind of outer or inner disturbance of the lovers, at least a distance that provides motivation for a discourse, a developing speech. For example, Schiller's *Don Carlos* begins only when the love between Carlos and Elisabeth is already doomed; whereas in Verdi's opera, there is no disturbance or distance in the love duet between Elisabeth and Carlos in the Fountainbleau act, which (significantly) precedes Schiller's drama. On the contrary, the lovers are in total unison: even their duet is *unisono* throughout several measures. There is no development; time stands still.

Even the two great love dialogues in the second and third acts of the quintessential love drama, Shakespeare's *Romeo and Juliet*, are excellent examples for the development of dialogue due to unfortunate outer circumstances. Shakespeare does not depict the presence of undisturbed love and bliss, but rather the situations before and after: fear and hope in the scene of the marriage promise, the refusal to realise that their happiness is fading ('It was the nightingale and not the lark'), and the pain of parting in the day song of the third act. How much less shadowed is the lovers' bliss presented in the *Romeo and Juliet* operas by Bellini and Gounod! But over and over, the moment of the greatest bliss and the moment of death are one and the same. How many deaths are died for love in opera, especially during the nineteenth century!

Not just the antagonism between love and death, but also the idea of their mystical unity, the delimitation experience melding *Eros* and *Thanatos* – linked with Romanticism and its successors via Wagner's eroticism of death to the *fin de siècle* – harken back to the humanism of the Renaissance and the mystic religions of Antiquity.[8] As Schopenhauer already remarked, Hellenistic and Roman sarcophagi are frequently decorated with erotic motifs, such as Leda and the swan. The topic is always the love of a god for a mortal: Dionysus loving Ariadne, Zeus loving Semele or Artemis loving Endymion. This antique constellation returns in the legends and fairy tales of love between humans and nature's sprites or demonic spirits, whether they are female figures, such as the mermaids Undine and Melusine – and finally Rusalka in Dvořák's opera, or the Little Mermaid in Andersen's fairy tale – or heroes who descend from a superhuman sphere to the humans, such as Lohengrin. Wagner explicitly interpreted the tragedy of Lohengrin and Elsa as a Christian-medieval variety of the myth of Zeus and Semele.

'Dying meant to be loved by a god and to partake of eternal happiness through him', Edgar Wind wrote in his famous book *Heidnische Mysterien in der Renaissance (Pagan Mysteries in the Renaissance)*.[9] The humanist Pierio Valeriano remarks that those 'who long for god and to be one with god are carried towards heaven and freed of their bodies by a death which is the deepest sleep. This form of death was called "the kiss" by the symbolist theologians.'[10] The Renaissance philosophers devoted innumerable works to the death kiss (*mors osculi, morte di bacio*). And more than any other music of the Renaissance, Gesualdo's art of the madrigal bears the marks of this death kiss, with its extreme harmonic experimentation that foreshadows much of music's future development and that appears to spring from a semantics of death's eroticism.

Verdi's *Otello* ends with a *morte di bacio*, stripped of its metaphysical symbolism; what is originally a kiss of love ultimately becomes a kiss of death: 'Un bacio ... ancora un bacio.' An *imitatio perversa* of the *mors osculi* is the kiss that Oscar Wilde's and Richard Strauss' Salome plants on the lips of the severed head of Jochanaan, who has refused to love her. Richard Wagner was closest to the concept of a kiss of death, reminiscent of the *Eros funebre*, the secret of the erotic decorations on the tombs of Antiquity, when he remarked in conversation with Cosima on August 15, 1869: 'The kiss of love is the first intimation of death, the boundary of individuality, and that is why one is scared so much by it.'[11] A similar thought is expressed in a poem by Friedrich Rückert (*After Dshelaleddin Rumi*):

> Thus, a heart trembles before love,
> As if threatened with doom.
> For where love awakens,
> Ego, the dark despot, dies.[12]

The unity of *Eros* and *Thanatos* as a mystical delimitation experience found its most powerful poetic expression in German pre-Romantic literature in 1773, in the final scene of Goethe's drama fragment *Prometheus*. Prometheus, whose titanic pathos is so much apparent in Goethe's famous hymn ('*Bedecke deinen Himmel, Zeus*' – 'Cover your skies, Zeus') and who also resoundingly opens the dramatic fragment; this defiant, egocentric Titan matures throughout this work to become a selfless mystic. Shaken, Pandora tells her father Prometheus how she observed a mysterious incident – a love scene that her childish innocence cannot comprehend. The lovers' swooning, their kisses and tears are unknown to her and deeply disturbing. 'Tell me, / What is all that, which shakes them / And me?', she asks her father. His lapidary answer: 'Death!'

PROMETHEUS
There is a moment that fulfills everything.
Everything we have longed for, dreamed of, hoped for,
And feared, my dearest. That is death.
PANDORA
Death?
PROMETHEUS
When, from your innermost depth
You feel everything, deeply shaken,

Everything joy and sorrow ever brought you,
When your heart swells as in a storm,
Wants to cry for relief and only deepens its flame,
And everything in you resounds and trembles and shakes,
And all your senses falter
And you swoon, and everything around you
Sinks into night, and in your innermost feeling
You grasp a world,
Then, a human being dies.
PANDORA (embracing him)
Oh father, let us die![13]

Who could overlook the foreshadowing of Novalis' *Hymns to the Night* and Wagner's *Tristan and Isolde* in these outrageous verses by the 24-year-old Goethe! The more Prometheus instructs the human beings to become themselves, the greater is their longing for a loss of self, a delimitation of the *principium individuationis*. They long for a condition in which death and love are one.

In relation to the kiss of death and the longing for a unification with God (which is projected onto ancient myths about the love between Gods and humans), Pierio Valeriano has utilised the image of the *assumptio* – the journey to heaven. Here, too, we can draw a connection to Richard Wagner, who compared his Isolde with Tizian's Venetian *Assunta*, which Wagner adored. In her diary entry of 22 October 1882 Cosima writes that Wagner denied 'that the Assunta is the mother of God, she is Isolde declaring her love'.[14] Wagner was intuitively aware that Tizian's painting dealt with the erotics of death, which preoccupied the Platonists of the Renaissance: the assumption of the mortal Mary into heaven means her ecstatic unification with God – a true transfiguration of love.

But Wagner no longer believes in the Christian metaphysical basis of love's transfiguration. Therefore, he relates it to Isolde and an erotics of death, which removes the theological background. In place of a love between Gods and mortals he foregrounds the experience of a loss of self emerging from pure human love, which can symbolically be connected to the old religious images of *Eros* and *Thanatos*. This becomes obvious, for example, in Isolde's final song referring to Tristan: 'Immer lichter / wie er leuchtet, / … / Stern-umstrahlet / hoch sich hebt: / seht ihr, Freunde, / seht ihr's nicht?' ('Brighter and brighter / how he shines, / illuminated by stars / rises high: / do you see it, friends, / don't you see it?'). The circle of stars is the usual symbol of the *Assumpta*. And when Tristan and Isolde sing in their love hymn in the second act: 'Ohne Gleiche! / Überreiche!' ('Without equal! / Overflowing!'), their words remind us of Gretchen's prayer to the *Mater Gloriosa* in the mountain scene of Goethe's *Faust*: 'Du Ohnegleiche, / Du Strahlenreiche' ('You unequalled, you richly radiant').[15] *Tristan and Isolde*'s world-immanent mystery of love contains images of the mysticism of Mary.

The *morte di bacio* in Wagner is no longer associated with an encounter between God and Man by means of which the human being enters eternal peace. This is also confirmed if we look beyond *Tristan and Isolde* to Wagner's other musical dramas. With the exception of the happy ending of the *Meistersinger*, love in Wagner is always connected to death, to a radical readiness for death. But love's telos is always a merging of lovers with each other, even when the heavens sanction such a release or deliverance (as, for example, in *Tannhäuser*). At the end of *Der fliegende Holländer* (*The Flying Dutchman*) man does not ascend to God; instead, the saved one and his saviour both experience their *assumptio* together: 'In weiter Ferne entsteigen dem Wasser der Holländer und Senta, beide in verklärter Gestalt; er hält sie umschlungen'[16] ('In the far distance the Dutchman and Senta, he embracing her, rise from the water, both transfigured'). This is a *morte di bacio* without transcendental–redemptive reference.

On the other hand, where God and the human being enter a love union no 'redemption' takes place either, as in the *Lohengrin*, for example, which, as Wagner pointed out, was informed by the myth of Zeus and Semele. There is such a deep alienation between Lohengrin and Elsa, between the divine and the human, that they can only destroy one another. Elsa dies without experiencing any metaphysical transfiguration. Lohengrin returns defeated to his solitude with the 'Geständniß seiner Göttlichkeit' ('confession of his divinity'), as we read in Wagner's *Eine Mitteilung an meine Freunde* (*A Communication to My Friends*) (1851).[17] After all, Brünnhilde is no longer a divine being when she is woken up by Siegfried. There has opened up an incurable rift between Gods and humans in the *Walküre*. The kiss with which Wotan sends his daughter into a kind of sleep of death is not a death kiss raising her to divine life but, to the contrary, he robs her of her divinity and lowers her to the level of the human. Therefore only a human will be able to awaken her from this sleep of death.

Tristan and Isolde is even more so a world without redemptive transcendence – it is Wagner's only musical drama without manifest Gods or God. In the powerful synaesthetic hymn which ends *Tristan and Isolde*, the *unio mystica* of the lovers is carried out in a pantheistic, spiritualised universe. Isolde, in her final ecstasy of death, feels herself enveloped by sounds, breezes, waves and fragrances. The German preposition and prefix '*um*' suggests an embracing elemental medium in which Isolde dissolves with Tristan. This dissolution is represented as: 'süß in Düften / mich verhauchen' – 'ertrinken / versinken' in 'des Welt-Athems / wehendem All' ('Sweet in fragrances / melt away' – drown / be engulfed' in 'the wafting Universe of the World-Breath' which mingles with the 'sweet breath' from Tristan's lips.[18] This *unio mystica* with the dead lover is a way of entering the divine totality. 'Love in *Tristan* is not to be understood in terms of Schopenhauer but in terms of Empedokles', Nietzsche writes in a posthumous note in 1875. Love is the 'sign and guarantor of an eternal unity'.[19]

Indeed, despite Schopenhauer's influence, *Tristan and Isolde* does not embrace his pessimism. Rather, pessimism makes way for an affirmation of the cause or essence of the world, which becomes manifest in powerful terms at the end of the musical drama. Isolde's *Liebestod* has nothing in common with the cessation of all desire in nirvana which, according to Schopenhauer, can be achieved only by means of a renunciation of worldly things. Wagner distanced himself from such a view in a letter to Mathilde Wesendonck on 1 December 1858, and also in an unposted draft letter to Schopenhauer himself. Wagner describes love as a way of salvation[20] which leads to a transcendence of the 'individual strength of will'.[21] In a sense, Wagner re-interprets Schopenhauer's 'Metaphysics of Sexual Love' in the spirit of his philosophy of death.

In the most important philosophical source for *Tristan and Isolde*, Schopenhauer's treatise 'On Death and Its Relation to the Indestructibility of Our Inner Nature' (1819), we read that death is that moment of 'deliverance from the one-sidedness of an individuality which does not constitute the inmost kernel of our being, but is rather to be thought of as a kind of aberration of it. The true original freedom re-enters at this moment, which, in the sense indicated, may be regarded as a restitutio in integrum.'[22] But for Schopenhauer *Eros* is diametrically opposed to this 'restitutio in integrum'. 'The sexual impulse also proves itself the decided and strongest assertion of life by the fact that to man in a state of nature, as to the brutes, it is the final end, the highest goal of life. Self-maintenance is his first effort.'[23] In Wagner, where the symbolic identity of the love and death potion in *Tristan and Isolde* is most significant, *Eros* removes itself from servitude to life and becomes one with a longing for death and sublation of the individual, a longing for the self's union with the universe ('even then / I am the world'[24]).

Death, according to Schopenhauer, 'is the great opportunity to no longer be I'.[25] This is also the goal of Tristan and Isolde's love, which can realise itself only in death. That is why they exchange their identities (Isolde: 'You Isolde / Tristan I / no longer Isolde!' Tristan: 'You Tristan / Isolde I / no longer Tristan!'), why they long for their sweet word 'and' which separates their names from each other, and which expresses that they are not yet one but still I *and* you. They want to experience their individual loss of self through each other. Not only death but also love – the death in love, the love in death – offer 'the great opportunity to no longer be I'. This is the message of *Tristan and Isolde* – in the spirit with and against Schopenhauer – which carries over an erotics of death from ancient mysteries, to Renaissance neo-Platonism via Romanticism into a world without transcendence.

The love potion of *Tristan and Isolde* is the abbreviation of a complex psychological process. He 'has discovered what had to become obvious', says Bangäne in Wagner's prose draft version of *Tristan*.[26] For it is not the love potion, the drug from the magic kitchen of Isolde's mother, which kindles Tristan and Isolde's love, but, because both believe to be drinking death – the poison which Isolde has ordered Brangäne to get from the mother's pharmacy and which Brangäne secretly swaps with a love potion – they confess to their repressed love, and the illusory values and defiant sense of self-protection which had separated them disappear. This is Wagner's re-interpretation of the medieval subject matter, the original meaning of which has been recovered in Frank Martin's oratorio *Le vin herbé*, based on a philological novel by Joseph Bédier. (In the medieval novel, whose traces both Bédier and Martin follow, it is the love potion alone that awakens the love between Tristan and Isolde. This love does not already exist beforehand.) In Wagner, it is only the supposed death potion which makes possible the complete confession of love. Magic no longer prevails; rather, to use the title of Calderón's play: *Love [is] the Greatest Enchantment*, but it is a love which has been created from the enchantment of death, an erotics of death which has distanced itself from its former religious context. The love between Gods and mortals is replaced by a purely human love on which the old religious sentiments of *Eros* and *Thanatos* are projected symbolically.

The maelstrom of erotic death in *Tristan and Isolde* is a recurring topic in the literature of decadence of the *fin de siècle*[27] and it is often associated with Wagner's own death in Venice, where, in 1858, he completed the second act of this night- and death-intoxicated musical drama. Wagner's death represents a myth of the *fin de siècle*, as, for example, in Gabriele d'Annunzio's novel *Il Fuoco* (1900), which describes a morbidly magnificent funeral procession of Wagner's body across the Canale Grande; and in Maurice Barrès' *La Mort de Venise* (1902) or Thomas Mann's *Tod in Venedig* (1912), with its rich allusions to art and the life of Wagner. In Mann's *Buddenbrooks* (1901) and his *Tristan* novella (1903), *Tristan and Isolde* constitutes the cause of death of its protagonists. Hanno Buddenbrook's amateurish metamorphoses of *Tristan and Isolde* on the piano foreshadow the death of this hyper-sensitive boy who is losing the will to life; and, in the novella, the consumptive Gabriele Klöterjahn dies from exaltation, having played Wagner's score on the piano. What is still a mystical union of love and death in Wagner becomes here an aestheticisation of hubris and cruelty.

There is no opera in the history of music where the theme of the kiss of death is as significant and overwhelming as in Jaroslav Kvapil and Antonín Dvořák's 'lyrical poem' *Rusalka* (1901), which contains many harmonic quotations of Wagner's *Tristan and Isolde*. Here, of course, the semantics of the *morte di bacio* are a reversal of the humanistic tradition. The prince has betrayed his love for the water nymph Rusalka, who represents the *femme enfant* or *femme fragile* – a popular type in *fin-de-siècle* literature – by falling passionately for a foreign duchess, a typical *femme fatale*; but at the end he returns, his soul broken, to the beloved natural being Rusalka and longs for her liberating, purifying kiss of death: 'Kiss me, oh kiss me, grant me peace! / I do not want to return to the circle of the world / kiss me, oh kiss me to death!' But Aquarius, king of the elements and fantastical Christian metamorphosis of Poseidon, shows that any hope for the liberating power of love/death is futile: 'He dies in vain in your arms / futile are all sacrifices / inconsolable, pale Rusalka! / Woe! Woe! Woe!' Rusalka is excluded from the world of Christian redemption, yet, hoping that her sacrifice of love will bring the mercy of God to her futile lover, she gives him the kiss of death. But in doing so she excludes herself from eternal salvation – like Lohengrin, and Wotan, who kisses Brünnhilde into a death-like slumber, which condemns them both to eternal sorrow.

One of the most profound continuations of the *Tristan* message may be found in the final scene of Hofmannsthal and Strauss' *Ariadne auf Naxos*, where the *unio mystica* of death and love returns to its sources in Antiquity. Having been abandoned by Theseus because the Gods have decided that Dionysus should be her husband, Ariadne expects nothing but death. Here, as always where love reigns absolute, death is the only force for which love may be traded in. And this trade-off, this deception, takes place in the encounter with Bacchus-Dionysus. Ariadne thinks that Death is coming for her on his boat – the boat of Charon. She confuses death and love, just as Goethe's Prometheus and Pandora identify both, and truly takes Dionysus as *Thanatos* and thus as a 'great god of the soul' who really 'is kin to Dionysus, to Venus' – as Death identifies himself in Hofmannsthal's early drama. She confides in Bacchus 'as one confides only in Death', Hofmannsthal writes in his great Ariadne letter to Richard Strauss in mid-July 1911. 'She gives herself over to him, as she thinks he is Death; he is death and life at the same time.'[28] That is the secret of the Dionysian element as the experience of the ego's delimitation. Death and the highest form of life, as it is revealed in the 'enormity of the erotic experience' (Hofmannsthal),[29] become one. That is also the theme of Hofmannsthal's fragment *Semiramis* of 1909: 'Semiramis and death: only when she knows she is dying is she able to feel love … only now does she live.' Only now does she realise that 'only he lives who has absorbed death'.[30] And only he who has absorbed death is capable of truly loving.

For love is as strong as death. We have traced this biblical message through the history of opera and noticed that the strength of love and death can be the result of a conflict – where death defeats the lovers in their worldly existence, but love has the power to transcend it – or of death and love's mystical unification. In the *Song of Solomon* God grants love a power equal to death, a power to survive life and even death. The Christian message establishes the redemptive power of love. God sacrifices his son out of love for humankind; Jesus accepts death in order to deliver us from evil: for love – through death. Love and death become one in the redemptive act of Jesus Christ; love finally triumphs over death. This metaphysical certainty of divine and redemptive love's victory over the power of all-consuming death disappears in our secular world. But it is transferred onto erotic love, as is evident in the message of redemption contained in modern erotic religiosity. The ending of Wagner's *Tannhäuser* is a classic example of an erotic love of redemption against a Christian background. This is also the case in Massenet's *Werther*. The dying Werther receives the Christmas message – a leitmotif of the work – and interprets love as a redemptive power which grants him eternal life. In *Rusalka*, the unfaithful lover is granted Christian mercy through the love of the pagan creature Rusalka, a mercy which she herself is excluded from. And every religious person keeps hoping that love is as strong as death, that love carries us beyond our individual frailness. This experience is given to us above all in music, which has the power to overcome the finality of existence, especially in those moments of happy love which Mozart, unlike any other composer, was able to create for us in his overpowering work.

One of the most moving aspects of Mozart's music is its ability to present moments which are so fulfilled that they make time stand still. This the condition of pure happiness, which Pamina and Tamino praise in song after the trial of fire and water: 'Thou Gods! What a moment! / We have received Isis' happiness!'[31] This condition of pure happiness is established in powerful terms when death stands in the background, as is the case in this trial of fire and water – the deadly threat of the elements – or in the duet between Belmonte and Constanze in the Abduction, in the moment when the lovers are convinced that they are going to face death. Beethoven has repeated this Mozartian 'experience of the moment' in his *Fidelio*, when Leonore removes Florestan's chains: 'Oh God! – What a moment!' In Beethoven, as in Mozart, the fulfilled, completely present moment is cherished as a moment of re-united love; a moment which does not lack anything because, in the words of the three boys in the

Zauberflöte: 'the world is a heaven / and mortals are like Gods'. In this moment of transcending the finite, Man becomes equal to the Gods. This is the experience of music and perhaps the deepest secret of opera.

Notes

1. Hugo von Hofmannsthal, *Gesammelte Werke*, ed. Bernd Schoeller (Frankfurt am Main, 1979), p. 288.
2. *Lessings Werke*, vol. VI, ed. Georg Witkowski, (Leipzig/Wien [no year]), p. 80.
3. Friedrich Schiller, *Sämtliche Werke*, vol. 1, ed. Albert Meier (München/Wien, 2004), p. 166.
4. See Jan Assmann, *Die Zauberflöte. Oper und Mysterium* (München/Wien, 2005), p. 69ff.
5. See Dieter Borchmeyer, *Mozart oder die Entdeckung der Liebe* (Frankfurt am Main and Leipzig, 2005), p. 83ff.
6. See Dieter Borchmeyer, '"El maestro vol cussi, e basta"! Verdi und die Struktur des Opernlibrettos', in Udo Bermbach (ed.), *Verdi-Theater* (Stuttgart/Weimar, 1997), pp. 117–40; p. 130f.
7. See Wulf Konold, 'Der festgehaltene Augenblick. Zur Dramaturgie von Verdis Opern', in Udo Bermbach (ed.), *Verdi-Theater* (Stuttgart/Weimar, 1997), pp. 141–64.
8. See Edgar Wind, *Heidnische Mysterien in der Renaissance* (Frankfurt am Main, 1981), pp. 177–97 ('Amor as God of Death').
9. *Ibid.*, p. 179.
10. Cited in *ibid.*, p. 179f.
11. Cosima Wagner, *Die Tagebücher. Volume I* (Munich, 1976), p. 140.
12. See Dieter Borchmeyer, *Das Theater Richard Wagners* (Stuttgart, 1982), p. 270.
13. *Goethes Werke*. Hamburger Ausgabe, 10th edn, vol. 4 (Munich, 1981), p. 186f.
14. Cosima Wagner, *Die Tagebücher. Volume II* (Munich, 1977), p. 1029.
15. See Borchmeyer, *Das Theater Richard Wagners*, p. 282f.
16. Richard Wagner, *Gesammelte Schriften und Dichtungen* (*Complete Works and Poems*), vol. I, 2nd edn (Leipzig, 1888), p. 291.
17. *Ibid.*, vol. 4, p. 296.
18. Wagner, *Gesammelte Schriften und Dichtungen*, vol. 7, p. 80f.
19. Friedrich Nietzsche, *Kritische Studienausgabe*, vol. 8, eds Giorgio Colli and Mazzino Montinari (Munich, 1980), p. 191.
20. Wagner, *Sämtliche Schriften und Dichtungen*, Volksausgabe, vol. 12 (Leipzig, 1911), p. 291.
21. Richard Wagner to Mathilde Wesendonk. Berlin 1904, p. 79f.
22. Arthur Schopenhauer, *The World as Will and Representation*, Part 2, Supplements to the fourth book, chapter 41, trans. R.B. Haldane and J. Kemp (London, 1909), p. 308.
23. *Ibid.*, Part 1, Book 4, §60.
24. Wagner, *Gesammelte Schriften und Dichtungen*, vol. 7, p. 45.
25. Schopenhauer, *The World as Will and Representation*, p. 307.
26. Wagner, *Sämtliche Schriften und Dichtungen*, vol. 11, p. 334.
27. See Erwin Koppen, *Dekadenter Wagnerismus. Studien zur europäischen Literatur des Fin de siècle* (Berlin/New York, 1973).
28. Richard Strauss/Hugo von Hofmannsthal, Briefwechsel (Letters), *Gesamtausgabe* (Zürich, 1964), p. 134.
29. *Ibid.*, p. 135.
30. Hofmannsthal, *Gesammelte Werke*, p. 565.
31. See Dieter Borchmeyer, *Mozart oder die Entdeckung der Liebe* (Frankfurt am Main, 2005), p. 35ff.

6

Eros/sex, death/murder: sensuality, homicide and culture in Musil, Brecht and the Neue Sachlichkeit

George Hunka

A still photograph of Marlene Dietrich in Josef von Sternberg's 1930 film *The Blue Angel* remains the most potent symbol of late Weimar sensuality. Leaning back while seated on top of a barrel, wearing a silver top hat and silver heels, revealing pale thigh and delicate ruffled undergarments, Lola-Lola shamelessly invites and displays male and female desire from the stage of a smoky beer-sodden cabaret. Even those who have not seen the film itself are attracted by the grey, potent image and can identify it as an expression of transgressive and female sexuality.[1] Dietrich remains an icon of the LGBT community even now, nearly a century later.

The Blue Angel was released only a few years before the end of the Weimar period. In 1933 Hitler's rise to the Chancellorship of Germany effectively led to the nullification of the republic's constitution, symbolised by the Reichstag fire in February. By then, Dietrich and von Sternberg were in Hollywood, and most of the representatives of the then-dominant *Neue Sachlichkeit* movement in the plastic arts and literature would soon follow them into exile.

Von Sternberg's film may represent an epitaph for the final flowering of female and transgressive sensuality represented by the movement. The theme of the film – the incompatibility of creative sexuality and sensuality with a bourgeois, militarist and conformist middle-class culture – left Emil Jannings' Professor Unrat for dead at the desk of his classroom in the final frames, and implied the revenge of the culture against the subversive energies that such a sexuality unleashed. The film's release, however, came at the end of a thirty-year period that began with the 1905 publication of Sigmund Freud's landmark *Three Essays on the Theory of Sexuality*, a book which posited the inescapable presence of transgressive sexualities within the irrational unconscious self. Freud's work, as it reached wider audiences through the next thirty years, constituted a profound threat to conventional bourgeois morality in the German-speaking world, as well as the Enlightenment project of a progressive, ameliorist human rationality. This realisation played itself out in aesthetics almost immediately, informing Schoenberg's monodrama *Erwartung* in 1909;[2] as Expressionism gave way to the *Neue Sachlichkeit*, the work of artists such as Otto Dix, George Grosz and Christian Schad and the early plays of Bertolt Brecht also evinced this realisation. A profound conflict between this morality and the emergence of the irrational sexual being revealed itself not merely in art and culture, but also in violent criminality that may have been the first individual, private vengeances against these realisations, a vengeance that was writ more culturally with the rise of twentieth-century European fascism. Although the *Neue Sachlichkeit* artists conceived of their project as a reaction against Expressionism, as a politically active and potentially revolutionary aesthetic that addressed the industrialised realities of the early twentieth century, the *Neue Sachlichkeit* also resulted in an explosion in the art of individual portraiture. In addition, the re-emergence of figurative rather than abstract graphical gestures in the works of these artists (who were profoundly influenced by the painters of the Northern Renaissance) also emphasised a new awareness of decay and sexuality within the individual bodies of the portraits' subjects: an extension into figurative art of the more abstract tropes of the Expressionists, rather than a complete repudiation of individualism.

The public sexual consciousness of the period has been examined more recently with the publication of books such as Mel Gordon's provocatively titled *Voluptuous Panic*, which chronicles the conflicts – between *Eros* and death, conformity and rebellion, sensuality and erotic self-denial – that emerged during the Weimar era. As a collection of ephemera that includes newspaper articles, photographs, magazines, postcards and other disposable erotica and pornography, the book underscores the presence of these conflicts as they emerged in the private consumption of the products of mass reproducible media. If Freud's theories retain any validity, the conflict between conformity and sexuality, middle-class domesticity and sensuality, remains valid a century later, and the conflict plays itself out within a culture that has expressed its conformist domination through administration rather than militarism: the totally administered society foreseen by Theodor W. Adorno.

To trace this association of eros and death, mass sexuality and mass murder, of which *The Blue Angel* was only a late exemplar, one can turn to *fin-de-siècle* Vienna and the closing years of the Habsburg dynasty for clues to Modernism's tragic end. While the years 1914–1933 marked the triumph of Modernism, they also signalled the triumph of forces that sought to undermine the erotic possibilities of transgressive sexuality through the pursuit of a stable bourgeois conformity: a conformity that reached its full emergence in the explicit bourgeois authoritarianism of the Second World War's axis powers and the implicit administered state of the allies.

Robert Musil: Eros, disaster and transgression

In the first volume of his monumental novel tracing the end of Austrian modernism, *The Man Without Qualities*, Robert Musil places a character named Moosbrugger at the centre of Vienna's journalistic culture in the years just before the First World War. Moosbrugger, whose gross and brutal sex murder of a prostitute has attracted enormous attention, has become a celebrity, his name on the lips of every visitor to cocktail parties, at every café table:

> For Moosbrugger had killed a woman, a prostitute of the lowest type, in a horrifying manner. The reporters described in detail a knife wound in the throat from the larynx to the back of the neck, also the two stab wounds in the breast that penetrated the heart, and the two in the back on the left side, and how both breasts were sliced through so that they could almost be lifted off. The reporters had expressed their revulsion at this, but they did not stop until they had counted thirty-five stabs in the belly and explained the deep slash that reached from the navel to the sacrum, continuing up the back in numerous lesser cuts, while the throat showed marks of strangulation. From such horrors they could not find their way back to Moosbrugger's good-natured face, although they were themselves good-natured men who had nevertheless described what

had happened in a factual, expert manner and, evidently, in breathless excitement. They hardly availed themselves of even the most obvious explanation, that the man before them was insane – for Moosbrugger had already been in various mental hospitals several times for similar crimes – even though a good reporter is very well informed on such questions these days; it looked as though they were still reluctant to give up the idea of the villain, to banish the incident from their own world into the world of the insane. Their attitude was matched by that of the psychiatrists, who had already declared him normal just as often as they had declared him not accountable for his actions. There was also the amazing fact that no sooner had they become known than Moosbrugger's pathological excesses were regarded as 'finally something interesting for a change' by thousands of people who deplore the sensationalism of the press, from busy officeholders to fourteen-year-old sons to housewives befogged by their domestic cares. While these people of course sighed over such a monstrosity, they were nevertheless more deeply preoccupied with it than with their own life's work. Indeed, it might happen that a punctilious department head or bank manager would say to his sleepy wife at bedtime: 'What would you do now if I were a Moosbrugger?'[3]

Musil's witty description draws a precis of the rise of the celebrity culture in Western media: Moosbrugger is not famous for being famous, perhaps, but he is nonetheless elevated to the status of media 'darling'. (In his criticism of Viennese media, Karl Kraus ridiculed the simultaneous titillation and puritanism of the coverage of sexual crimes and prostitution in the Austrian press; some of his strongest writings of the period argued for sexual freedom and the legalisation of prostitution, arguing that its continued repression inevitably resulted in violence.) No doubt there had been sex murders earlier, but the emergence of industrialised media, as well as the recent ability of publishers to reproduce photographs in rotogravure press, laid the groundwork for a new fascination with such murders. (The 1888 Jack the Ripper murders of Victorian London pre-dated the fictional Moosbrugger by about twenty-five years, but even there, the sex crime was concomitant with the new photographic journalism, and the killer himself acknowledged the new mass status of the press by writing to the daily newspapers himself.)

Both Moosbrugger and Jack the Ripper locate this particular confluence of sex and death within the economic relationship of women to men: a pleasure purchase enacted within a professionalised service economy. While prostitution may be the world's oldest profession, until the rise of the industrialised press it may also have been one of the most private and intimate: an economic and sexualised encounter between a man and a woman. The rise of the photographic mass press brought the prostitute–client relationship into a brighter light: no longer private, it became a centre of community attention. The perversity of the relationship, however, is what reaches the front pages of these newspapers, not its ubiquity through history. The reportage associated with Moosbrugger and his crime is simultaneously sensational and didactic: it provides a moral warning ('This is what happens to women who transgress sexually, seeking in business the pleasures that should be found only within sacred matrimony') and at the same time an acknowledgement of the darker forces at work within the power relationships that govern sexual partnership and pleasure ('What would you do now if I were a Moosbrugger?').

Moosbrugger remains a peculiar figure at the fringes of *The Man Without Qualities*: a symbol of extreme reaction against the urgings of the unconscious, a reaction which defies rational explanation even as the figure presents himself as just another Viennese. 'The psychiatrists … had already declared him normal just as often as they had declared him not accountable for his actions'[4] – a chilling indictment not only of Moosbrugger but also of the dynamics that lead to deterministic social, political and economic explanations for the wars of the twentieth century. The bestiality of the murder, as well as its direct relationship to an illicit sexuality, hangs over the novel like a grey cloud, until Ulrich and his sister Agathe find a potential release from meaningless anxiety in transgressive sexuality[5] in volume 3 of the unfinished work:

It's the ancient longing for a doppelgänger of the opposite sex, for a lover who will be the same as yourself and yet someone else, a magical figure that is oneself and yet remains magical, with the advantage over something we merely imagine of having the breath of autonomy and independence.[6]

Musil's dual aesthetic intent – to provide a satiric portrait of the Austria of the pre-First World War period and to attempt a novel that more ambitiously charts the metaphysics of that culture and the forces that led to its decay – writes the private on the public, the intimate on the cultural. The public's fascination with the Moosbrugger case occurs within a culture and a media that hesitate to grapple with the larger socio-political and nationalistic ideologies that would eventually lead to the assassination of Franz Ferdinand and the mobilisation of France and Germany (and, finally, to the mass slaughter of the war). Moosbrugger's fantasies of control and murder in the bedroom lead to the fantasies of power, subjugation and violent death on the battlefield: the participants in which are also 'normal' and 'not responsible for their actions'.

From Musil to Brecht/from sex to politics: Expressionism to the *Neue Sachlichkeit*

Of the two streams of post-Kantian philosophy represented by Schopen-hauer and Hegel, the philosophy of Schopenhauer and Kierkegaard served as inescapable influences in the work of Wittgenstein and other Viennese artists during the pre-First World War years: philosophies which found artistic outlet in the journalism of Karl Kraus, the music of Schoenberg and Webern, the paintings of Gustav Klimt and Egon Schiele and the psychology of Freud and his followers.[7] But the war years were accompanied by the initial success of the Russian Revolution of 1917, which fired the imaginations of politically aware artists with a radical progressivism that drew Hegelian and Marxist dialectic once again into common cultural currency. The catastrophe of the war, especially among the vanquished German-language nations, seems to have given rise to a recognition of the necessity for radical, violent if necessary, political change. In the wake of the war Soviet-style coups took place in a number of German localities – none of which entirely succeeded, but which informed the composition of the Weimar constitution, which itself exemplified a delicate and ultimately unsustainable balance among the radical left-wing and radical right-wing government powers, as well as the capitalist ownership and working classes.

The months of late 1913 and early 1914, during which *The Man Without Qualities* was set, also marked a development in aesthetics in German-language countries. Expressionism was already on the wane, evolving instead into the less abstract but no less experimental forms of the *Neue Sachlichkeit*. The hysteria that might have been assigned to *Erwartung*'s 'Woman' was no longer assigned to a generalised humanist abstraction but inhered now in individualised figures.[8] The *Neue Sachlichkeit* movement, however, did not lead to forms of photorealism in painting, despite the 'objectivity' that '*Sachlichkeit*' implied. The explosion in portraiture that accompanied the rise of the movement in painting now provided recognisable and identifiable facial and physical features in the human body, but, like the work of Expressionism, these portraits provided them in exaggerated forms. The *Neue Sachlichkeit* portraitists may have looked to the work of the sixteenth-century Northern Renaissance for compositional reference and inspiration – as in the Dutch portraits of burghers and government officials, the posed figures were surrounded by artefacts of their professions, livelihoods and social status – but perspective was deliberately flattened, rendering minor inanimate objects and secondary figures in the portraits of equal status to the subjects.

Sexual and spiritual identity in these portraits was thereby foregrounded by the status of these subjects as individual bodies. No longer an abstract quality to be plucked from the air and trees of the forest that surrounded *Erwartung*'s 'Woman', desire gained a face, a torso and a name. And while Christian Schad concentrated on the sensuality of the Weimar Republic in which he worked, Otto Dix looked back to the suffering of the First World War, George Grosz forward to the economic and cultural disaster that followed in the wake of Germany's defeat.

In the drama, the young Bertolt Brecht paid allegiance to no specific movement in the first decade of his career (1918–1928, approximately comprising the plays from *Baal* to *Dreigroschenoper*), although his first stage works were deliberately antagonistic responses to the Expressionism of Georg Kaiser and Hanns Johst.[9] Johst's *Der Einsame* served as direct inspiration for *Baal*, the earlier play arousing Brecht's wrath towards Expressionism's 'invocations of Humanity with a capital H', as John Willett has characterised the Expressionist drama.[10] For Brecht during these years, there was no Humanity, although there were Baals, Andreas Kraglers, George Gargas, Schlinks and Edwards; and, too, there were Johannas, Anna Balickes, Jane Gargas and Mortimers. Although the first stage productions of these plays apparently drew upon Expressionist scenic and directorial techniques, it rapidly became clear that the Expressionist *weltanschauung* would not support the individual agencies of the characters that populate the plays, who acted on their own behalfs and in their own interests rather than as representatives of larger cultural or metaphysical entities.

In part this was the result of the growing emphasis on urbanisation that also placed the city of Vienna at the centre of Musil's novel as an organic force of its own. Although *Baal* contains scenes set in forests and on riversides, these are alternated between scenes set in the small city of Augsburg and may well be justified as satiric and parodic commentaries on the natural world in which the Expressionists attempted to locate their abstracted human figures. Certainly the two plays that followed *Baal*, *Drums in the Night* and *In the Jungle of Cities*, are unquestionably urban works, their sexual and power dynamics located not among trees and rivers but in concrete buildings and on asphalt streets. Once these dynamics are extracted from forces outside the human collective and placed within the autonomous individual agent, they acquire a new and more dangerous energy: rather than a shared concern they become discrete within the bodies that contain them, antagonistic towards each other as autonomous identities rather than as representatives of a common humanity.

The range and spectrum of sexuality in Brecht's early plays would not be equalled in his later career, and the close relationship of *Eros* and death remains a central dynamic of these dramas. There are two explicit deaths within *Baal*, with both heterosexual (Johanna) and homosexual (Ekart) overtones, and the conflict described in *In the Jungle of Cities* is a 'fight to the death' between two men, one of whom tells the other 'I love you' during their final confrontation. *In the Jungle* also features depictions of miscegenation and prostitution, and the adaptation of Marlowe's *Edward II* does not tone down the homoerotic attraction between Mortimer and Edward, a transgressive sexuality that leads to an all-out civil war. There are murders in all three plays in which sexuality and eroticism are significant and compelling motives.

These early plays coincided with the crushing economic and cultural defeat of post-First World War Germany, a society pauperised first by the reparations demanded by the Versailles treaty and then by the global economic collapse of the late 1920s. In his satire of the soldier's homecoming play *Drums in the Night*, composed in 1919 and produced in Munich in 1922, Brecht opposed the autonomous individual Kragler to both the bourgeois ideology of the Balicke family and the communist ideology of the early German Soviets and found them both wanting; Kragler regains his former fiancée Anna Balicke and therefore a sexual identity and energy only when he repudiates both ideologies in the final moments of the play, the surviving soldier ironically confessing that he is not up to the game:

> The bagpipes play, the poor people die in the newspaper district, the houses fall on them, the day dawns. They lie in the street like drowned cats. I'm a stinker, and the stinker goes home. ... The shouting will all be over tomorrow morning, but I'll lie in bed tomorrow morning and multiply, so as not to perish from the earth. ... Drunken foolishness! Now's the time for bed, for the big, white, broad bed. Come![11]

Kragler's final monologue is played out in an energetic, physical fury against the sentimentality of both progressive ideology and bourgeois comfort; a final stage direction reads '[Kragler] staggers around and throws the drum at the moon which turns out to be a Japanese lantern. Drum and moon fall in the river, which has no water in it.'[12] Both Realism and Expressionism are contained in the moon and river, which in the end are revealed to be theatrical illusions: neither the bourgeois conformism of the Balickes nor the political radicalism of the revolutionaries in the newspaper district are, for Kragler, satisfying personal responses to the post-catastrophic culture of 1920s Germany.

As Germany's economic and cultural crisis deepened throughout the 1920s, Brecht turned more to politics. The 1926 *Man is Man*, a comedy satirising colonialism and instrumentalist conformity, is a fevered farce that careens energetically towards nihilism. But with the rise of German nationalist political parties and the destruction of the radical left through those years, Brecht was compelled to a study of Marxist economics, a study that began to find its way into his work in plays immediately preceding and following *Dreigroschenoper*, his most commercial success. For Brecht, nihilism was a dead-end. In lieu of hallucination, political commitment acquired new status.[13]

The tragedy of commitment: Brecht's *The Decision*

Among Brecht's plays the *Lehrstücke* are the most radically experimental in form and radically political in content; the best-known, *The Decision*, is a spare austere revelation of individual sacrifice for a social ideal. Four Communist agitators from the West travel to China to incite revolution; along the way, they gain another party functionary, the Young Comrade. In China the functionary, in demonstrating compassion and anger at the inhumanity he witnesses, makes a series of 'mistakes' – including his attempts to alleviate individual suffering. Finally, on the run from the police, at risk of arrest and execution themselves, they shoot the Young Comrade and toss his body into a lime pit, with his acquiescence.

It must be noted that Brecht, even before his Marxist period, dismissed the idea that his work was 'tragic' in any sense of the word. In a subtitle, he called *Drums in the Night* a comedy, and as he became more politically committed he had less concern for a form which, he believed, lacked value for a revolutionary politics – neither of the Aristotelian values of terror and pity were acceptable, unless 'by terror were meant terror before human beings, and by pity, pity for human beings, and if the theatre were to cooperate in removing these conditions among human beings that generate mutual fear and necessitate mutual pity. For the Fate of Man is now Man himself.'[14] But more broadly speaking, some qualities of tragedy still inhered. As in many tragedies, the story of *The Decision* is either well-known to its audience or telegraphed to the audience in the first scene or two; the rest is the journey to the tragic end. The dedication to a radical progressive point of view constitutes the bizarre motive for the murder/suicide; and because the Young Comrade's death is mentioned in the second line of the play ('We have to report the death of a comrade. ... We killed him. We shot him and threw him into a lime pit'), mortality hovers over the events of all the successive scenes.

It is a curious piece of agit-prop, and from the time of its premiere performance in Berlin in 1930 it was met with a deep ambivalence, much to Brecht's chagrin. In a 1956 letter to Paul Patera, who planned a production of the play in Sweden, Brecht wrote: 'In my experience, public performances of it inspire nothing but moral qualms, usually of the cheapest sort. Accordingly, I have not let anyone perform the play for a long time.' (Editor John Willett notes that Patera apparently planned an anti-Communist production of the play.)[15]

The discomfort that Brecht describes, those 'moral qualms', arises from the very fleshed nature of the Young Agitator's death: he is shot, then thrown into a lime pit, in which his skin melts away from his body – a painful fleshed sensuousness of violence. Although desexualised, the bodies in Brecht's *Lehrstücke* are not unfleshed: in lieu of sexual experience leading to a painful mortality, however, political experience leads to the same agonising self-eradication. Perhaps not sexual, the death remains sensual: a self-erasure of the body. Sexuality, sensuality and eroticism continued to play a significant role in Brecht's later works, but the body and its flesh were now a far more distant concern than in the early plays or even, as demonstrated above, the *Lehrstücke*. While Brecht's later plays cannot easily be charged with misogyny, it is also true that the sexual and the feminine became profoundly simplified. Prostitutes continued to populate Brecht's plays through the end of his career, but other women in the plays tended towards a strange virginal purity (always with the exception of Mother Courage, a profoundly ambivalent figure). Grusha, Shen Te and Kattrin, while permitted sensuality, are only marginally sexual figures, although Kattrin's character begins to display an erotic awakening in the scenes leading up to her death. This is an unfortunate neglect, since the prostitute as a figure in popular culture combines transgression, economics and sexuality, but in marginalising these figures Brecht neglects the opportunity of examining this nexus, perhaps because a Marxist and socialist political commitment found the dynamic difficult to contain or utilise in the progressive revolutionary project. Given the early plays, it is hard not to read some of Brecht's later dramatic work as a sublimation, if not purgation, of the elements of transgressive sexuality that informed his early drama. In exploring the aesthetic 'use of commitment' in the artist's work, the transgressive and erotic body – a vehicle for the autonomous individual and his or her imagination – is erased from the theatrical map. Humanity with an H once again becomes a central feature of the plays.

After the wars: and before the next?

As one traces the erotic mortal body through the work of Musil, the New Objectivists and Brecht to the films of von Sternberg and Pabst,[16] it is hard not to recognise the historical tension that lay beneath the dynamics of that body, especially with the hindsight of history and in the knowledge of Auschwitz and Hiroshima. In addition, in the totalising administered society that attempts to somehow unlearn this knowledge and seeks to become blameless once again, fascination with the Weimar era partakes of a titillation dissociated from the liberating project of Weimar's artists: the doom of that culture seems pre-ordained when viewed with the same historical hindsight. But this is mere historical determinism. The self's dive into the sensually metaphysical erotic body always toyed with mortality; drowning within darkness of ecstasy was possible, perhaps at some level desired, but never was that drowning necessarily pre-ordained. Auschwitz and Hiroshima may not have been the end of one chapter of human experience; they may have been the beginning of a second. As bodied entities, we continue to explore the same trajectories of *Eros* and mortality.

Sexuality and murder, *Eros* and death, remain a part of our culture even as the grisly violent details remain more fully sublimated in the Culture Industry, including its theatrical outlets, than ever. A New Puritanism not only constrains the reproduction of sensational photographs and graphics relating to sex murders in the electronic media, but continues to repress transgressive sexual imagination and creativity as well, while the totalising social project, in the name of progressive liberal democracy, paints a new myth of community and individuation. This Puritanism conceals the Lola-Lolas; it conceals the violence not only of war but of sexual frustration, as the Culture Industry suppresses these depictions in the name of the greater moral good; it also conceals the depiction of a wasted mortality at the front of Professor Unrat's classroom. What it ultimately cannot suppress is the creative energy of this sensuality, and the communitarian ideology, and urging to revenge and violence, that opposes it.

Note: I am indebted to Marilyn Nonken for information pertaining to the libretto of *Erwartung*.

Notes

1. A note on vocabulary here. Far from being an attempt to equate 'female' and 'transgressive', this phraseology reveals an issue integral to this paper: the desire to discuss an experience of sexuality that extends beyond received cultural norms to other forms of erotic, metaphysical and political possibility. I also considered the use of the word 'alternative', but this term is saddled with an assumption that one is discussing the sexual practices of the LGBT community; the issues discussed in this paper have their applicability in the realm of heterosexual male/female sensual dynamics as well (and, perhaps, even primarily). But one must get on with it: because 'transgressive' does indeed imply an exploration of sexuality beyond received cultural norms, no matter what the gender or sexual identity of the subject, I shall use it here.

2. The libretto for *Erwartung* was commissioned by Schoenberg from Marie Pappenheim, a Viennese physician; in 1928 she founded the Socialist Society for Sexual Counselling and Sexual Research with Wilhelm Reich.

3. Robert Musil, *The Man Without Qualities*, trans. Sophie Wilkins (New York, 1995), pp. 67–8.

4. *Ibid.*, p. 68.

5. Musil underscores the transgressive nature of this desire in his subtitle for volume 3, 'The Criminals', describing Ulrich and his sister Agathe.

6. Musil, *The Man Without Qualities*, p. 982.

7. Allan Janik and Stephen Toulmin's *Wittgenstein's Vienna* (New York, 1973) traces Schopenhauer's influence on these artists and writers and others. The absence of Hegelian or Marxist thought in Freud's work is demonstrated in the index to the *Standard Edition*, in which references to Schopenhauer's work appear nine times, Hegel's only once, and Marx's not at all. It is also notable that Schopenhauer was the first modern Western philosopher to place the sexual and sensual instinct at the centre of his metaphysics.

8. *Erwartung* is a 40-minute monodrama for orchestra and solo female vocalist depicting the dreamscape of a sexual and metaphysical hysteria that accompanies the character's discovery of her lover's dead body in the midst of a dark forest at night. Neither the character nor the locale have a name, set instead in an abstraction of a mental state.

9. It is of some interest that Johst, one of Expressionism's most popular dramatic representatives, later rose to the position of President of the Writer's Union during the Nazi years. It was in one of his plays, *Schlageter*, that the saying 'When I hear the word culture ... I release the safety on my Browning!' appeared, a phrase later falsely attributed to Hermann Göring.

10. Bertolt Brecht, *Collected Plays, Volume 1*, eds Ralph Manheim and John Willett (New York, 1971), p. xvii.

11. *Ibid.*, p. 106.

12. *Ibid.*

13. Later in his career Brecht did not repudiate or suppress these early plays. Editions that appeared in his lifetime were often revised over time, as were indeed his mid-period and later plays, and on occasion he tried to infuse these early works with Marxist and socialist significance. But these revisions were unsuccessful, as he himself realised. 'I admit (and advise you)', Brecht wrote in a late preface to *Baal*, 'this play is lacking in wisdom.' (Brecht 1971, p. 346.)

14. Bertolt Brecht, 'Die Einfühlung' in *Der Messingkauf*. Cited in Frederic Ewen, *Bertolt Brecht: His Life, His Art, His Times* (New York, 1967), p. 232.

15. Bertolt Brecht, *Collected Plays: Three* (London, 1997), p. 347.

16. Pabst's 1929 *Pandora's Box*, compared to *The Blue Angel*, drew the parallel between sex and death even more sensationally – at the close of the film, Lulu is murdered by Jack the Ripper (rather anachronistically, given the time scheme) – but the von Sternberg film remains more politically prescient.

7

The living corpse: a metaphysic for theatre[1]

Dic Edwards

I

This essay will look at the power of theatre to transform. In attempting to show how I think it does this I will hope to bring some insight into my intention as a creative writer of theatre. Theatre has the power to transform because it speaks to us from beyond the temporal parameters that would seem to define it. I will hope to show what I mean by reference to several of my own performed plays.

In the first place, theatre transforms time into space (hereafter referred to as *the space*). It is its ability to do this that gives dramatic expression its unique power and creates transformation in the audience. What I mean by this is that theatre can transform our conscious state into one that has deeper insight into reality; that it can transform our lives from the essentially passive to the arguably creative. This is not so much to argue this power as unique to theatre but rather to make the claim for theatre in order to emphasise the particular authority attendant on that place where we act out the deepest concerns that preoccupy us. I have developed the notion of the *living corpse* as the catalyst for this transformation, embodying as it does the ultimate paradox of life in death and becoming a kind of talisman for the essential nature of drama, bearing in mind that whatever death may be, the dramatic aesthetic is always the profoundest expression of its presence. It is worth saying at this point that, beyond the much discussed relationship between sex and death, I would argue for these as agents of the living corpse and relate them to my theatre in this way: sex implies the embracing of an impossible language for the characters focused on here – Casanova (in *Casanova Undone*), Gary Gilmore (in *Utah Blue*) and

Baudelaire (in *The Pimp*) – it is the language of ecstasy and, in relation to this, the combination of what they say and their place within the action of the play become proto-expressions of a language of death, that which the language of drama aspires to. These things I will come back to but it is worth saying here, without qualification (that too will come later), that in this way we can believe that the dramatic aesthetic is beauty revealed by the embracing of death's discourse and that the agent of that is the living corpse.

Let me say a little more about the time/space dichotomy. Time confines us by an order that appears rigid and unavailing of any meaningful reinterpretation of that order. Because the laws that govern time may be rigid we can learn them and this may lead us to perceive what appears to be a pleasing harmony or what we may call the beautiful. Our relationship with space, on the other hand, is much more one in which we intuit arrangements which suggest beauty and we have to use our creativity in order to imagine what those arrangements, in an aesthetic sense, might be. For example, I want to argue that that which is limited by temporality and its laws cannot be beautiful, unless we mean that kind of beauty which we may feel, at any random moment, qualified to witness. I cannot think that it is beauty in this sense that we are talking about. For me, to say that beauty is in the eye of the beholder, for example, is nonsense just as it is nonsense to say that someone unfamiliar with the language of music might declare, say, a Bach partita ugly or, worse, boring. For me it is meaningless to say that the look of a person is beautiful. A person's beauty does not exist in time but in space in the sense that beauty is not made of what we see superficially but what is made by deeper realities. The language of beauty exists beyond boundaries – those boundaries which are created by arguable law – which have to be crossed similarly to those boundaries that exist between our quotidian contact with expression and true creativity. This, in a dramatic sense, is the boundary between temporality and death. And, as with all art, to access the aesthetic – the metaphysic of beauty and absolute harmony – theatre has to seek transformation.

These arguments about beauty are important when we consider that the philosophy of beauty – aesthetics – very much determines the defining criteria for our public expressions of creativity.

Theatre takes us beyond those orders imposed by time. The space that is transformed time is, in concept, not unlike Wittgenstein's silence. For him, we cannot speak about those things of most importance because of the limits, as he saw it, imposed by what I would call *temporal* language. It is here in the consequent silence – in the space – that beauty resides; where creativity meets the aesthetic. This is where transformation takes us. In view of this, it is worth saying something here of a more detailed nature about creativity and with particular reference to David Bohm's thinking found in his book *On Creativity*.

If everything were unified by a set of ultimate, unchanging rules (everything in the universe) one could only discover what these rules are; one could not imagine anything beyond them. It would be meaningless to imagine new structures of order. But this is what a theoretical scientist does. Because the universe is not so absolutely ordered, he is able to imagine *new orders* which are then tested for credibility. In this way the scientist is creative because he has imagined something new. The universe only appears to be unified. In fact, all things, from the smallest particles that make up matter, find their place in phenomena as a result of what Bohm calls the 'similar difference' and 'different similarities'[2] things have, one with the other. There is a space between these two which is the territory in which great creative thinkers such as Einstein can imagine new orders and new rules. In the absence of certainty, they imagine relationships and these are then tested scientifically. It is a similar situation with artistic creativity.

So in the scientific context unity, and the beauty it implies, is perceived through an intense process of investigating recognised laws or ways of seeing things in order to discover new arrangements that will lead to new laws which brings the scientist and, in the other context, the creative artist closer to what he intuits, in Bohm's words as 'a certain oneness and totality, or wholeness constituting a kind of harmony that is felt to be beautiful'.[3]

So it is for all creativity: it is as if there is a space between similar differences and different similarities – an uncertain space not constrained by laws – in which we can imagine new constructs which will bring us closer to beauty and its philosophy, the aesthetic. Thus we find another account of the space that is transformed time which is now very much connected, as we have seen, with those principles of creativity for which

Bohm argues so powerfully. It is not simply that theatre has this power of transforming but that theatre will not achieve its aesthetic without it.

Most importantly for me, the space transformed of time by theatre is inhabited by the living corpse. The living corpse as an emissary of transformation will embody my arguments. My plays contain characters that also embody these arguments and consequently they become exemplars of the living corpse.

I have tried to show that this power of transforming is linked very closely to arguments I make for creativity. The expression of these arguments in a dramatic context is to be found in the language of my plays. At this point I will look at the nature of the language of theatre with particular reference to those plays of mine previously cited.

The language of the space is akin to the language of death. If we imagine that an understanding of death cannot be accessed ordinarily by the language of temporality then we might also imagine that we need a language of death to do it. But if death is akin to the space then a language of the space, which we might imagine imagining, should suffice.

The language of death is a language we have no knowledge of but if we can imagine that the notion of death, like fear of death, is determined by the temporal nature of our lives, then we may say that the space may include the embodiment of the negation of notions of death and fear of death because it is the absence of time. Consequently, the language that is not limited by time becomes a language *to be imagined*: a language that exists in the realm of the impossible (much as the architectural achievements of, say, the Renaissance were manifestations of the impossible to the Renaissance man in the street). This notion of the impossible as something for creativity to aim for is very important to keep in mind as a means to understanding what it is I want to say. In my play *Wittgenstein's Daughter* (1993), Wittgenstein's Ghost and all that he says is the embodiment of this. Wittgenstein's Ghost is also the dramatic representation of the famous, haunting last line of Wittgenstein's *Tractatus Logico-Philosophicus*: '*Wovon man nicht sprechen kann, darüber muss man schweigen*' – 'whereof one cannot speak one must remain silent'.[4] If the living corpse inhabits the space and the language of the space is the language of death then this is the language of the living corpse.

The space, as we have seen, is also the temple of the aesthetic and the creative and is beyond definition. It cannot be defined because the language that could define it is the language of our imagination which is a language subject to the impossible. This is similar to dramatic language; we have to understand dramatic language as being something beyond the merely spoken but a language subject to and caused by theatre's aesthetic and its transforming power. In other words, when death and eroticism meet in the dramatic conceit of the living corpse, we are afforded access to the most profound languages of the theatrical aesthetic that have the power to transform us.

And so, when we speak of death with regard to theatre and drama, we speak of it in an entirely different way from the way we speak of it in a temporal context; in the same way, theatre cannot be understood using only that language confined by temporality – which is why what Wittgenstein's Ghost has to say in my play *Wittgenstein's Daughter* is not meaningless and impossible but necessary to the unfolding of the drama.

Drama is about crossing boundaries. The living corpse is our agent in that endeavour.

II

To turn to the plays, I should say to begin with that the examples I give do not *prove* my thesis that theatre transforms, but do indicate the ways in which we seek as writers, creatively, to fulfil theatre's transforming potential. I do this playfully in *Casanova Undone* (1992) and much more seriously in the other two plays, and I directly argue the case in *Casanova Undone* by having Casanova himself produce arguments for the notion of creativity embracing the impossible, as in this example:

> You do not understand what it is to be great! For example, a great lover, as I've tried to show knows that you don't need the intercourse to enjoy the conquest. This is a revolution in thought that I am responsible for! Why can't you respond to its aesthetic charm? It's quite different from all that noisome pumping.[5]

Casanova is speaking to the character Sophie in a quarrelsome moment in which his status as the great lover has been questioned by her. Not only does Casanova make these direct arguments but the play itself is an argument for what this paper is seeking to contend. In the play it is the time of The Terror[6] and Casanova is impotent. He is writing his memoirs and it is imperative that he maintains his reputation. This is achieved with the help of his woman companion, Sophie, masquerading as the man Costa, armed with dildos and deception, who services the aging Duchesses and other flotsam of the *Ancien Régime* who come to Casanova to relive for an evening the sexual miracle of his and their youth. The argument I am making is expressed in this configuration of Sophie's *impossible* role as a surrogate Casanova achieved with the aid of sexual tools and doing successfully, as a woman pretending to be a man, what Casanova is unable to do as the greatest male lover. On the other hand, when he says to the beautiful Angelique, whom he would seduce:

> Today, I'm going to surprise you, excite you in a most unimaginable way: Bring you, perhaps, to the point of death and, as I lay upon your coffin wherein I've driven my nails, you'll sigh with the deepest sigh of gratitude that you came. For you will come.[7]

he is aware of the limits on his physical ability and is speaking here, actually, of a menu he is about to deliver verbally to the young woman, in place, as it were, of the sex. (She has come for a meal; he *impossibly* feeds her with words.) In this moment he invokes the language of sex as death-act – for he has always recognised the companionship of death and eroticism – and with food becoming the sustaining metaphor of his sexuality in the face of his impotence, he becomes the living corpse: drama's messenger. Continuing his and my theme, he says:

> When I eat *beef*, as you know, I eat it raw. My white bread soaks up the red blood. When I drink wine I drink the heaviest blood-like red. When I eat cheeses, I like best the cheese that's in a state of putrefaction. In my life I live one step away from death. One step the wrong way and I'm dead. In the practice of my life I don't fool myself that there's no such thing as death. That's why, when I eat and drink, I eat and drink – as Christ himself advised – the blood and the body. I despise a person who hides from death. In death I see that life is active because life includes death. A life without death would be like a dream without sleep.[8]

For Casanova it should be in 'the nature of man that he's able to eat in the face of death'.[9] He could be saying that it is in the nature of man to have sex in the face of death as though the one were an essential prerequisite of the other, as he might argue when he goes on to say:

> The man who remembers his menus is like a great lover. The great lover has to recall and remember his many conquests for the sake of his reputation. In gastronomy, a host who is unknowledgeable about the finest meats and cheeses will leave his guests with no experience of love just as he would leave his mistress with a belly ache. In fact the two things are so closely connected that only a man who remembers what he's eaten can leave his mistress feeling full after sex![10]

Bubbling beneath the surface of the play is Casanova's belief in his powers as an alchemist which becomes a further metaphor for creativity and transformation. Sophie puts this into context when, for the sake of a stratagem she has embarked on to save herself and Casanova from death at the hands of the agents of The Terror, she says to Angelique, the architect of the plot, who has doubts about Casanova's abilities:

> He is a great magician. Daily, I tell you, duchesses, marquises ... even, I've seen it, some women from the Convention, come here and he ... I don't know ... He's able to make of his room what it's not! It's as if it becomes a theatre and they're not only the audience but also the actors! If I may be blunt: Monsieur Casanova's whole reputation is rooted in this phenomenon: that while others – lesser lovers and all mortals, struggle to achieve climax, Casanova has climax, as it were, put at his disposal. Climax in the case of Casanova, is a concept created by his reputation rather than the reward of a lover's perseverance.

If we assume that what appears as reality in our everyday lives is not that real then it makes sense for Casanova to say:

> I am the first example in history of the most basic truth about the world moulded into a philosophy: that nothing's what it seems to be.[11]

and so remind us of what I said about theatre speaking beyond the parameters that seem to define it.

Gary Gilmore's imagining of death in my play *Utah Blue* (2000) has become palpable for him. He says to his brother Mikal:

> When I was a kid, death would whisper into my ear at night. That's how I got to sleep. And as I grew up, death would walk with me to school. Yeah! In school I learned with death: in the playground I played with death; when I played hooky, I played hooky with death. Death was in my schoolbag; in my lunchbox; in my pencil case: with my paint brushes. Death came down the chimney at Christmas and death lit up the Christmas tree. I ate at the table with death and left the table with death. When I was a baby I cuddled death. I sucked on death's teat. *(Pause)* I saw death in my judges and death in my juries and death in my screws. When I went to the gas station I was with death; when I went to a motel I was with death. When I humped a chick I was with death and when I kissed I was with death. Death taught me love. Death taught me life. Death taught me to see just as death taught me to paint. I was death's artist.[12]

The play is about Gary, the murderer who, in 1977, was executed by firing squad after insisting on it, and Gary's Body – a character in the play – is a clear representation of the living corpse. It is necessary for the drama that he is dead in order that he may commit the audience to the sharing of the erotic aesthetic displayed.

The play is as much about Gary's brother Mikal and Nicole, Gary's lover, and in the second half of the play, after the execution of Gary, Nicole and Mikal have an affair. Gary's Body in his interventions with Mikal and Nicole provides the shared eroticism with the audience in which we more clearly understand the language of sex. Paradoxically, Gary, as his own dead body reveals this language, is reduced to silence by dramatic necessity in the sense that in order to speak his language of dramatic truth he must be confined by death. The dramatic thrust of Gary as living corpse is that his connection with Nicole in death is truly erotic.

We get intimations of this early on. When Gary first meets Nicole, it is as if they've met before beyond the gates of the grave: not unlike we might imagine Gretta in Joyce's *The Dead* suddenly waking to the realisation that the dead Michael Furey is standing in the street beneath her window. Gary has met Nicole where the snow may paint eternity. He knows he cannot do it; cannot perform the physical act. He says:

> It's the beer, baby. The beer and the Fiorinal which I gotta take every day for my headache.[13]

Of course it is not the booze or the drugs, it is life. He tells his brother about Spinoza, whom he has studied in jail, and how, according to Spinoza, everything is one substance and all substance is included in the notion of God, who is infinite substance. For Gary the most important aspect of this substance is the power of death to make changes to it; the power of death to transform. Prison, for Gary, is death's ante-room and while he cannot make it with Nicole outside prison, inside they make volcanic love. He says:

> For me, doing it in here is like other people doing it in a five star hotel. But doing it out there man is like doing it in jail. For me. That was my problem babe. If I coulda done it whenever I wanted to out there instead of being blasted on booze and uppers and downers I wouldn'ta done that murder. It's related see? Fucking is creative like painting: if you can't be creative you get destructive![14]

Even more powerfully, after he is dead, while Mikal and Nicole are asleep, Gary's Body, in a moment of total dramatic eroticism, gets between Nicole's opened legs and inverts the necrophilic act: the dead possesses the living.

Before his execution, Gary has made a tape which he calls Utah Blue. It is music without musical notation. On it he says:

> Blue is what I lived with in my earlier lives and it's what I lived with from the moment I came into this one, which is why I'm taking steps to beat the karma rap in advance of the next one baby. It's Spinoza. It's all part of the one substance ... I love you baby, from out here in the blue.[15]

Nicole and Mikal make love as the tape plays. We are confronted with the haunting eerie music of eroticism and while in its strange chords we may find recognition of the hollowness of our lives, erotic or otherwise, in his death song we perceive a truth-hymn to dramatic sexuality. As living corpse he gives us the opportunity to access the dramatic sexuality by opening the door to our creativity.

In my play *The Pimp*,[16] the poet Baudelaire, after raping his long-time partner Jeanne Duval, becomes a living corpse as a result of which, paradoxically, he is able to see into the noumenal world of eroticism which is the world of *his* creativity and with such depth that he makes profound moral connections between drama and science. Baudelaire is the great moral poet whose music is so strange, so creative, that he was long mistaken for the Devil's most profound advocate. In an early poem he wrote:

> I love the thought of ancient, naked days
> When Phoebus gilded statues with his rays.
> Then women, men in their agility
> Played without guile, without anxiety …

'without guile and without anxiety' – innocent eroticism.

David Bohm, in his book *On Creativity*, points out that the ancient Greeks:

> regarded the key or essential difference as being between the imperfection and corruption of earthly matter and the perfection and purity of heavenly matter (and who thus generalised the moral notion of difference between imperfection and perfection as the fundamental one, relevant for the whole of existence). The complicated movements of earthly matter were taken as revealing its imperfect nature. On the other hand, heavenly matter should express the perfection of its nature by moving in a circle, which was considered to be the most perfect of geometrical figures.[17]

Where the Greeks saw imperfection as a template against which to judge activity that may be called moral or otherwise, they also saw disorder. In other words, when one acts apparently immorally it is because of the flouting of moral codes and this is disorder. For Bohm there is no such thing as disorder but, rather, more complex kinds of order which suggests that moral judgements cannot be so simple as those offered by codes, but are subject to more complex realities. In *The Pimp*, Baudelaire, as though anticipating Bohm, searches for a language that pictures these more complex species of order: for that creativity in which lies boundless, almost unimaginable beauty. The outcome of his searching is dramatised in this way: Baudelaire is being prosecuted for six poems that appear in his major work *Les Fleurs du Mal*, which the authorities have deemed obscene. In the play he sees this as good news as the consequent notoriety, he reasons, is bound to make him a substantial amount of money which will free him from the debts he had incurred over a lifetime. In the unfolding of the drama he comes to see the six poems as the truest expression of his creativity, as though in these poems he has discovered previously hidden complex forms of order. He says:

No, Mother! *(To ANCELLE)* Sir, I have come to see that these six poems are much more than simply an argument with our society's authority and decorum. They are the essence of me as a writer. They embody my liberation. You have argued that double entry bookkeeping is liberating because it frees the movement of capital from the breakdown of bad accounting. But this is nonsense to the artist though I myself, for too many years, have been subject to its confining boundaries. And I see this clearly now. Those boundaries present a challenge to me. Beyond them lies the world of my creating imagination but to get out there, to cross the boundary involves conflict and we are taught from childhood to avoid conflict. So we ourselves reinforce the boundaries. I may have thought when I took Jeanne as a lover that I was breaking out of my confinement but I wasn't. It was just fashionable to have a whore on my arm. So I failed to see the meaning of Jeanne. I supported her out of duty when I should have seen that she was the means to my freedom. Now I see the beauty in her; in this corrupted being. She is the obscenity in me. The six poems. To have sex with her as the body decays, as the lips of her vagina dry up and crack and her clitoris break off and her breasts lay on her ribcage like drained fruit skins ... Don't try and escape, Mother! This is the truth! We are nothing if not corruptible

– out-pourings of the most violent decadence. That is why, when a child dies, the offensiveness of it lies not in the death of youth but that it was denied the journey to heaven it should have made: flesh fallen from exposed bones, inseminated as the odour of rot rises. I will not plead with the Empress! It's not my poems that are the threat, it's capitalism. Capitalism needs boundaries and they threaten creativity.

This is a speech of transformation: he is ironically invoking Bohm's Greek dichotomy by recognising, in a sense, his own disordered existence, but, paradoxically, is describing new orders of beauty – paradoxically because his invoking of the Greek dichotomy enables him to describe a creative beauty and a new moral status beyond the boundaries of the Greek position. Baudelaire has found in the creative place a new aesthetic for eroticism. Or, put another way: what enables the transformation into the world of theatrical aesthetic and that most beautiful ethic accessed only through creativity is the connection the living corpse has with these more complex species of order – a species of order which, through the language of theatre and its aesthetic, produces this paradox: that the most awful of crimes he has committed on his partner have purified him. Unfortunately for Baudelaire in the play, he abandons his authority as living corpse and writes to the Empress in response to a demand to do so from his mother and from Ancelle, the family solicitor, the act of self-betrayal in which lies the seeds of his tragedy within the drama.

I think of Baudelaire as the French Wagner and his *oeuvre* as an enormous *Liebestod*, which, like theatre, transforms time into space. In the Wagner opera Isolde sings the *Liebestod* (translated as Love Death) over the body of the dead Tristan. Wagner wrote that Isolde 'as if *transfigured* sinks ... onto Tristan's corpse'. Isolde is transfigured to meet Tristan erotically in death in a way that can only be understood by applying the philosophy of the living corpse and its power of revelation to this manifestation of Wagner's creativity. Isolde, like Gary, Baudelaire and the aged Casanova is an exemplar of the living corpse, transfigured and transformed by the theatrical aesthetic, that aesthetic which has to exist beyond the boundary of temporal reality. This, as I have argued, is the realm of creativity.

In conclusion, let me say that the theatrical aesthetic embodies this paradoxical necessity: that erotic activity and imaginings – the most profound proof of living – imply and need for their fullest expression the electric touch of death; that these meet in a crucible of rhapsodic transformation that is our creativity. That, in fact, for theatre not to inhabit this realm is a misuse of its own purpose and that purpose is what we cannot escape as sentient beings: to confront the realm of death and its archive of truth wherein the modes of existence we structure from mediocrity are annihilated to be replaced by the language of infinity. The inconsolable sadness of solitude, which is how the living often appreciate death, is the absence of creativity or, we may say, the absence of any flirting with impossibility.

Notes

1. This essay first appeared in *The Nature and Culture of the Human Body*, ed. Peter Mitchell, *Trivium*, 37 (Lampeter, 2007).
2. David Bohm, *On Creativity* (London, 2002), p. 7.
3. *Ibid.*, p. 13.
4. Ludwig Wittgenstein, *Tractatus Logico-Philosophicus* (London, 1961), p. 150.
5. Dic Edwards, *Casanova Undone* (London, 1992), p. 42.
6. The Reign of Terror (5 September 1793–28 July 1794) or simply The Terror (French: *la Terreur*) was a period in the French Revolution characterised by brutal repression.
7. Edwards, *Casanova Undone*, p. 45.
8. *Ibid.*
9. *Ibid.*, p. 48.
10. *Ibid.*, p. 47.
11. *Ibid.*, p. 45.
12. Dic Edwards, *Utah Blue* (London, 2000), p. 25.
13. *Ibid.*, p. 17.
14. *Ibid.*, p. 31.
15. *Ibid.*, p. 59.
16. *The Pimp,* produced at The White Bear Theatre Club, London, 2006.
17. Bohm, *On Creativity*, p. 13.

8

Flirting with disaster

David Ian Rabey

Emotional entanglements

Plato, in his work *The Republic*, considers theatre (as a paradigm for art in general) as something which has to *earn* its place in his ideal world. Aristotle, in his work *Poetics*, similarly regards theatre as dangerous, and best constructed as a *conductor* of danger, in terms which Joe Kelleher identifies as 'homeopathic': 'less likely to lead to a change in the political state of things than to a recognition of those feelings that need to be kept in check for the sake of the common political good', thus providing 'a means of running off, as if through a drainage channel or short-circuit, any generative charge, any static electricity in the politics of performance that threatens the status quo'.[1] In Aristotle's political programme, 'no less authoritarian' than Plato's, 'the theatre is a means of channelling, or purging, or appropriating, its dangerous emotional material'.[2] However, theatre's innate unpredictability and estrangements make it resistant to instrumentalism. Kelleher notes theatre's distinctive tendencies to interrupt 'whatever is taken for granted as "the political"' and give 'form to the new',[3] as when it makes 'the invisible visible';[4] this *mercurial* quality of theatre means that the aforementioned dangerous material 'remains, in a sense, infectious and a destabilising influence on political organisation', intimating that theatre still harbours 'within itself, whatever the political agenda at hand, the constant promise – or threat – of *another* politics'.[5]

Nicholas Ridout, following Peggy Phelan, suggests that one possible manifestation of this 'promise – or threat – of *another* politics' might be re-cognised through the philosophical writings of Emmanuel Levinas, who proposes the centrality of (not God, nor social control in the name of rational enlightenment and modernisation, but) the encounter with the 'other', which can make manifest a sense of responsibility 'in a recognition of our mutual vulnerability which encourages relationships based on openness, dialogue and a respect for difference'.[6] Phelan, like Kelleher, links this with the idea of the invisible made visible: 'The condition of witnessing what one did not (and perhaps cannot) see is the condition of whatever age we are now entering': an age which might be called 'post-postmodern' or 'the age of terrorism', but is 'characterized both by an intimate reawakening to the fragility of life and a more general sense of connection to one another that exceeds simple geophysical, ideological, or cultural proximity'.[7]

This paradigmatic reference to Levinas has its problems when, as Ridout acknowledges, some of Levinas's observations seem to distrust the category of the aesthetic (in which we would locate theatre, drama and performance) as dark, obscurantist and evasive.[8] Phelan's 'general sense of connection' may also be used to advocate a generalisation of pluralistic liberalism which is vague and merely sentimental. I venture that this idea of the encounter, and its characteristic *theatricalities*, may find more precisely subversive development through reference to two other philosophers: Alphonso Lingis and Anne Dufourmantelle. Lingis, a former translator of Levinas, develops earlier concepts of existentialism and phenomenology to the eminently theatrical sense of significant encounters within 'the community of those who have nothing in common' thrown together through confrontations with eroticism and death. Dufourmantelle's book *Blind Date: Sex and Philosophy* traces some exclusions, evasions and points of contact in characterisations of erotic sexuality and philosophical thought, their provocations of traversal and exile, their promises of dis/orientation, which may be extended to drama, theatre and performance.

Lingis, in his book *Dangerous Emotions* (2000), proposes: 'Despite the Aristotelian theory of catharsis and the Freudian theory of cathexis, emotions are not dissipated in being released, but escalated';[9] and further, that the rationalist distrust of emotions conceals a fearfulness regarding their ability to contest issues and spaces of power:

Our emotions reorient others, disturb their trains of thought, seep through into the blueprints of their projects, contest them, and afflict them with misgivings and self-doubt. Power among humans is not simply the physical force with which one material body may move another; it is the force to distract, detour, maneuver, and command. Every pleasure we indulge in and every pain we suffer exerts power over others.[10]

So it may be erroneous to consider or identify emotions as passive or reactive in opposition to the avowedly primarily conceptual or intellectual initiative, the imperative of linear progression, which may strategically adopt the mask of 'engaging with reality' (often a smokescreen for a despotic demand that one give a rationally justified account of oneself according to imposed terms of surveillance) or invoke an alliance with the populism of 'common sense' (merely a duplicitously judgmental aloofness from articulation, which sees meaning progressing in and through only one direction). Lingis's description of emotional dynamics is significantly dramatic: both filmic and theatrical:

> An emotion isolates an object or event and brings it into focus: it dramatizes ... The emotion frames, crops, views that object or event from a distance or in extreme close-ups, views it from an odd angle or through a slightly open doorway, as reflected on the surface of a pond or in a mirror, in the mist or in the shadings of twilight. The emotional energies charge that object or event and make it shine and glower, purr and howl. The active force of emotions makes us act in the romance, comedy, tragedy, cosmic or mercantile epic, melodrama, or sitcom they improvise as they go.[11]

This model of the human consciousness as distinctively dramatic and often theatrical has some affinities with my propositions (following William Simon, Katharine Liepe-Levinson and others) that sexuality can be informatively figured in dramatic and theatrical terms.[12] Anne Bogart asks, in *A Director Prepares*: 'How do you awaken what is asleep? ... You turn it slightly till it awakens.'[13] This is close to the task of what Lingis identifies as a primarily *emotional* intelligence and imagination: 'Laughter and tears, blessing and cursing break through the packaging and labelling of things that make our environment something only scanned and skimmed over'; they claim a right to be identified as 'the forces with which we impact on nature, which we had perused only as the text of the world', the 'forces that seek out and engage reality'[14] more responsively than the accusatory separatism of despotic control. These more courageous emotions 'seek out what is incoherent, inconsistent, contradictory, countersensical; they endorse what is unpredictable, unworkable, insurmountable, unfathomable'.[15] I suggest that the more courageous forms of drama and theatre do the same.

Eroticism, philosophy and speculative theatre

Anne Dufourmantelle's *Blind Date: Sex and Philosophy* (2007) proposes that the elusive, mercurial disobediences of sex and philosophy can be traced to the intrinsically common qualities of astonishment and hunger: 'Sex and philosophy share a desire to taste a truth that no one can have predigested for them, whether it be corporeal or conceptual.'[16] Her use of the term 'sex' here and elsewhere seems to be primarily associated with erotic sexuality (rather than sexuality in general), as in her identification of what she terms 'Dionysian Life', which is manifested in specifically theatrical imagery:

> From Plato to Jan Patočka, sex has been perceived as *furor* and rapture, a state of being drawn outside the self ... Through the figure of the god Pan and other avatars, we see Dionysian sexuality displayed on stage – on all stages – as a device for knowing and overturning identity ... Dionysus is a dangerous god, radically foreign to the order deployed by the world according to *logos*.[17]

Dufourmantelle proposes that eroticism 'goes to extremes to defy the ennui of existing'; and, similarly, philosophy 'embodies thought's supreme effort to think the world and thus to transgress the constraints imposed by the illusion of the senses and the misleading games of consciousness', to present an 'eagle's-eye-view ... that comes from the territory of the dead'[18] to inform the living (a Faustian excursion into impossibility that reminds me of the necromantic compulsion expressed by the narrator of Bob Dylan's song 'Silvio', compelled to travel to find out something only dead men know). As Dufourmantelle notes elsewhere, 'What alters a subject

126

is what s/he does not know. It is that place where s/he cannot go and by which s/he is nevertheless obsessed.'[19] I would also suggest that drama and theatre offer an imaginative, yet interpersonal, encounter with that which lies beyond the literally and immediately available.

Philosophy's particular forms and habits of interrogation appear in their most Platonic and Aristotelian armoured forms when 'intent on strengthening us against emotion', making 'rules designed to discern what *compromises* us in emotion', 'whatever carries us away, in short whatever mixes thought with something other than itself'.[20] The consternation of emotion may be characterised as an 'event' animating 'what we do not know about ourselves when the world approaches'.[21] However, Dufourmantelle maintains that philosophy will and must take account of desire, the encounter with an unbidden emotional truth, as an experience central to life; though philosophy 'uses concepts as if they were so many magic little rungs from which a timeless ladder could be constructed', the ladder will always lead to the particularly perilous step constituted by 'desire'.[22] On the one hand, contemporary social life presents us with the 'simultaneous effect of rejection and overexposure of sex', an avoidance of the catastrophic potential of desire occurring under the cover of 'a diffuse sexualization of all the consumer objects (human beings included) of our society'.[23] On the other hand, Dufourmantelle suggests, erotic sexuality, 'the subterranean fiction that makes us pledged to "the other"', 'runs through everything, including the most resistant concepts, those that form the armature of metaphysics, like so many metallic ribs: Time, Truth, Measure, Politics, Appetite, Being, Infinity, Face, Causality'; 'none emerges unaffected' from a confrontation with erotic sexuality.[24] We might make a link here with Baudrillard's vision of seduction as a power that subverts power by demonstrating the possibility of reversibility: similarly, Dufourmantelle suggests the emotional charge of erotic sexuality has the power to 'undo the workings of philosophical concepts one by one and tilt them gently toward the incomprehensible'[25] – again recalling Bogart's formulation of 'awakening' work in rehearsal and theatrical performance.

While sex is widely commoditised, Dufourmantelle maintains that it nevertheless remains ultimately and inextinguishably transgressive: alternately ignored, demonised and effaced, erotic sexuality is nevertheless a primary 'philosophical aporia'.[26] In consequence, much effort has been expended to deny the intelligence of eroticism, 'so that the enigma of desire can be reduced to the expression of a mechanical need',[27] in the fearfully defensive reflex of all forms of totalitarianism. However, even this will fail to account for and manage entirely the persistent human impulse to be unsettled, even profoundly, which may attend and inform the exposure of the self to art and sexual chance ('One spends one's life waiting for … an encounter; and fearing it, too'[28]) – just as anxiety may constitute an important element of the theatrical encounter. There is a (correctly identified) threat to our security here, a sense of things actually or potentially being 'taken away': 'true knowledge appears in the form of dispossession, divestment, encounters'.[29] We might make a link here with Derrida's proposition that the gift gives time: the gift does not give itself as a commodity to be possessed or consumed but promises a future moment in excess of the present: 'temporality, delay, a calculation of timeliness';[30] the difference between a gift and every other operation of exchange is that the gift gives a 'delimited time', a rhythm 'that structures [time] originally'.[31] Dufourmantelle identifies both eroticism and philosophy as responses of defiance to conventional manifestations and pressures of time – and perhaps we might add theatre as a third, and similarly purposed, force, which 'suspends time for as long as the conjunction of bodies lasts … as long as we remain caught up in the sway of the moment and the act'.[32] Theatre's physicalisation of an essential imaginative volatility may exacerbate the effect of time, erode apparently fixed concepts and thus reveal the instability of received truths. But theatre also aims to take, and ordain, *its* time, time to make its point: it offers complex experiences which demand time to be unfolded and orchestrated, and insists on the *right* to this time, 'the here and now deployed absolutely', which shows how the terms of real life and conventional time become *open to question.* Dufourmantelle associates this moment of 'the here and now deployed absolutely' with the Greek term *kairos*, the opportune moment,[33] in forms which are performative in action and dramatic in effect.

If erotic sexuality promises the *kairos*, the perfect instant that steps outside conventional time, its shadow side might be trauma, which Dufourmantelle characterises as that which 'freezes time for all the descendance to come';[34] however, this seems to question her notion of sex as an 'absolute freedom' that opposes subjection.[35] Traumatisation might appropriately be considered as a one-sided orchestration, taking and imposition of *time*. She herself adds the important refinement and *caveat*:

> But sex is not outside of time. No more than thought is. Sex is in time, caught up in time's glue from the outset: expectation, desire, delay, regret, avoidance, failure, pleasure, difference, caress, absence – everything speaks to us of time that passes too quickly or too slowly but that does pass; everything speaks of the lag that accentuates and figures the very space there is between you and me.[36]

Moreover, I would suggest that that which 'accentuates and figures the very space there is between you and me' is one working version of *the theatrical*. Dufourmantelle proposes that erotic sexuality is 'not what "is done" between two beings, but the universe that pulsates between them like blood, lodged in the space of language'.[37] This also works as a model of the spatial dynamics of poetic theatre and drama, where intensity burgeons in the space and distance negotiated and contested *between* characters, which conducts heat in a specifically hypersensitised theatrical way, opposed to the convention of filmic and televisual naturalism which would construe intimacy in terms of more literally depicted and conventionally recognisable forms of physical proximity. Like eroticism, speculative drama may also offer a 'constellation of gestures never made',[38] in the literally referential or representational terms of the world (history) outside of the theatre (encounter); nevertheless, these fictional and metaphorical (real/ not real) gestures propose 'an act, a relation, and a language' which (as Dufourmantelle claims for erotic sexuality) demands an unusual degree of abandonment so that 'something can begin'.[39] Perhaps we might also say of speculative theatre (what Barker terms The Art of Theatre[40]), as Dufourmantelle does of erotic sexuality, that it 'does not raise the question of the world'; rather it seeks a moment of *kairos* which 'cuts into it, wounds it, responds to it by creating it',[41] manifesting something which was, previously, literally never there. This links to Dufourmantelle's notion of enchantment, following on from Jan Patočka (which in turn recalls Baudrillard's world of seduction, in which one moves 'in an enchanted world'): Patočka suggests that when we are in the 'exceptional' mode (as opposed to the ordinary, the everyday), 'we are *enraptured* ... Here we are not escaping from ourselves, but, rather, we are surprised by something, taken aback, captivated by it, and that something does not belong among things and in the ordinary day in which we can lose ourselves among the things that preoccupy us ...':[42] thus, rather than the exceptional offering 'escape from ourselves' it offers encounters with others, and thereby with ourselves, in surprising forms. Hence the wariness of philosophy towards the suspensions and distortions of a theatre which may trouble rational logic and refute the organisation and objectification of political power because it insists on, and demonstrates, the possibility of reversibility.

Eroticism in tragedy

In Barker's *The Europeans* (written 1987, staged professionally 1989), the violated and disfigured protagonist Katrin insists on the public performance of her pain and its consequences: 'I wish to hold on to my agony, it's all I have.'[43] Katrin is deliberately catastrophic/catastrophist in her insistence on continued and excessive life, which mocks conventional social and political forms of work, reason, sanity and function. More classically tragic protagonists, such as Racine's Phèdre, Shakespeare's Timon, John Whiting's ennobled nihilists, are irrevocably death-bound, gathering their pain into themselves as a means of transport beyond a world which is nevertheless emptied of meaning by their departure. However, in all cases, these figures claim and insist upon their suffering, writing and reading a narrative of their own lives out of the social confusion they compulsively re-present. As Lingis reminds us, there can be joy in suffering:

> let us beware of setting out to alleviate a suffering that another needs and clings to as his or her destiny ... To be afflicted with another's suffering requires that we care about the things the sufferer cares for ... In the midst of grief and torment there is an upsurge of force that affirms the importance and truth of what one is tormented by, of what one grieves over.[44]

Through publicly framed persistence (Katrin) or dissolution (Timon), these dramatic characters discover a power in vulnerability and disconnection, and similarly invite their witnesses (on and off the stage) to let go, to abandon plans and remember how every emotion is a surrender 'of the supports and the implements, a giving way of the ground under our feet, a vertigo'.[45] As Barker notes, the tragic protagonist 'observes her own life without *asking to be saved*' for more of the inadequate life that she has already repudiated,[46] suggesting that death, like eroticism, may become 'a necessity, a perfection', belonging not only to 'the old, sick and fatigued' but to 'the strongest':[47] a crucial refinement of *style*. These characters relinquish their moorings and become 'naked and *disastrously free*'[48] from others' terms; hence, tragedy seduces death itself: 'it *arranges* death as a lover might arrange the veil of his bride, so she might be *seen to advantage* ...'.[49] This image promptly conjures for me the last movement of Shakespeare's erotic tragedy *Antony and Cleopatra* (specifically, Charmian's adjustment of Cleopatra's crown), as does Dufourmantelle's characterisation of erotic sexuality as 'excess par excellence', that which 'does not seek to be satisfied', and insists on a 'radical absence of God'.[50]

In the tidal rhythms of Shakespeare's *Antony and Cleopatra*, in a world where Cleopatra proclaims 'My oblivion is a very Antony' and all form tends towards dissolution, we find another scenario which supports Dufourmantelle's propositions: eroticism is 'a magnificent, essential power to forget', 'a practice of oblivion' which forgets 'that it has already taken place and will take place again and always'; rather, it seeks 'a constantly reiterated first time'.[51] Antony and Cleopatra's bids to 'mock the midnight bell' aim to slow time to a succession of intensely present moments. Cleopatra makes hunger where most she satisfies, creating on the horizon of desire a reappearing 'indefatigable craving for what does not allow itself to be entirely destroyed by our hunger'; hence 'the hunger experienced as desire is accompanied in human beings by all the appetites, including murderous ones'[52] – as dramatised when Antony flares up in violent resentment of her power over him. Finally the couple brave the opacity of death by infusing it with a willed eroticism, which discards the world and revisions the afterlife in terms which do indeed suggest a radical absence of God, who is Himself effectively forgotten. They dramatise and demonstrate (and remind us of) what Lingis terms:

The force to forget that melancholy succession of mortifications that is the history of each of us is the great power that makes us able to love tonight as though we had never made love to anyone before, to make love tonight as though there will never be anyone again; it is the ecstasy that says I was born to be here, in your arms, I could die now.[53]

As Charmian Savill has remarked, the positive face of encountering death, pain and suffering is 'the intensification of your relationship with the people you love'.[54] In theatre, as in life, we are not usually attracted to, or fascinated by, people on account of how reasonable they are. Lingis observes that if 'we open a conversation with someone, [or perhaps attend the theatre with them?] it is because first we see him or her as someone with whom we could laugh and grieve';[55] crucially, the impulse to 'enter into contact with someone' is not reducible to a conceptual grasp of his or her identity or respect for 'his or her boundaries and inner space'.[56] Indeed, there is the possibility that, in both theatrical tragedy and in life, the terms of our fascination may involve an exacerbation, rather than an attempted relief, of someone's will to pain, which renders them extraordinary. If, as Lingis suggests, we are attracted to those 'who face what happens, what is, and who suffer',[57] any neo-choric spasms of pity may attempt to diminish their charisma, to avert their apotheosis, to reclaim them for what they would elude: such is the *awkwardness* of The Last Supper (both the Biblical scene, and Barker's 1988 play of that title).

Death's ellipsis

Edward Bond's drama aims to show how violence 'is not produced by an upsurge of animal impulses in individuals, but by recurrence of institutions',[58] and how, significantly, these institutions propagate their effects through restricted forms of language which deny their citizens tools for analysis of their social situation. Lingis's *aperçu* could be a kernel image for several of Bond's recent plays for young people: 'There is never a perfect fit of words on the things they designate; they are GI uniforms pulled over the gawky bodies of adolescent recruits.'[59] In Bond's drama the discrepancy between the human body and the social uniform imposed upon it figures the space of cultural death in terms of regimentation: the deformation of conformity.

Sarah Kane's drama configures and approaches the pressures of death and time differently, notwithstanding Bond's acknowledged importance to her work. Kane's work increasingly forsakes the clarifying elaboration of values (with which we might still associate Bond's drama) for an anxious theatrical practice of insomnia and non-consolation. Here, sex might initially seem to offer a meaningful response to the anguish of death; however, as Dufourmantelle reminds us 'Sexus in Latin … signifies what is separated':[60]

> What is separated always manifests itself to us in the present, in the time of crisis, the time of the insurmountable, in order to preserve the broken identity … What is 'separated' is experienced as such only in the pure present … we call for the dream of another self more intimate than our own self, we evoke the absent brother, the loved being, the lost love; we navigate between absence and terror.[61]

This sounds eerily like the world of Sarah Kane's *Cleansed*, in which Grace's sense of separation calls forth the ghost of her lost and absent brother until she is drawn into a dream of lost unsundered intimacy, as she and the lovers in the former university turned concentration camp 'navigate between absence and terror', forced into a 'concentration' on either vicious loss or a ghastly present undiluted by the significance of time. *Cleansed* presents a world over which a merchant of death presides, refuting and containing every bid for a grand gesture such as sacrifice; a heightened image of a world of inquisitional transparency, which 'no longer makes death the final mystery of the world, the ultimate liberation, it no longer makes death a proof of mad love, of extreme love, there is nothing left for it to do but consume the product of death',[62] bathetically re-presented as a bottomless box of chocolates. The bid to sense, reclaim, explore this 'final mystery of the world' in a way that eludes bathos appears to be the increasingly dominant impulse informing Kane's plays *Crave* and *4.48 Psychosis*, in which several voices seek to 'prove' or substantiate an 'extreme love' which may be termed 'mad'. *4.48 Psychosis* in particular might be viewed in the light of Dufourmantelle's image of the intimate nocturnal struggle between rationalised 'thinking' and 'wild thought', in which the apparent psychiatrist represents the mechanism of thinking, incarnating a 'machine for swallowing wild thought'; however, wild thought 'wins in secret; it takes refuge in folded papers, twisted words, dreams, stammerings emanating from the memory of the dead', generating apparent 'thoughts without a thinker' which 'submerge our ability to think them our patiently consolidated beliefs, our ego'.[63] Part of the power of *Crave* and *4.48 Psychosis* may be their ability to make manifest the overwhelming appeal of these 'thoughts without a thinker', which Kane's dramatic form refuses to manifest in single or finally reducible embodiment.

The articulation of the indefinite is truly artful. Dufourmantelle suggests transgression 'both reminds us of death's ineluctability and allows us to avoid it',[64] by which I think she means that transgression exposes the terms of life, and death, in a somewhat Promethean victory which refutes the clamour for life at any price (what Cordella in my play *The Back of Beyond* refers to as 'The cowardice of flesh. Hanging on to repetition as if it were hope'[65]). Dufourmantelle goes on to identify a sacrificial quality in erotic sexuality, a dislocating and relocating restlessness which transcends mere repetition; in its repeated 'last resort' to reach '[a] final limit continually readjusted', '[s]ex repeats that "once and for all" against death endlessly.'[66] This is strikingly close to what the protagonist of my play *The Contracting Sea* glimpses in the rhythm of that sea: 'Its / Persistent / Final / Bid'.[67] *The Contracting Sea* proceeds from one of the relatively rare moments when someone conceptualises themselves as mortal through a sudden shattering illumination (in this case, the death of a partner) of the human condition which, like the sea, has a horizon that frequently appears 'immobile'; indeed, Dufourmantelle wonders, '[i]f this strange forgetfulness were to abandon us, if we were hurtled all at once into knowing exactly when and how we would die, what would become of desire?'[68] My protagonist wryly suggests we'd 'make a much better job of / Everything ...'.[69]

In his essay 'Joy in Dying', Lingis notes:

> In the world of work and reason, every moment is subordinated to a future moment. The sense and direction of every present depends on a future, on a conclusion or result. But there are moments when the grip of a projected result on one's present eases, and the present lights up and burns in a surge of liberation and exultation ... At the moment when none of the anticipated words are there, we are held in the present, a present disconnected from the chain of word-vectors of the past and from the anticipated conclusion.[70]

This moment of *ellipsis* ('...') recurs in Howard Barker's dramatic and theoretical texts as a moment of legible *dying*, of dissolution and opening, which indicates a desirous route to death and prefigures it with surprising and paradoxical vitality. These are moments when words 'that are more meaningful, more significant than the words we anticipated provoke the mind to anticipate a further, broader range of possibilities beyond the statement we had expected' so that the mind is driven 'to strive more, work more, to seriously survey the field into which the sentence is leading'.[71]

Dufourmantelle's proposition 'For there to be ecstasy ... nothing suffices if there is not in the body an immediate absolute response to death'[72] could provide an epigraph for Barker's *Gertrude – The Cry*, a play which indeed locates sex in 'the history of a cry, a rhythm, a syncope, a word wrenched from the body, scorched by *jouissance*',[73] in a pursuit which Claudius calls 'killing God', which requires neither afterlife nor satisfaction. Dufourmantelle's recognition that '[d]esire always displaces the very thing it desires, moves it farther out of reach'[74] is the deregularising axis of this world. In a memorable dramatic elaboration of this, Gertrude's servant Cascan discourses on the compulsive lure of ecstasy, 'a haunting mirage on the rim of life': 'All ecstasy makes ecstasy go running to a further place that is its penalty we know this ... still we would not abolish ecstasy'; and if 'eventually it lures us over a cliff', Cascan wonders 'is a cliff worse than a bed a stinking bed inside a stinking hospital no give me the cliff'.[75]

Barker's play *The Fence in its Thousandth Year* offers further dramatic expression of the fascinated intimation that erotic sexuality 'is not without danger ... It is whispering in the dark, walking backward, groping blindly along an unknown boundary line ... With that particular dark night comes the whole question of limits ... What are our limits? ... When desire is served up for the taking, it becomes apparent that what constitutes a limit is the boundary that separates and unites *jouissance* and horror ...'.[76] In Barker's play, the fence is consciously identified as not beautiful but nevertheless 'the condition of beauty'.[77] It is a self-dramatising denotation (and only partial container) of excess (like the art of theatre itself) which becomes the site of ritual provocations, violations and reconfigurations. Barker's protagonist is a duchess who repeatedly loses and recovers herself in a series of exposures and copulations which occur at, and through, the wire; around which the play depicts other characters' compulsive impulses and actions of *discovery*, in which the characters are frequently drawn through transgression as a doorway to a further, broader range of possibilities beyond those they, or the audience, might expect. This brings us to a final wordless tableau of the duchess, who can and indeed does stand 'naked and disastrously free': a moment of silence akin to those further developed in Barker's compendium of short plays, *The Forty* (written 2006), which characteristically bring characters and audiences towards the negotiation of a wordlessness. *The Forty* takes us into a realm of transgression which has much in common with the initiatives and effects identified by Alexander E. Hooke:

> To transgress means to recognize and dare certain limits or boundaries. Yet transgressing also requires more than a careful reflection or intellectual grasp. It is fuelled by passions that make one moved by or toward another. Insofar as this movement circumvents the demand to verbalize one's reasons, there is a silent component central to transgression. Yet this silence is hardly negative, for it presents the moment when collaborations and associations are developed, when other possibilities of social and political life are created or risked.[78]

Courage

Courage, summoned by both eroticism and death, is an emotional force which itself demands a transgressive disconnection from what one has previously known (about oneself, the limits of one's powers, the viable odds of success). Harold Pinter, in *Party Time* (1991), dramatises a man forcibly marginalised through political imprisonment, sundered from the politely vacuous social chat which constitutes the linguistic currency of the ostensibly 'free' elsewhere in the play; reduced to carrion, the prisoner nevertheless discovers in his sole and final speech what Lingis terms a corresponding 'carrion utterance': in his very distance from the cocktail parties, roadblocks and exclusive health clubs, he discovers a power and resource in his very abjection, something of 'the clamour of the toads over the swamps stinking with the effluvia dripping out of the pipes of industry and of the swarming of centipedes and rats over the ruins' which 'stirs in him and reverberates in the resistance in him':[79] 'I sit sucking the dark ... It's the only thing I have. It's mine. It's my own. I suck it.'[80]

Defying political authoritarianism requires one form of courage; attending the dying requires another. If, as Lingis suggests, to be 'given the chance to accompany the dying is to be given the most passionate, the most extravagant of gifts', it is also true that it carries a substantial toll: 'To be admitted into the company of one who is dying is to risk our own integrity, our health and our sanity, our courage.'[81] At this point, one is 'called upon to be there when the other is at the limit, and also at the origin, of the virtues, the power, that a life can have', and one finds oneself correspondingly 'at the limits of the power of language'.[82]

I propose that tragic and catastrophic forms of theatre give us opportunities to rehearse our courage through their courage. Barker suggests:

> Nothing *said* about death by the living can possible relate to death as it will be experienced by the dying. Nothing *known* about death by the dead can be communicated by the living. Over this appalling chasm tragedy throws a frail bridge of imagination.[83]

Barker also writes elsewhere that he does not intend the audience member to be 'without a guide': rather, 'by sheer bravery', the actor 'becomes the focus of hope and the source of security that cannot, in my work, be found in the usual forms of the message or the verisimilitude', with the intention that in 'the actor's courage, the audience individual finds his own'.[84] The tragic actor unfolds and enters a fictional scenario in which his character is 'at the limit, and also at the origin, of the virtues, the power, that a life can have', and correspondingly 'at the limits of the power of language' – and, I suggest, must memorably perform *not only* the language and action specified *but also* the sense of being at its limits, sensing its spasmodic inefficacy, its hopelessness, and yet the obligation and compulsion to persist (which is also their literal task, if they are not to abandon a performance part way through – which, despite the ubiquitous discomfort, is unusual). The (fictional) risk, defiance and persistence of the character find their (more literal, yet also imaginatively necessary) analogue in the risk, defiance and persistence of the actor (who puts in hazardous play his reputation, his professional prospects, his emotional equilibrium and perhaps his physical safety). The tragic protagonist may indeed be bound for nowhere, the place where there is, if not nothing to see, then nothing with which to report from it. This is a fictional rehearsal of what Lingis terms the 'limit-situation':

> This is not where the necessity of language ends in silence, but where it is no longer what has to be said that is the essential ... now you have to be there and have to speak. You have to say something – something that language cannot say, something that language cannot say, something that is not in the resources of common discourse to be able to say, and something that is, in the end, inessential. It is the saying that is imperative.[85]

For me, this invokes the situations of Samuel Beckett's characters, 'drowned in dreams and burning to be gone',[86] compelled to speak in order to attempt to put an end to speaking and being; conscious of the likely inefficacy, yet obliged to persist; strangely and surprisingly courageous (perhaps not least to themselves) at the limits of the powers of language. Beckett's theatre offers an experience akin to the time of dying, where dying 'takes time; it extends a strange time that undermines the time one anticipates, a time without a future, without possibilities, where there is nothing to do but endure the presence of time'.[87]

Lingis notes how artists 'cease to be artists and turn into entertainers and illustrators, simply by repeating themselves'.[88] However, the artist may remain existentially authentic by offering not 'a *true account*' (in a literal or journalistic sense) but 'a spectacle of utterance, the utterance born of an ordeal':[89] the persistence with action and utterance which is indeed a risk and ordeal for the actor, even though one less literally and consumingly than that of the character. The character (in the literal terms of the narrative fiction) and the stage actor (in his apparently excessive investment in an event scheduled to be repeated) show every sign of embracing the (conventionally avoided) once-in-a-lifetime encounter 'which one senses that one will never again have the ardour to live through'[90] (or re-perform so thoroughly). Barker brilliantly captures this sense of theatre's transaction with death:

> The play only appears to be about the living because the actors are living. The *characters* have never lived, nor by the same token, can they

ever be said to be *dead*. Theatre is situated on the bank of the Styx
(the side of the living). The actually dead cluster at the opposite side,
begging to be recognized. What is it they have to tell? Their mouths
gape ...[91]

Similarly, Lingis identifies death with an abyss in the interstices of the
world, 'that shows through as we advance, that opens our understanding,
indefinitely, beyond the things within reach and the ground upon which
we stand, make our stance vertiginous and without repose in itself, and
makes our existence action ... Action risks impotence, to materialise
its forces'[92] (the theatrical and sexual resonances of this assertion seem
entirely appropriate). Dufourmantelle also highlights an awareness of
inefficacy, the foreboding of a day in which the world will be emptied of
oneself: 'Sex is the business of living beings haunted by the fear of no
longer being present, of no longer being loved, the fear that nothing – acts,
words, exchanges of all sorts – has been of any use'; however, 'it may be
that the joy that is discovered in this process is more intimate, more real,
than our fear.'[93] If that notion implies that we should not despair, another
of Dufourmantelle's *aperçus* suggests we should not presume: 'The taboo
on thinking and the taboo on loving may lie at the foundation of the social
body ...'.[94] Or, to refocus this assertion: perhaps our predominant social
managerial organisations of time enveigh purposefully, fearfully and
justifiably, against encounters, theatrical and otherwise, with eroticism
and death?

Lingis perceives opportunities for encounters more meaningful than
those offered by these predominant social managerial organisations of
time in experiences of an initial disconnection from social promise:

It is not in elaborating a common language and reason, in collaborating
in transpersonal enterprises, that the human community takes form.
It is in going to rejoin those who, fallen from the time of personal
and collective history, have to go on when nothing is possible or
promised.[95]

However, the tragic, catastrophist and speculative forms of theatre to which
I have linked Lingis and Dufourmantelle's proposals are indeed at least

to some extent collaborative, and innately transpersonal. They therefore offer, in their distinctly startling forms, ephemeral yet potent formations of communities of those who have nothing in common.

'To *admit death* … to know *now* what you knew but were denied consciousness of … that *all* is predicated on death … is this political?'[96] Oh, yes …

Notes

1. Joe Kelleher, *Theatre and Politics* (Basingstoke, 2009), p. 50.
2. *Ibid.*, p. 54.
3. *Ibid.*, p. 73.
4. *Ibid.*, p. 75.
5. *Ibid.*, p. 54.
6. Nicholas Ridout, *Theatre and Ethics* (Basingstoke, 2009), p. 54.
7. Peggy Phelan, 'Marina Abramović: Witnessing Shadows', *Theatre Journal*, 56 (2004), p. 577; quoted in Ridout, *Theatre and Ethics*, p. 60.
8. Ridout, *Theatre and Ethics*, p. 55.
9. Alphonso Lingis, *Dangerous Emotions* (Berkeley, CA, 2000), p. 70.
10. *Ibid.*, pp. 17–18.
11. *Ibid.*, p. 69.
12. David Ian Rabey, 'The Theatrical in the Sexual, the Sexual in the Theatrical', *Essays in Theatre/Études Théâtrales*, 21(1 and 2) (2002/2003), published 2008, pp. 63–78.
13. Anne Bogart, *A Director Prepares* (London, 2001), p. 53.
14. Lingis, *Dangerous Emotions*, p. 78.
15. *Ibid.*, p. 80.
16. Anne Dufourmantelle, *Blind Date: Sex and Philosophy*, trans. Catherine Porter (Urbana, IL, and Chicago, IL, 2007), p. 12.
17. *Ibid.*, p. 45.
18. *Ibid.*, p. 60.
19. *Ibid.*, p. 55.
20. *Ibid.*, pp. 18, 20.
21. *Ibid.*, p. 21.
22. *Ibid.*, p. 17.
23. *Ibid.*, p. 82.
24. *Ibid.*, p. 6.
25. *Ibid.*, p. 17.
26. *Ibid.*, p. 9.
27. *Ibid.*, p. 12.
28. *Ibid.*, p. 7.
29. *Ibid.*, p. 32. Compare my delineations of Howard Barker's theatre in terms of offering 'gifts of loss', rather than the reinscriptions of institutionalised knowledge, in David Ian Rabey, *Howard Barker: Ecstasy and Death* (Basingstoke, 2009), pp. 3–17.
30. Elizabeth Grosz, 'The Time of Violence', in Scott Lash, Andrew Quick and Richard Roberts (eds.), *Time and Value* (Oxford, 1998), p. 42.
31. Jacques Derrida, quoted by Grosz in *ibid.*, pp. 42, 43.
32. Dufourmantelle, *Blind Date*, pp. 16–17.
33. *Ibid.*, p. 24.
34. *Ibid.*, p. 41.
35. *Ibid.*, p. 80. Unsurprisingly I question Dufourmantelle's assertions elsewhere on this page: 'Sex is the space of sacrifice par excellence … a zone of perpetual danger for anyone who seeks to subject others … Nothing has a hold on sex except the desire for sex itself … in the absolute freedom that it opposes to subjection'. This seems to be an absolutist (rhapsodic?) idealisation of sex, which chooses to ignore its potential role in the dynamics of power which inform domination and abuse.
36. *Ibid.*, p. 42.
37. *Ibid.*, p. 88.
38. *Ibid.*, p. 88.

39. *Ibid.*, p. 43.
40. Howard Barker, *Death, The One and the Art of Theatre* (London, 2005).
41. Dufourmantelle, *Blind Date*, p. 65.
42. Quoted in *ibid.*, p. 46.
43. Howard Barker, *Plays: One* (London, 2006), p. 99.
44. Lingis, *Dangerous Emotions*, pp. 50, 51.
45. *Ibid.*, p. 81.
46. Barker, *Death, The One and the Art of Theatre*, p. 33.
47. *Ibid.*, p. 44.
48. *Ibid.*, p. 105.
49. *Ibid.*, p. 94.
50. Dufourmantelle, *Blind Date*, p. 26.
51. *Ibid.*, pp. 99–100.
52. *Ibid.*, p. 81.
53. Lingis, *Dangerous Emotions*, p. 107.
54. In conversation with the author.
55. Lingis, *Dangerous Emotions*, p. 98.
56. *Ibid.*, pp. 99–100.
57. *Ibid.*, p. 101.
58. Alphonso Lingis in Mary Zournasi, 'Foreign Bodies: Interview with Alphonso Lingis, 1996', in Alexander E. Hooke and Wolfgang W. Fuchs (eds), *Encounters with Alphonso Lingis* (Lanham, MD, 2003), p. 94.
59. Lingis, *Dangerous Emotions*, p. 97.
60. Dufourmantelle, *Blind Date*, p. 57.
61. *Ibid.*, p. 58.
62. *Ibid.*, p. 63.
63. *Ibid.*, p. 53.
64. *Ibid.*, p. 102.
65. David Ian Rabey, *The Wye Plays* (Bristol, 2004), p. 43.
66. Dufourmantelle, *Blind Date*, p. 59.
67. David Ian Rabey, *Lovefuries* (Bristol, 2008) pp. 41–2.
68. Dufourmantelle, *Blind Date*, p. 102.
69. Rabey, *Lovefuries*, p. 28.
70. Lingis, *Dangerous Emotions*, p. 165.
71. *Ibid.*, pp. 165–6.
72. Dufourmantelle, *Blind Date*, pp. 102–3.
73. *Ibid.*, p. 47.
74. *Ibid.*, p. 59.
75. Howard Barker, *Plays: Two* (London, 2006), pp. 84–5.
76. Dufourmantelle, *Blind Date*, p. 56. Other passages in Dufourmantelle's book have a notable pertinence to Barker plays: notably the way that sacrifice leaves an unearthly, sublime 'remainder', which is 'not the body itself, nor the feeling of being alone; it is rather a hollowed-out space', the symbolic form of desire (Dufourmantelle, *Blind Date*, pp. 79, 80); this echoes the action of Barker's play *The Brilliance of the Servant* (published in his *Collected Plays Vol. 5*, (London, 2001)), in which a servant sacrifices himself for his mistress and returns from the enemy encampment literally viscerally hollowed out. Also, Dufourmantelle's disquisition on the term 'blind date', which speaks of the blind person feeling her/his way, 'speaks of sex and the words that surround it in order to avoid it, to obsess it, to put it in the wrong' (Dufourmantelle, *Blind Date*, p. 103), might serve as a summary of the initial premise of Barker's *The Twelfth Battle of Isonzo* (staged 2000, and published in the same collected volume).

77. Howard Barker, *The Fence in its Thousandth Year* (London, 2005), p. 17
78. Alexander E. Hooke, 'Silent Communities: Foucault and Lingis on the End of Philosophy', in Hooke and Fuchs, *Encounters with Alphonso Lingis*, p.69.
79. Alphonso Lingis, *The Community of Those Who Have Nothing in Common* (Bloomington, IN, 1994), p. 192.
80. Harold Pinter, *Plays: Four* (London, 1993), p. 314.
81. Lingis, *Dangerous Emotions*, p. 185.
82. Lingis, *The Community*, p. 108.
83. Barker, *Death, The One and the Art of Theatre*, p. 1.
84. Howard Barker, *Arguments for a Theatre*, 3rd edn (Manchester, 1997), p. 206.
85. Lingis, *The Community*, p. 113.
86. Samuel Beckett, *The Complete Dramatic Works* (London, 1986), p. 222.
87. Lingis, *The Community*, pp. 173–4.
88. *Ibid.*, p. 162.
89. Barker, *Death, The One and the Art of Theatre*, p. 11.
90. Lingis, *The Community*, p. 164.
91. Barker, *Death, The One and the Art of Theatre*, p. 20.
92. Lingis, *The Community*, p. 161.
93. Dufourmantelle, *Blind Date*, p. 103
94. Dufourmantelle, *Blind Date*, p. 12.
95. Alphonso Lingis, *Abuses* (Berkeley, CA, 1994), p. 236.
96. Barker, *Death, The One and the Art of Theatre*, p. 8.

9

Howard Barker's 'monstrous assaults': eroticism, death and the antique text

Graham Saunders

In a 1994 essay, 'Murders and conversations: the classic text and a contemporary writer', the dramatist Howard Barker addressed what he called 'conversations with dead authors',[1] and asked 'what compels an author – at various moments in his progress – to engage in this literary necrophilia? ... [within] the charnel house or the pantheon of European drama'.[2] Such dialogues have been a long-running strand throughout his work and have included *(Uncle) Vanya* (1992), Barker's reconception of Anton Chekhov's *Uncle Vanya* (1900); and *Minna* (1994), his take on Gotthold Lessing's *Minna von Barnhelm* (1767). Yet it has been Elizabethan and Jacobean tragedies that have most occupied Barker (albeit intermittently) throughout his career. The first encounter began with a BBC radio play, *Henry V in Two Parts* (1971), while the style and content of early plays such as *Cheek* (1970) and *No One Was Saved* (1970) saw his inclusion among a group of playwrights termed by John Russell Taylor 'the New Jacobeans'.[3] Others, including Edward Bond, Peter Barnes and Howard Brenton, shared features that Russell Taylor identified as a self-conscious theatricality, a fascination with violence and the grotesque and an anarchic sense of black humour.

However, it was not until 1986, and Barker's self-styled 'collaboration' with the Jacobean playwright Thomas Middleton in the rewriting of *Women Beware Women* (*c.*1612–27), that his work directly engaged with the drama of this period. These encounters have continued over nearly a twenty-year period and have included *Seven Lears* (1989) and most recently

Gertrude – The Cry (2002), a reconception of Shakespeare's *Hamlet* (*c.*1601).

However, Barker's engagement with classic texts does not express any comforting agreement with their professed 'universalism' or liberal humanist values. Quite the contrary, in fact: for Barker, locked deep within the architecture of the classical text lurks material that potentially offends what he calls our present 'age of social hygiene'.[4] Such material is elusive, however, existing between half-glimpsed interstices and significant absences. Crucial to this, classical texts – and here Barker refers only to tragedies – are potential repositories for *secrets* which can profoundly repulse and disturb received ideologies upon which contemporary society relies. Yet the texts themselves do not give up their secrets so easily. Barker's approach has been to carefully expose and extrapolate significant gaps in order to 'glimpse the original for the frail and naked exposition of feeling, tender and afraid'.[5]

These acts of exposure through rewriting include a new ending given to *Women Beware Women*; the restoration of the missing queen in *Seven Lears*, who, as Barker notes in reference to Shakespeare's *King Lear* (*c.*1604–05), 'is barely quoted even in the depths of rage or pity';[6] and an exploration of transgressive female sexuality in *Gertrude – The Cry*. These plays, while still related to their classical sources, go beyond the palliative measures of adaptation or ideologically driven 'corrective' readings. Out of this state of benign neglect, 'consigned to the realms of cultural archaeology' through the process of canonisation, Barker's rewritings attempt radical acts of reclamation, ones that seek to 'identify the pleasures and dangers of the classical text'.[7] By 'dangers', Barker refers chiefly to the liberating, yet potentially destructive, *eroticism* that lies inert within these plays. The new texts, by being tangentially related to the old, attempt to impel enervating new forms of desire that have formerly been repressed. Suppression might have come through direct censorship by the authorities at the time (as Thomas Middleton points out in his fictitious 'conversation' with Barker[8]), or be the result of self-imposed censorship by the dramatists themselves. This, together with the forces of history following the Enlightenment, can lead to a play such as *King Lear*, which began as a fractious and deeply troubling work, being reduced to what Barker calls a 'placid story'.[9]

The repression in Shakespeare's Lear can be sensed in his misogynistic outbursts in response to female desire ('Down from the waist / They're centaurs, though women all above.' IV.v.120–1),[10] and its political consequences through the outbreak of civil war, during which Lear's daughters Goneril and Regan vie for Edmund's sexual attention. As with the ending of Middleton's *Women Beware Women*, female sexual appetite is shown to lead to destruction. Shakespeare the moralist in *King Lear* even displays onstage the bloody knife and the two dead sisters as a warning and an education to his audience about the dangers of unbridled desire (V.iii.195–209). Yet this capitulation to a prescribed form of morality pulls against the play's more radical impulses that question ideas of leadership and monarchy. Barker calls the ending of *King Lear* 'smothered genius',[11] and in his prequel *Seven Lears* the patent artificiality of the moral order Shakespeare imposes becomes far more understandable through the introduction of Lear's queen, Clarissa: she is, Barker argues, although a speculative character, part of the architecture of *King Lear*; just as 'we have slowly re-learned that architecture is about emptiness as well as substance',[12] her absence inhabits *King Lear* as a play. By comparison, the analogy of architecture to embody absence is used even more literally in Harold Pinter's *The Homecoming* (1965), where the dead matriarch Jessie is mentioned in the same breath as the removal of a wall and a door in the family home following her death.[13] Aspects of this figure also recur in the eponymous figure of Gertrude, discussed later in this essay.

The consequences of prescribed morality, together with historical processes that lead to inclusion within the canon, ultimately neuter impulses that can be thought of as radical forms of desire. Barker believes that Jacobean playwrights such as Thomas Middleton have never fully enjoyed acceptance in the pantheon of English drama because they somehow continue to transgress established order.[14] Subsequently the forces of conservatism seek to resist such impulses – be it in the form of self-censorship on the part of the dramatist or state censorship by the authorities: either way, such constraints attempt to displace and smother what is potentially liberating or troubling to established moral order. Hence the elaborate mass slaughter that ends Middleton's *Women Beware Women* is, for Barker, 'transparently inauthentic',[15] little more than an elaborate theatrical smokescreen that crudely attempts to reinforce a sense of moral obedience among its Jacobean audiences. Such parroting of a conservative orthodoxy (such as the Cardinal's final speech, 'Sin, what thou art these ruins show too piteously … So where lust reigns, that prince cannot reign long' v.ii.224–7),[16] which Barker describes as 'a genuflection of imagination to legality, a debt paid by an artist to a semi-tolerant state',[17] paradoxically helps to reveal equally powerful contradictory moral forces. These are mostly played out in Middleton's *Women Beware Women* through the sexual relationship between the young clerk Leantio and the older aristocrat Livia; yet the liaison hints towards a form of sexuality that is not defined by the simple belief, forcefully articulated elsewhere in the play, that desire is synonymous with moral corruption.

In contrast, Shakespeare's *Hamlet* displays an almost constant *vigilance* for stirrings of unruly female sexuality. This is exercised most keenly on Ophelia, who becomes the focus of both her father's and brother's anxieties. Laertes, for instance, urges his sister to 'keep within the rear of your affection / out of shot and danger of desire' (i.iii.34–5), while Polonius reinforces this advice, 'be somewhat scanter of your maiden presence' (i.iii.121). Hamlet's simultaneous attempts to provoke Ophelia into a sexual response, together with his violent repression of it in the (in)famous 'Get thee to a nunnery' (iii.i.70–152) speech ultimately seem to drive her to madness; yet the snatches of bawdy song with which Ophelia regales the court show potential at any moment to become a conduit through which uninhibited desire might erupt.

Howard Barker's most realised expression of feminine desire as an enervating, yet destructive, force has been his reappropriation of the figure of Gertrude from Shakespeare's *Hamlet*. This reclamation of a well-known Shakespearian character also makes possible a reconsideration of well-known events that take place within the play. These include Gertrude's hasty remarriage to the king's brother Claudius so soon after her husband's death, but it is Hamlet's behaviour, and particularly the well-known expressions of disgust at his mother's new union, that give rise to the suspicion that Shakespeare is repressing something terrible: namely that Hamlet's misanthropy is nothing more than a futile attempt to block the new calling his mother now finds with Claudius. In Barker's play, this is expressed through the moment of overwhelming sexual fulfilment known as the Cry: its presence in *Gertrude – The Cry* is exactly that which is silenced (but hinted at) in Shakespeare's *Hamlet*. The Cry is first heard during Gertrude's involvement in the murder of her husband, an act Barker describes as 'a three way moment of ecstasy, intercourse and murder'.[18] Significantly, in *Hamlet* the actual murder is never shown, but artfully choreographed via the Players' enactment of *The Mousetrap*. Yet its absence in Shakespeare makes the act even more compulsively fascinating, whereby in *Gertrude – The Cry* the inclusion of the murder becomes a new map by which to reinterpret *Hamlet*.

It also offers an alternative solution to T.S. Eliot's famous essay 'Hamlet and his problems'; namely anxieties over what Eliot terms the missing *objective correlative*. Eliot argues that Hamlet's disgust at his mother's remarriage is not sufficient cause to set in motion the chain of events that leads to the tragic *dénouement* of the tragedy. Indeed, Eliot himself almost stumbles upon the buried objective correlative in his observation that had Shakespeare 'heightened the criminality of Gertrude [it] would have been to provide the formula for a totally different emotion in Hamlet'.[19] In turn, Barker acknowledged that Eliot's dissatisfaction with the play and his intuitive speculations on Gertrude's involvement in the murder of her husband led to his re-vivification of the queen as 'passionate, defiant and more authentically tragic than the adolescent prince himself'.[20]

Howard Barker has called *Gertrude – The Cry* his 'greatest play'[21] and, more specifically, 'his greatest work on love'.[22] However, it is perhaps more accurate to say that *Gertrude – The Cry* emerges out of Barker's own long-running interrogation of *desire* within Elizabethan and Jacobean drama. In retrospect, the architect Krak's appalled question 'Where's cunt's geometry?'[23] in Barker's 1985 play *The Castle* is returned to over fifteen years later in *Gertrude – The Cry*, and, with it, the potential threat that female desire poses to established order. In his version of Middleton's *Women Beware Women* (written a year after *The Castle*), two principal themes which distinguish Barker's appropriation of Elizabethan and Jacobean drama are established – both the aforementioned nature of female desire and with it the fetishisation of the older woman.

With regard to the former, *Women Beware Women* becomes the theoretical basis of Barker's 'Theatre of Catastrophe', where the desire of characters such as Livia, Leantio and Sordido to experience forbidden knowledge leads to profound moments of ecstatic truthfulness.

Nevertheless, this first real engagement with Jacobean drama still displays vestiges of Barker's earlier incarnation as a 'political' dramatist throughout the 1970s. Here, Livia recognises that her coupling with Leantio has wrought changes that make her renounce her former life as a witty court schemer. Sexual desire and political transformation come together in Livia's Brechtian-tinged speech: 'The world hates passion … All hate your lives and change the world!'[24] Barker's Cardinal also recognises that Livia's newly emergent selfhood represents 'another sex … Something which unlocks the discipline of the civil state' (35). This culminates in a savage disruption of a public spectacle – namely the Duke and Bianca's marriage – through Sordido's rape of Bianca. This is not only a sexual attack, but also an assault on the state itself embodied through Bianca, who is complicit in what David Ian Rabey calls its 'voyeuristic pageantry'.[25] Livia sees Bianca's personal salvation coming out of her rape by Sordido, but it will also have politically liberating consequences whereby Sordido's savage act of violation will 'rock the state off its foundations, which is erected on such lies as ducal marriages' (51).

Barker's next engagement with the drama of this period was with Shakespeare. In *Seven Lears*, a prequel to Shakespeare's *King Lear* and written three years after *Women Beware Women*, the impulse that drives sexual transgression towards liberating political change is absent. Here, the adulterous affair between Lear and his wife's mother is shown through a seven-part process that transforms the idealistic young king with an innate need for justice at the beginning of the play into the politically corrupt figure of the ending. At this final incarnation, Lear is ready to step from the Barkerian stage onto the Shakespearian one. Prudentia is the very antithesis of Livia in Barker's version of *Women Beware Women*, who challenges Leantio by pointing out that 'my flesh is not a pond to drown your fears in' (50). In *Seven Lears* such advice is disregarded and the potential of desire as an agent for political or moral revelation lost through Lear's blind sexual obsession with Prudentia. In Barker's rewriting, Lear's infatuation for his wife's mother becomes part of his political mis-education.

These countervailing strands between moral liberation through the erotic as well as its capacity to corrupt distinguish Barker's interrogation of classical drama from this period. Partly this comes from his observation that, because of its smothering ubiquity in contemporary Western culture, the pornographic obliterates the erotic.[26] This is why Prince Hamlet in *Gertrude – The Cry* mistakenly locates the source of his mother's sexuality entirely by the length of her skirt, provoking his grandmother Isola's derision: 'He thinks a short skirt's sex' (24).[27]

As mentioned, an exploration of the erotic's potential to disrupt order is a recurring theme through Barker's conversations with Shakespeare and his contemporaries. In *Gertrude – The Cry*, Isola – the former queen – engineers her daughter-in-law's downfall by corrupting the nature of her sexual ecstasy. Like many of Barker's characters, Isola's attitude to Gertrude veers from wonder to hatred. Consequently, Isola both understands her son Claudius' infatuation and by inference the need to murder his own brother for possession of the Cry. Yet Isola also wishes to corrupt this source of passion and attempts to inveigle Gertrude into sexually betraying Claudius with the young Duke of Mecklenburg. Gertrude recognises these attempts at subverting her powerful sexuality into the mundane. This is made evident in the scene where Gertrude calls for her 'PROSTIUTE'S COAT' (38). Again, this is reminiscent of Harold Pinter's *The Homecoming*, in which the powerful eroticism that the figure of Ruth displays both fascinates and appalls the all-male household she inhabits. Their solution is to break Ruth's power by setting her up as a Soho prostitute – what Gertrude calls 'my vocation' (39). There is a sense in both *Gertrude – The Cry* and *The Homecoming* that a fragile boundary exists between the power that resides in the erotic and its potential to be despoiled.

This corruption is also shown in other ways. Just as Lenny in *The Homecoming* is obsessed about the origins of his own paternity, Claudius also challenges his mother – who he calls 'a whore in her own time' (50) – to name his brother's father. Isola, too, is reminiscent of the dead matriarch Jessie from Pinter's play, who is described as 'a slutbitch of a wife' by her husband (25). Barker sets up an extreme juxtaposition between Gertrude's power to kill men 'with those legs inside those stockings' (35) to the tawdriness of her prostitute's coat that is 'belted / To draw a line at violation … And thin / To hint at poverty' (39). The presence of this item of costume onstage makes clear the difference between the erotic and the pathetic tawdriness of the sexual transaction. This echoes Livia's belief in Barker's version of *Women Beware Women* that 'the world hates passion. Fornication's all its taste' (34).

Gertrude also marks a break in the relationship between the libidinal and structures of political power that occupy *Women Beware Women* and to a lesser extent *Seven Lears*. Instead, one gets the impression that Barker is more concerned with revealing moments of terrible ecstasy within *Hamlet* – moments that have become obscured by history, theatrical tradition and canonisation. It is the sexually transgressive figure of Gertrude who not only reveals these formerly buried impulses within *Hamlet*, but also comes to represent Barker's current thinking on the relationship between the erotic and death. Whereas his fictional 1986 conversation with Thomas Middleton is tinged with a sense of utopianism whereby his version of *Women Beware Women* 'insist[s] on the redemptive power of desire',[28] by the time of *Gertrude – The Cry* in 2002, the erotic has become a terrible and destructive force. Andy Smith (with reference to Julia Kristeva) terms the figure of Gertrude 'the "death mother", poised between *Eros* and *Thanatos*'.[29] In fact, as the play progresses the shift is irrevocably towards the death drive.

This is made explicit in the opening scene where Gertrude and Claudius copulate over the expiring body of her husband. Here, the erotic does not reside in the act of sex itself, but rather the moment of old Hamlet's death being its catalyst. While this scene is highly 'Barkerian' in its merging of both violent and erotic imagery (alluded to in young Hamlet's grim joke that Gertrude 'choked' his father 'with a view'),[30] the physical representation of erotic ecstasy – Gertrude's 'Cry' itself – is both highly ambiguous and complex. It both represents Barker's latest thinking concerning the relationship between erotics and death while also revisiting several of the key ideas from *Women Beware Women* and *Seven Lears*.

For instance, Livia's assertion in *Women Beware Women* that 'desire's truth' continues through Gertrude's refusal to fake the Cry for her lover's gratification (22), yet its origins also lie in cruelty. Gertrude recalls that she first heard the Cry as a child when her mother-in-law Isola, the former queen, would couple with one of her subjects while his blind and crippled wife was forced to listen to the infidelity taking place (21). In a moment of brutal clarity, Gertrude recognises that betrayal – such as her later unfaithfulness against Claudius – is the destructive origin of the Cry (44). But the Cry is at its most intense in the presence of death; and Gertrude's two most intense ecstasies come from the death of her husband old Hamlet, and her son, the prince. At this latter point Gertrude is less of a Kristevian 'death mother', and more subject to an overwhelming erotic force that leads to the destruction of others. As Gertrude's servant Cascan asserts, 'All ecstasy makes ecstasy go running to a further place ... Eventually it lures us over a cliff' (10–11). This speech, delivered immediately after Claudius and Gertrude have murdered old Hamlet and experienced the Cry for the first time, foretells of the catastrophe to come. By now, the intercession of Claudius is no longer necessary (80), and death is no longer in equilibrium with the erotic: it now holds sway completely in what Barker sees as 'the erotic secret of tragedy', namely 'those moments of immaculate exposure to seduction/destruction'.[31]

Here it is interesting to compare Barker's current thinking about the nature of desire with his 1986 version of *Women Beware Women*. In this play, the Cardinal names 'another sex' (35) for the relationship between Livia and Leantio, and which is contrasted against the rapacious sexuality of Middleton's/Barker's Florence. This can be attributed in part to the political and social climate of Britain in the 1980s, with the production at the Royal Court taking place at the height of Thatcherism's economic reforms. Caryl Churchill's *Serious Money*, the major play of the following year, revealed a clear vogue for 'city comedies' that drew from history in order to comment on what Barker in 1986 called 'a money and squalor society'.[32] However, by *Gertrude – The Cry* in 2002 not only has the relationship between societies based on power, sex and money entirely disappeared from his work but in its place a more private and profoundly *tragic* relationship has taken its place, based on what Barker calls 'the prospect of personal destruction'.[33] This stands in opposition to Aristotelian tragedy, which fulfils a quasi-social function of pacifying and morally assuaging its audience. In Barker's plays, the tragic is always profoundly disturbing because it is predicated on 'the threat of annihilation that hovers about the margins of all passionate encounters'.[34] With the possible exception of Sarah Kane, Barker is almost unique among contemporary dramatists in his desire to interrogate the disturbing yet transformative qualities that can be found in Elizabethan and Jacobean tragedy.

By the time of *Gertrude – The Cry* and, later, in his 2005 book *Death, The One and the Art of Theatre*, Barker had refined what he believes to be the inviolable secret of classical tragedy: namely the relationship between eroticism and death. Like many of the tragic protagonists of Shakespeare and his contemporaries, Barker's characters venerate death because of an innate recognition that 'tragedy … intends no good to man. But intending no good to him, it enhances him.'[35] Because modern theatre has 'ceased to make death its subject', it has resulted for Barker in a 'surrender[ing of] its authority over the human soul'. Instead, it has become involved with 'mundane projects of political indoctrination and social therapy'[36] that are opposed to the very nature of the tragic experience. Barker criticises modern theatre's 'hatred of the dark, the obscure, the unexplained, above all the private, the enclosed, essentially that which disdains justification, function, utility'. However, the one thing that defines modern culture above all else in Barker's eyes is 'its loathing of a secret'.[37] We can also add to this Terry Eagleton's observation that tragedy with 'its ontological depth and high seriousness … grates on the postmodern sensibility … As an aristocrat among art forms, its tone is too solemn and portentous for a streetwise, sceptical culture.'[38]

However resistant modern 'streetwise' culture might be to tragedy, it still has its own venerated subjects – chief among these is the enshrinement of youth. It is significant that Barker's *Women Beware Women*, *Seven Lears* and *Gertrude – The Cry* stand as provocative refutations to this ethic through their insistence on the erotically desired older woman. This radical reorientation of female sexuality not only sets out to puzzle and offend contemporary sensibilities but does the same to received opinion from the Elizabethan and Jacobean age. In *Hamlet*, for instance, the Prince's disgust at Gertrude's remarriage is also mixed with a sense of bewilderment that his mother still desires and is desired: 'You cannot call it love; for at your age / The heyday in the blood is tame, it's humble / And waits upon the judgement' (III.iv.69–71). In Middleton's *Women Beware Women* this bafflement is replaced by stern moral warnings and finally retributive punishment. At one point the Mother tells Livia a story concerning a woman of 'nine-and forty' who had been robbed by a former younger lover as 'fair warning to all other women / That they live chaste at fifty' (II. ii.169–70). Livia's murder in the final scene only serves to underscore what happens to women who attempt to go against the natural order of things.

However, Howard Barker aims to completely overturn this mixture of disgust and bewilderment. For instance, in his version of *Women Beware*

Women Leantio proclaims, 'no woman under forty is worth entering!' (32). This rejection of youthfulness – the coltish Isabella in Barker's version is described by the Ward as 'full of grimy sweetness, like a toffee left in pockets' (36–7) – is born out of a recognition that the state attempts to impose its ideologies quite literally through control of the body politic. Barker argues that youthfulness as an ideal is synonymous with the practicalities of fecundity, but in making youth its ideal, the state 'effectively locates sexual charisma at the shallowest point'.[39] In *Gertrude – The Cry*, even this shibboleth of youth and fertility is ruptured when the queen's transgressive powers of the erotic reside in her pregnancy at the age of forty-three.

Barker also makes the important distinction between *beauty* and *desire*. In *Arguments for a Theatre* he points out that it is manifestly foolish to believe Homer's account of Helen's physiognomy provoking the Trojan War: 'a beautiful woman cannot launch a thousand ships, whereas we suspect a desirable woman might.'[40] This is recognised by the Cardinal in Barker's *Women Beware Women*, who sees in Livia and Leantio's public displays of rebellious carnality a challenge to the status quo – 'Let the population copulate … whelps and growls from upper storeys … satisfaction and quiescence everywhere'. Instead, Livia's example 'might lever up whole pavements and turn fountains red' (35). Here, Barker draws attention not only to revolutionary change coming out of a recognition that desire extends beyond child-bearing age but also the perverse pleasure it affords by offending against the accepted order of things – such as Leantio deliberately choosing to 'lick experience out of [Livia's] wrinkles' rather than 'girls tight in their skins on every pavement!' (35).

Yet in *Seven Lears* Barker also shows the potential of such unions to produce a sense of sterility and neglect. Here, the affair between Lear and his mother-in-law Prudentia is shown as one of the milestones in his political corruption ('all wrongs are right with you' (22)) and the beginning of his descent into infantile madness. In contrast, his younger wife Clarissa is clearly shown to be the fittest to rule in his place.

The figure of Hamlet has also at times been appropriated into modern culture's obsession with youth, as with, for example, productions of the play during the latter part of the 1960s where characterisations of the Danish Prince drew upon aspects of the rebellious and hedonistic counterculture.[41] Yet Hamlet's squeamishness over matters sexual, especially his dealings with Ophelia, have never made this association particularly convincing. In *Gertrude – The Cry* Barker is keen to emphasise Hamlet's infantilism – for example, dressing him in the original 2002 production as an English public schoolboy – and the misogynistic repulsion towards female sexuality that is omnipresent in Shakespeare's play. Barker's Hamlet, described by his grandmother Isola as 'a bore and a prude' (23) exhibits these traits all too clearly during a soliloquy that takes place while examining the face of his dead father:

> I expected to be more moved than this...
> Never mind these things will come later when I least expect them
> in bed with a bitch or on a horse eyes full of tears ... I'll get off the
> bitch off the horse have you a handkerchief
> (*He laughs briefly*)
> Horses don't have handkerchiefs but bitches might to wipe their
> crevices that stinks
> I'll say stinks of filthy copulations am I to wipe my eyes with that yes
> wipe away and fuck your finicky fastidious and
> (*He laughs, shuddering*)
> WOMEN ARE SO COARSE (13)

Andy Smith's analysis of this passage argues that it projects Hamlet's prudery and misogyny 'into the very *raison d'etre* of the character',[42] and also serves as a nexus point between the two plays: here it would be easy to imagine the Hamlet of Shakespeare who speaks of 'the rank sweat of an enseamed bed / Stewed in corruption, honeying and making love over the nasty sty' (III.iv.83–4) at the same time time discoursing about bitches and horses. In *Gertrude – The Cry* the underlying fear that motivates such outpourings is also realised in Hamlet's vision of Elsinore being rebuilt in glass. While this whim for complete exposure might at first seem the very antithesis of a prudish condition, it in fact confirms it. This is because, in Barker's reckoning, profound moments of erotic desire are engendered under conditions of darkness and secrecy. Just as the neon lights of modern cities have practically obliterated the stars in 'a dazzling scrutiny of transparency', for Barker modern society itself 'abhors the shadows' which are breeding grounds for the unsettling and the transgressive.[43]

Hamlet's project to eradicate desire itself in *Gertrude – The Cry* makes him literally an architect for what Barker calls 'The Illuminated Society'.[44] The endeavours to eradicate the potency of secrecy and darkness, elements that so permeate Shakespeare's *Hamlet*, also give rise to the profound moments of erotic power that trouble Shakespeare. But arguably it is these very qualities that succeed in making *Hamlet* one of the greatest tragedies of the Western canon.

Yet the garrulous moralising of Shakespeare's Hamlet, while retained at the beginning of *Gertrude – The Cry*, becomes progressively reduced to 'saying less' (54) as the full extent of his mother's terrible sexuality and abandonment of familial bonds reveals itself. Here one can detect the compulsive need that exists in so many of Barker's characters to speak truthfully. Hamlet himself realises that once he has moved beyond the 'purgatory of adolescence' (15), and with it the desire to simply shock, he will be more fit to rule. Gertrude also acknowledges 'an insidious attraction' as her son attempts to tread a precarious path within the 'maze of manners' (25) that sustains court life at Elsinore.

In this essay, I have tried to show that Howard Barker's engagement with Elizabethan and Jacobean drama has been an ongoing interrogation 'to identify the pleasures and dangers of the classical text'.[45] In *Women Beware Women*, *King Lear* and *Hamlet*, these spaces and evasions, as well as the half-glimpsed moments of profound erotic desire, are exposed by Barker in order to renew a sense of the tragic within a contemporary theatre that promulgates entertainment, social relevance and accessibility as its chief functions. John Russell Taylor's classification of Howard Barker as a 'new Jacobean' at the start of his career is perhaps more true now than it was back in 1971. Whereas Russell Taylor's use of the term denoted a tendency towards a dramatic style that was vivid, anarchic, violent and macabre, Barker has subsequently become Jacobean in far more profound ways. In his 1996 essay 'Love in the museum: the modern author and the antique text' Barker speaks about his encounters with Thomas Middleton and William Shakespeare as being akin to walking in a darkened room with 'powerful invisible allies in that devastating contest with new orthodoxies that characterizes the artistic life'.[46] Yet, writing elsewhere, Barker has also noted that the Jacobean playwrights, 'far from being [seen as] great flourishing of the English genius', were in fact 'rapidly extinguished by the Reformation and the subsequent waves of humanism, utilitarianism, socialism, Methodism, and all the moral enthusiasms that constitute the English soul'.[47] Considering Barker's own marginalised position in British theatre, it is not too much of an overstatement to place him in an analogous position with his Jacobean predecessors. While the late Sarah Kane's assessment of Howard Barker as 'the Shakespeare of our age' has been frequently cited in relation to his work,[48] in a formerly unpublished interview Kane also observed that '[i]n a few hundred years Howard will be like Shakespeare. No one will really understand what Howard Barker's done until he's been dead for a long time.'[49] The two assessments are both laudatory and pessimistic in that they seek to locate the work in a continuum begun by his Jacobean predecessors but also point towards his continuing neglect. Nevertheless, Barker's attempts to unlock the radical potential of erotics and desire within classical texts show that a more productive reassessment of these plays will have taken place.

Notes

1. Howard Barker, *Arguments for a Theatre*, 3rd edn (Manchester, 1997), p. 154.
2. *Ibid.*, pp. 153–4
3. John Russell Taylor, 'British Dramatists. The New Arrivals', *Plays and Players*, 18 (1971), pp. 24–9.
4. Barker, *Arguments for a Theatre*, pp. 182–9.
5. *Ibid.*, p. 157.
6. Howard Barker, 'Introduction' to *Seven Lears* (London, 1990).
7. *Ibid.*, p. 173.
8. Barker, *Arguments for a Theatre*, p. 25.
9. *Ibid.*, p.155.
10. William Shakespeare, *The Tragedy of King Lear*, in Stanley Wells, Gary Taylor, John Jowett and William Montgomery (eds), *The Oxford Shakespeare: Tragedies* (Oxford, 1987), p. 1298. Further references to *King Lear* and *Hamlet* will use this edition of the text.
11. Barker, *Arguments for a Theatre*, p. 155.
12. *Ibid.*, p.154.
13. Howard Pinter, *The Homecoming*, in *Plays: Three* (London, 1997), p. 29.
14. Barker, *Arguments for a Theatre*, p. 154.
15. *Ibid.*
16. Thomas Middleton, *Women Beware Women*, in Bryan Loughrey and Neil Taylor (eds), *Five Plays* (London, 1988), p. 286. All further quotations will use this source.
17. Barker, *Arguments for a Theatre*, p. 98.
18. Howard Barker, Programme Notes, *Gertrude – The Cry* (The Wrestling School, London, 2002).
19. T.S. Eliot, *The Sacred Wood: Essays on Poetry and Criticism* (London, 1922), p. 86.
20. H. Barker, Letter to Andy Smith. Cited in Andy Smith, '"I am not what I was": Adaptation and Transformation in the Theatre of Howard Barker and The Wrestling School,' in Karoline Gritzner and David Ian Rabey (eds), *Theatre of Catastrophe: New Essays on Howard Barker* (London, 2006), pp. 48–9.
21. Howard Barker and Eduardo Houth, *A Style and Its Origins* (London, 2007), p. 19. In a letter to Andy Smith, Barker has also commented, 'I regard *He Stumbled* and *Gertrude* as major works, and in this climate, revolutionary works.' See Gritzner and Rabey, *Theatre of Catastrophe*, p. 53.
22. *Ibid.*, p. 116.
23. Howard Barker, *Collected Plays Vol. 1* (London, 1990), p. 241.
24. Howard Barker (with Thomas Middleton), *Women Beware Women* (London, 1989), p. 34. All subsequent references to the play will use this source.
25. David Ian Rabey, *English Drama Since 1940* (Harlow, 2003), p. 185.
26. Barker, *Arguments for a Theatre*, p. 187.
27. In recent work, such as *Gertrude – The Cry* and *Dead Hands* (2004), the female protagonist's penchant for wearing high stiletto heels locates the erotic in these fetishised objects. For a more detailed discussion see Helen Iball, 'Dead Hands and Killer Heels', in Gritzner and Rabey, *Theatre of Catastrophe*, pp. 70–82.
28. Barker, *Arguments for a Theatre*, p. 25.
29. Smith, '"I am not what I was"', p. 52. In much of her later work Kristeva identifies the maternal with Freud's notion of the death drive Thanatos. For an informative introduction to Kristeva's ideas in this area see Janice Doane and Devon Hodge's *From Klein to Kristeva: Psychoanalytic Feminism and the Search for the 'Good Enough' Mother* (Ann Arbor, MI, 1993), pp. 53–78.

30. Howard Barker, *Gertrude – The Cry* (London, 2002), p. 17. All subsequent quotations will use this edition as its source.
31. Barker, *Arguments for a Theatre*, p. 160.
32. *Ibid.*, p. 26.
33. *Ibid.*, p. 160.
34. *Ibid.*, p. 175.
35. *Ibid.*, p. 186.
36. Howard Barker, *Death, The One and the Art of Theatre* (London, 2005), p. 2.
37. Barker, *Arguments for a Theatre*, p. 171.
38. Terry Eagleton, *Sweet Violence: The Idea of the Tragic* (Oxford, 2003), p. ix.
39. Barker, *Arguments for a Theatre*, p.195.
40. *Ibid.*
41. The best-known example being Peter Hall's 1965 Royal Shakespeare Company production with David Warner as Hamlet.
42. Smith, '"I am not what I was"', p. 50
43. Barker, *Arguments for a Theatre*, p. 182.
44. *Ibid.*, p. 184.
45. *Ibid.*, p. 143.
46. *Ibid.*, p. 178.
47. Howard Barker, 'The Ethics of Relevance and the Triumph of the Literal', in Margarete Rubik and Elke Mettinger-Schartmann (eds), *(Dis) Continuities: Trends and Traditions in Contemporary Theatre and Drama in English* (Trier, 2002), p. 86.
48. Dan Rebellato, 'Sarah Kane: An Appreciation', *New Theatre Quarterly*, 15(3) (1999), p. 280.
49. James Christopher, interview with Sarah Kane. Cited in Graham Saunders, *About Kane: The Playwright and the Work* (London, 2009), p. 48.

10

'Welcome to the house of fun': Eros, Thanatos, and the uncanny in grand illusions

Michael Mangan

Every great magic trick consists of three parts or acts. The first part is called the Pledge. The magician shows you something ordinary: a deck of cards, a bird or a man. He shows you this object. Perhaps he asks you to inspect it to see if it is indeed real, unaltered, normal. But of course ... it probably isn't. The second act is called the Turn. The magician takes the ordinary something and makes it do something extraordinary. Now you're looking for the secret ... but you won't find it, because of course you're not really looking. You don't really want to know. You want to be fooled. But you wouldn't clap yet. Because making something disappear isn't enough; you have to bring it back. That's why every magic trick has a third act, the hardest part, the part we call the Prestige.

The Prestige (2006)

We asked noted magician The Great Amazo why it is that we never see 'Sawing a Man in Half'. Amazo answered, 'Who would want to saw a man in half?'

Mallusionist – Stage Magic Explained (website)

The origins of an illusion
The conjuror's routine which is commonly known as 'Sawing a woman in half' is one of a large family of stage illusions which involve a pattern of symbolic, or apparent, death and resurrection. It is also one of conjuring's

most iconic tricks, one of those which define the art in the popular imagination, as 'natural' a part of the image of the conjuror as the rabbit and top hat or the fanned deck of cards. Most histories of magic record that its originator was the British illusionist Percy Thomas Tibbles, who worked under the stage name of 'Selbit' and who first sawed a woman in half at the Finsbury Park Empire, London, on 17 January 1921.

However, Selbit's claim, like so many other claims to originality in the history of magic, is a contested one. Because the specifics of an illusion, and the mechanics of how it is effected, are so basic to the economics of their profession, magicians have, understandably, tended to guard their trade secrets with some care. One result of this has been the well-known magicians' code of secrecy, and the sanctions which organisations such as the Magic Circle have carried out against those who break that code. Another has been a great emphasis within histories of conjuring on the question of who first originated a particular trick. In terms of establishing provenance, however, the magician is caught in a double bind: if he invents a new routine – or a significantly new version of an old routine – he naturally wants to benefit from his invention. But if he patents his routine, lodging the details of its mechanism with the Patent Office, he simultaneously reveals it, since he has placed those designs in the public domain. Yet if he does nothing, he gains no credit for it. This was Selbit's problem. His sawing illusion was an immediate commercial sensation, and almost equally immediately it was copied by a host of other magicians. The most successful of his competitors was Horace Goldin, who performed a version of the sawing illusion in the US in June 1921 to the American Society of Magicians at the McAlpin Hotel in New York – a version which he then *did* patent, and thereafter claimed to have originated. Goldin's account of his own 'invention' of the trick in his autobiography[1] makes no mention of Selbit by name, but bears the traces of the bitter legal battle which the rival magicians fought over the rights to the illusion. Goldin successfully defended his patent on the grounds that the means used to effect the illusion were not exactly the same as Selbit's, although he spent a very large amount of money on legal fees in the process. Nonetheless, the illusion was a lucrative one for Goldin: at the height of its popularity, his fees would sometimes amount to more than two thousand dollars per week, while overall the Keith theatrical circuit, for whom Goldin toured, earned more than a million dollars from the trick.[2]

There are other suggestions about the illusion's origins, although the most commonly cited – that the trick was invented by Torrini, the mentor of the great nineteenth-century illusionist Robert-Houdin[3] – is certainly false, since Torrini was a fictional character invented by Robert-Houdin himself to enhance his own narrative.

Certainly, though, the sawing illusion has numerous predecessors in the form of tricks in which humans and animals have various body parts cut off and then restored. Decapitation is the most popular of these, and the first-ever recorded magic trick, performed at the court of Cheops, builder of the Great Pyramid at Giza in the twenty-sixth century BCE, involved decapitating various farmyard animals, culminating in an ox. In the sixteenth century CE, Reginald Scot's *Discovery of Witchcraft* famously provided illustrations showing how the decapitation of John the Baptist was performed on stage. And in the late nineteenth century the illusionist Dr Lynn had had great success with his 'Palingenesia', a comically horrific routine which involved cutting off the victim's legs and arms as well as his head.

Selbit's unique contribution to the dismemberment sub-genre, however, operated at two levels. Firstly, at the technical level, he invented a new way of effecting the illusion, using the coffin-like wooden box. Secondly, at the 'narrative' level, or the level of presentation, he foregrounded the gender of the victim: in his version of the trick it definitely becomes sawing a *woman* in half. There are good practical reasons for a conjuror to use a female assistant for the routine, of course: its successful performance depends upon the victim being small enough and flexible enough to squeeze their body into unexpectedly small spaces. On a symbolic level, however, Selbit's innovation was to take a familiar magical narrative whose theme was *Thanatos*, and re-present it in terms of *Eros*.

Selbit, who had had a successful career in magic since the 1890s, seems to have had a fascination with the elements which led to the sawing illusion long before his 1921 triumph. In his 1901 volume *The Magician's Handbook*, in a chapter entitled 'Death, Decapitation and Resurrection', he gives details of 'a practical magical act that can be accomplished with comparative ease by performers with or without much knowledge of the magician's business'.[4] It involves, as the chapter title suggests, the cutting off and restoration of a head, and Selbit adds that 'It is most suitable for clowns to perform, as they can combine their delightful buffoonery with the terrible tragedy that is apparently enacted.'[5] He also describes a trick he has seen (and which, ironically, he credits to Horace Goldin as having introduced to the English stage) which he calls the 'New vanishing lady': a burlesque comic narrative in which a lady is chased by police and hides in a cabinet. As the pursuers approach,

> the front curtain only comes half way down, this leaving of course the lower half of the lady visible. By means of a rope suspended from a pulley, this improvised cabinet is hoisted from the floor just as the police open the door and walk in to search for the girl. Of course they discover her, or at least they see her dress in the cabinet, and pull down the other half of the curtain, thereby covering her up entirely; but just at that moment the performer fires a pistol and the curtains collapse and fall to the ground, showing that the lady has vanished, leaving the cabinet suspended in the air, quite empty.[6]

While sundry variations on the vanishing lady illusion were standard fare for the late-nineteenth-century magic show, this particular twist on the story, in which half the lady remains visible, is interesting considering the nature of Selbit's later triumph. Even more apposite is another recent trick which he describes: 'The new half-lady illusion'. This is, he explains,

> an illusion of a very mysterious nature. It was nothing short of a half lady, who was announced to float above the audience … resting in a sort of cup on the trapeze bar which is fixed to the balloon instead of the usual car. Presently the balloon begins to move forward, and it is pulled by ropes completely over the heads of the people in the stalls towards the gallery, the lady tossing flowers right and left all the while, and gracefully revolving in her cup which works on a pivot.[7]

The secret of this trick, it transpires, is that there is no secret: '*The girl in the balloon*', he reveals dramatically, '*had no legs*. It is believed that she had the misfortune to lose them both in a railway accident, and some ingenious entertainer saw a fortune in her loss.'[8] Death, decapitation, resurrection and half-ladies: Selbit's imagination was primed, twenty years before the sawing illusion was realised, with all its key elements.

It must be acknowledged that the genealogies of magic tricks, and the compulsive obsessions of conjurors and magic historians concerning who invented which magical illusion, may be of limited interest to anyone outside the professional fraternity of conjurors. In this case, however, it is worth considering the original circumstances of production. These specifics have a wider cultural resonance, since one of the elements which contributed to the trick's popularity was its contemporary social and political resonance. Selbit's sawing trick was first performed shortly after the passing of legislation which provided for partial female suffrage in the UK; following years of struggle for emancipation, the British suffrage movement had won significant victories with the granting of the vote to women over thirty in 1918. In America, the story was more complex, with different states passing emancipatory legislation at different times; there, too, however, the beginning of the 1920s was a time marked by significant shifts in gender relationships: the US Congress ratified the Nineteenth Amendment, which prohibited gender-based restrictions on voting, in 1920.

In both America and Britain resultant male anxieties about the new-found political, social and economic power of women found a range of cultural expression, from novels and plays through to music hall and vaudeville jokes and comic songs. Selbit's hugely popular routine should be seen as part of this anti-feminist backlash. Magic historian Jim Steinmeyer records that

> When Selbit introduced the Sawing in 1921, one of his earliest publicity stunts was to offer Christabel Pankhurst [one of the leaders of the British women's suffrage movement] twenty pounds a week to serve as a permanent sawing block for his illusion ... When Selbit challenged Christabel and Sylvia Pankhurst, he was challenging the women who had faced off with the government and frightened society with their goal ... 'What a chance for Selbit!' a review concluded. 'To be able to say he has actually "sawn off" the redoubtable "Sylvia"!'[9]

'My lovely assistant'
In fact, Selbit's gibe at the Pankhursts was only one of several examples of male magicians who used the suffrage movement as foils or butts, and it was

a comparatively late one: like many alert popular entertainers, conjurors had always been ready to weave topical references opportunistically into their acts. Thus, long before the parliamentary emancipation bill, David Devant and Charles Morritt had both performed routines in which they made suffragettes appear and disappear,[10] while in 1908 Harry Houdini (with rather greater courtesy) had successfully risen to the challenge from a group of London suffragettes to 'allow us to secure you to a mattress, with sheets and bandages; and think that we will be able to fasten you, so that you will not be able to effect your escape'.[11]

Thus, although the specifics of the historical situation in 1921 (the successes of the suffrage movement, the prospect of new social and economic freedoms for women and subsequent male anxieties) certainly provide a social and historical context by which to understand the immediate success of the sawing trick, it is important not to overstate its significance. The illusion of sawing a lady in half also belongs to a larger pattern of nineteenth- and early-twentieth-century cultural misogyny (visible, too, in films, plays and novels) which inscribes the woman as the victim, as the passive figure who is acted upon rather than acting, and who is the subject of persistent patterns of symbolic or actual violence and abuse. So when Jim Steinmeyer goes on to suggest that Selbit's 1921 performance marks the point at which 'the image of the woman in peril became a specific fashion in entertainment',[12] he greatly overstates the case. Both in the specific world of conjuring, and in the wider realms of culture, the damsel in distress was hardly a new motif.

The female assistant, it is true, is a comparatively late addition to the standard conjuring act. An assistant of *some* kind has always been an essential part of the set-up, not least because very often it is the assistant rather than the conjuror who actually makes the trick work; and conjurors during the sixteenth, seventeenth and eighteenth centuries tended to follow the standard practice of a male-dominated entertainment industry by employing male assistants. However, throughout the nineteenth century, as women gained greater employment in music halls, vaudevilles and variety shows, the female assistant became increasingly common. Not infrequently this, like many of the acts of the nineteenth-century music hall and popular theatre, was a family affair, with the role of the assistant being taken by a wife, daughter or sister. There is a particular advantage for the conjuror in keeping things within the family, of course, since the 'assistant' is necessarily privy to the operation of the apparatus and complicit in the working of the tricks: family members are less likely to abscond with the trade secrets. Thus John Henry Anderson, The Great Wizard of the North, performed with his daughter Lizzie, while half a century later Harry Houdini toured with his wife Bess, who nightly escaped from a trunk at the climax to their famous 'Metamorphosis' routine in the 1890s. The male conjuror/female assistant configuration was well established as a showbiz cliché by the late nineteenth century. More to the point is the kind of role the female assistant began to take in the show: like that of her male counterpart, much of her job involved bringing on and taking off props, handing them to or taking them from the conjuror – and in the process either distracting the audience's attention from something happening elsewhere on stage, or secretly operating the trick herself. Increasingly, however, as we can tell from bills, reviews, books and published descriptions of magicians' routines,[13] it was a female rather than a male assistant who was preponderantly being used for the kinds of tricks which involved symbolic death and resurrection: being put to sleep, hypnotised, incarcerated, levitated and made to vanish in various ways.

Will Goldston's 1912 volume *Stage Illusions*, for example, features plenty of these, of which perhaps the most spectacular is a cremation illusion in which

> a girl, with her arms bound to her sides, is brought on from the wings, and lashed with ropes to the post. Assistants now bring in four bundles of faggots, which are piled round her .. The curtain ... is now lowered, and a brazier brought on to the stage, over which the performer chants incantations and then lights the torch, which he thrusts under the canopy; a blaze of fire immediately starts inside, coupled with agonised shrieks from the victim. This part of the illusion gives great scope for acting on the part of the performer, and, should it be desired, the effect can be considerably increased by lighting red fire in the wings, and weird band music, such as that of the Mephistopheles Scene from 'Faust'. These sounds gradually die away, until, amidst dead silence, the canopy is raised.[14]

Selbit, then, was by no means the first to torture a woman onstage in the name of magic. And in other areas of art and entertainment, too, the passive and victimised female had long been a cliché. It was a staple of popular theatre and film, from the melodrama of the previous century through to the emerging cinema serials of the twentieth. It was a frequent motif of eighteenth-century Gothic literature, drama and painting, and also of its nineteenth-century derivatives, including the theatre of excess that was the French Grand-Guignol.[15] Meanwhile, at the level of high culture, the Victorians' fondness for the image in painting and sculpture as the expression of a cultural fear of female vitalism is well documented.[16] It may be truer to say that Selbit's routine took a well-worn cultural cliché and translated it into terms that the conjuror could exploit, revitalising the cliché by changing its context. At the very least, it appears to have spoken to a particular audience with particular pertinence: on what Roland Barthes termed the level of myth, Selbit's trick may well have been doing, in its own time, some very powerful cultural work. 'Myth', according to Barthes,

> has the task of giving an historical intention a natural justification, and making contingency appear eternal ... Myth does not deny things, on the contrary its function is to talk about them; simply, it purifies them, it makes them innocent, it gives them a natural and eternal justification ...[17]

The sawing trick, then, both performs and celebrates cultural misogyny, and by presenting it as entertainment, it also naturalises it, making the idea of violent revenge (in Barthes' ironic inflection of that term) 'innocent'.

Spectatorial pleasures: the uncanny gaze

One of the main functions of cultural criticism post-Barthes has been to *de*mythologise – to dismantle and analyse seemingly innocent or value-free cultural practices and to reveal their ideological implications. Few areas of scholarship have been more effective in this than film criticism, and (given the proximity and occasional convergence of their interests) it is perhaps strange that the methods, frameworks and approaches of film theory and criticism have generally had comparatively little impact on performance studies. A partial exception to this is the work of Laura Mulvey. Her 1975 landmark essay 'Visual Pleasure and Narrative Cinema'[18] is generally recognised within film studies as 'the most thoroughgoing and explicit introduction of neo-Freudian psychoanalytic theory to feminist film studies, and the most inescapable reference in the field',[19] and some of its key points have been taken up and applied by influential performance theorists.[20]

Mulvey's analysis presupposes a predominantly male, or male-identified, spectatorship, and one whose pleasure is derived from a dominant perspective. Using Lacanian and neo-Freudian theory, her essay focuses on the way in which 'pleasure in looking has been split between active/male and passive/female' so as to neutralise the threat posed by the image of the woman:

> The scopophilic instinct (pleasure in looking at another person as an erotic object), and, in contradistinction, ego libido (forming identification processes) act as formations, mechanisms, which this cinema has played on. The image of woman as (passive) raw material for the (active) gaze of man takes the argument a step further into the structure of representation, adding a further layer demanded by the ideology of the patriarchal order as it is worked out in its favorite cinematic form – illusionistic narrative film.[21]

Mulvey's argument, to be sure, has not been without its critics within film theory,[22] and Mulvey has to some extent modified her position in her own later writings. It must be acknowledged, too, that while 'gaze theory' seemed initially attractive to performance theorists and theatre historians, it became increasingly apparent that it does not translate particularly easily to discussions of live performance. It was, after all, first intended to analyse a culturally specific art form at a very particular historical moment – the Hollywood narrative movies of the mid-twentieth century – and Mulvey's model is so centrally concerned with the way the gaze is constituted by means of the camera that it begins to look unhelpful once the camera itself is removed from consideration, or once one begins to deal with a live performance situation where the gazed-at 'object' can look back, and meet the spectator's gaze head-on.

Even so, the terms by which Mulvey characterises the gaze do seem particularly appropriate to certain forms of live performance, and to specific tropes within those forms – not least to the conjuror's grand illusion. The conjuror, like the cinematographer, is particularly adept at manipulating the angle of the spectator's perception in order to limit what 'he' sees. Moreover, at the level of gender ideology, it is hard to deny – although some have tried[23] – that many grand illusions tend to turn the woman into 'the (passive) raw material'[24] for a gaze which sees her victimised in very literal ways.

And if, as Mulvey suggests, patriarchy's favourite cinematic form is the illusionistic narrative film, it might be added that its favourite theatrical form should be the conjuring act. The overwhelming majority of stage conjurors have been – and still are – male. For the last 200 years or so Western theatre has been comparatively hospitable towards any number of female actors, singers, dancers, acrobats and other kinds of performing artist, but female magicians have always been in the minority: even today 'of the 7,000 members of the Society of American Magicians, the largest magic organisation in the country, 479 are women ... In the organisation's 157-person New York chapter only two are women.'[25] But more important is the way in which the whole structure of the traditional conjuror's act has been predicated on a display of masculine power. As John F. Kasson puts it, '[b]y performing amazing feats of mastery over objects and situations, the magician became an exemplary masculine figure to complement the strongman. Both spoke to dreams of dominance and authority in the modern world ...'.[26] Dressed (often) in a costume which signified both class and gender privilege, the male conjuror has acted out some fairly grotesque fantasies on the body of his lovely assistant. Even if the end result involves reunification, resurrection or restoration – even if, as Cutter says in *The Prestige*, 'making something disappear isn't enough; you have to bring it back'[27] – the imaginative journey towards that restoration is a gruesome one which may involve not only sawing the woman in half, but locking her into trunks, stuffing her into baskets, piercing and impaling her with swords, daggers, spears and knives, making her disappear, decapitating, dismembering, drowning or incinerating her.

The analytic framework which Mulvey articulates seems particularly appropriate to the conjuror's act. The often-repeated cliché of the conjuror's mutilation of the lovely assistant looks very much like some kind of masculine revenge fantasy against the woman. Writing of the horror movie genre, Linda Williams talks directly about the way in which these movies 'punish' women for the exhibiting of their own sexual potency and desires.[28] If the sawing illusion also represents a form of cultural punishment, the crime that was being punished was perhaps not so much that of sexual potency as that of political assertiveness.

The uncanny

Mulvey's political argument is rooted in the psychoanalytic theories of Freud and Lacan; she seeks to articulate the relationship between voyeuristic scopophilia and sadism, arguing that

> pleasure lies in ascertaining guilt (immediately associated with castration), asserting control and subjecting the guilty person through punishment or forgiveness. This sadistic side fits in well with narrative. Sadism demands a story, depends on making something happen, forcing a change in another person, a battle of will and strength, victory/defeat, all occurring in a linear time with a beginning and an end.[29]

Gaze theory, I am suggesting, provides an appropriate way of thinking about such conjurors' routines as the sawing illusion. It is also, however, a limited one, since (unlike a movie by Hitchcock or von Sternberg) the sawing illusion wears its punishment motif on its sleeve. To develop the analysis a stage further, then, it is useful to turn to another term – one which has a powerful resonance both in psychoanalytic theory and in film criticism, and one which, again, has immediate resonance for the analysis of conjurors' performances: the 'uncanny'.

'The uncanny' is a complex term. In an everyday sense it might be said that most conjuring tricks aim to produce an effect which we might broadly describe as 'uncanny'. The underlying fiction of the entertainment is that the audience will witness an event which operates somewhere within the nexus of dictionary definitions which are generally offered for the word: 'weird, supernatural; (of, e.g., skill) much greater than one would expect of an ordinary human being; unsafe to associate with ...'.[30] In contemporary cultural theory, however, the word has a particular resonance: one which derives from an argument within psychological studies in the early years of the twentieth century, as psychologists attempted to offer rational scientific explanations for those subjective impressions of supernatural unease which the English language labels 'uncanny' and the German language calls 'unheimlich'.

The first explanation, proposed by Ernst Jentsch in an essay entitled 'On the Psychology of the Uncanny' (1906), was that feelings related to the uncanny arose from a sense of uncertainty about the borders of life and death, animate and inanimate.

> Among all the psychical uncertainties that can become a cause for the uncanny feeling to arise, there is one in particular that is able to develop a fairly regular, powerful and very general effect: namely, doubt as to whether an apparently living being really is animate and, conversely, doubt as to whether a lifeless object may not in fact be animate – and more precisely, when this doubt only makes itself felt obscurely in one's consciousness.[31]

The second explanation, propounded by Sigmund Freud thirteen years later, traced the sensation to repressed sexuality. It is in the interplay between these two theories, rooted as they are in the twin themes which are the subject of this volume, that an understanding of the uncanny should be located.

Freud's essay on the subject (and later psychoanalytical scholars' readings of his essay) eclipsed Jentsch's account, and established the importance of the uncanny in contemporary cultural theory,

> plant[ing] the idea of 'the uncanny' in the very ground of contemporary art and representation ... [It] has been hugely influential; admired and torn to shreds in equal measures but it has certainly instituted 'the uncanny' alongside the sublime or the absurd as the generic effect of a certain kind of art in any medium.[32]

In his explanation and analysis of the term Freud refers specifically to images of the kind we have been considering:

Dismembered limbs, a severed head, a hand cut off at the wrist, as in a fairy tale of Hauff's, feet which dance by themselves, as in the book by Schaeffer which I mentioned above – all these have something peculiarly uncanny about them, especially when, as in the last instance, they prove capable of independent activity in addition.[33]

Freud's frame of reference is narrative literature and the folk tale (Hauff and Schaefer) rather than popular theatrical entertainment, but he could just as well be describing the stage acts of Selbit, Goldin, Dr Lynn and a host of other European and American conjurors of his own age, conjurors whose performances, as we have seen, made impressive use of images such as these, adopting the motifs from folk literature as the motifs of popular conjuring illusions. But Freud's theorising of the uncanny has resonances far beyond either literature or popular entertainment. If his essay established the importance of the term it also, at the same time, defined 'the uncanny' in a very specific way. Immediately after the above quotation he adds that 'this kind of uncanniness springs from its proximity to the castration complex'[34] – and, indeed, the central argument of the essay is that a sense of the uncanny derives from these repressed anxieties. It is on this level that the essay has been so influential – giving rise, for example, to an established body of film scholarship which interprets the effects of horror films in terms of castration anxiety and the 'return of the repressed'.[35]

This is not the place to explore the details of Freud's argument with Jentsch, although it is worth noting in passing that his intellectual victory over his opponent depends on a rhetorical sleight-of-hand which might have impressed Selbit, Goldin, Dr Lynn or Robert-Houdin. More important, perhaps, is *why* he feels it so important to replace Jentsch's explanation with his own: that is, the underlying, and unresolved, disagreement between the two about what it is that underpins that sense of unease and uncertainty which they both recognise as characterising the uncanny. For Freud, its source is to be found in (suppressed) sexuality and its anxieties. For Jentsch it is to be found in (the ambiguities) of life and death, the animate and the inanimate – in the mysteries which the major world religions have traditionally sought to address. The rhetorical purpose which underlies Freud's essay is deeply embedded in Freud's own developing theories of psychoanalysis and his beliefs about civilisation and culture. Scholars and editors of Freud's work have tended to categorise his essay on the uncanny as belonging to a series of essays on 'art and literature'.[36] It is more plausibly seen, however, as part of his longer-term project to provide a scientific explanation for the phenomenon of religion and religious belief. Throughout his career, Freud regarded both established religion and folk beliefs in the supernatural as delusional, comparable to a childhood neurosis,[37] and arising from an attempt to control the Oedipal complex. He also saw them as a serious enemy to scientific and rational inquiry. 'Of the three powers which may dispute the basic position of science', he said in his *New Introductory Lectures on Psychoanalysis*, 'religion alone is to be taken seriously as an enemy ... [it] is an illusion and it derives its strength from its readiness to fit in with our instinctual wishful impulses'.[38] Freud's writings include several books devoted primarily to a scientific inquiry into religious belief.[39] This shorter essay on 'The Uncanny', addressing the experiential element of such folk beliefs in the supernatural, can be seen as a part of this longer-term project to rationalise the irrational.

This, then, is why it is so important to Freud that he should establish a new paradigm for thinking about the uncanny, one which renders Jentsch's explanation redundant and which stresses suppressed sexual feelings rather than confrontations with death. By directly comparing Freud's essay with Jentsch's we can see the suppressed dynamics which have determined the way in which the term has been understood as a repeated theme in popular culture and its theory. And the point is not that Jentsch was right after all, and Freud wrong. Rather, it is that a complex understanding of the uncanny should be located at the intersection of Jentsch's concern with questions of life and death and Freud's with sexuality – the space which Selbit's illusion inhabits.

Saw II – III – IV ...

Like the seemingly endless contemporary horror film franchise, the success of Selbit's original illusion ensured that it was imitated, adapted, repeated and developed by countless conjurors, from Goldin onwards. While some of these variations are largely of technical and mechanical interest to professional conjurors, others have more to do with the kinds of cultural meanings with which we are concerned. These meanings are contingent and continually changing. If Selbit's illusion had a historically specific significance in the 1920s, it also articulated a more generalised and underlying cultural misogyny, the roots of which may be described psychoanalytically. But then, when that 'same' illusion is revived and repeated for later generations and audiences, its changed historical situation generates new and different meanings. These then interact both with those earlier historically specific meanings, and also with the general ones.

Thus the sawing routine has been repeatedly repackaged by different generations of conjurors in ways which allow it to be read in ways rather different from those of Selbit's original performance. Sometimes this has been done in order to downplay any sense of cruelty: Mark Wilson developed a version of the routine on his American television shows in the 1950s and 60s in which the tone of the presentation worked hard to counter the sense of violence which was inherent in the structure. Cheerful and non-threatening, Wilson's approach was perfectly tailored for the newly popular medium of commercial television, and for a show whose target audience was the nuclear middle-American family, and whose content and mood was strictly controlled by sponsors and advertisers in a socio-economic context of a cultural climate of high conservatism and high consumerism.[40] At the other extreme, the South American illusionist Richiardi and his son Richiardi Jr used a buzz-saw for the sawing illusion in his live shows in a version which emphasised all the horror of the routine, spraying stage and audience liberally with stage blood and fake entrails.[41]

Moreover, while popular entertainment tends frequently to reproduce the dominant ideologies of its day, it will just as frequently articulate the shifts and the emergent elements of those ideological formations. In recent years, for example, there has been an increasing and predictable tendency for what few female magicians there are to perform the sawing illusion with the help of a male assistant/victim and to foreground the gender implications of this role reversal. The gender conflict of Selbit's original illusion is knowingly reframed in terms of post-feminist gender politics – or, as one promotional website proclaims, 'Your guests will be blown away as Sue-Anne, dressed in black, skintight PVC, fulfils the fantasies of women everywhere by sawing her husband in half with a real live chainsaw.'[42]

More complex and more ludic, though, than such simple reversals are the postmodern performances of the more recent generations of conjurors, who enter into knowing collusion with the audience in terms both of the tricks they perform and of the ideological work which those tricks undertake. One of the first of these was the British conjuror Simon Drake, whose work provides a fitting conclusion to this exploration of conjuring history in relation to psychoanalytic film theory. During the 1990s Drake conducted all manner of sawings and decapitations – frequently with himself as the victim – in an act which attracted a large cult following by knowingly combining the conjuring techniques of the classic grand illusion, the narrative techniques of the rock video and the visual imagery of the horror movie. In his own live shows, in his late-night TV series *The Secret Cabaret* and on tour with the heavy metal band Iron Maiden Drake employed lighting, set, costume and music which worked together to evoke the world of the vampire movie, the slasher movie, the supernatural thriller or the apocalyptic horror. His routines featured darkly erotic figures and the ever-present threat of gruesome death. He – or sometimes, more conventionally, his assistant – was repeatedly tied to sacrificial altars and dissected by guillotines, axes and chainsaws on sets and equipment which looked like high-camp versions of *The Devil Rides Out* or *Mad Max*.[43] Playing to a predominantly young audience who were well-educated in such conventions of popular culture, Drake invited them to read his illusions intertextually, and to conflate the pleasures of the horror film with those of the conjuring performance, pleasures which involved a complex series of different levels of 'gaze'. On the one hand the audience was invited into the fantasy world of the horror movie, in which the spectator's gratification lies in a complex interplay of 'spectator-positions', in which the sadistic pleasure of watching the horrors unfold on the body of the victim is intertwined with the masochistic one of identification with the victim himself or herself. On the other hand, the audience was simultaneously being challenged – as a conjuror's audience is typically challenged – to work out how it is done. Drake's illusions were ironic reflections on illusion itself, and on the nature of the fantasies through which the horror movie engages its audience. In them, Simon Drake took to playfully subversive extremes the relationship between *Eros*, *Thanatos*, and the uncanny.

Notes

Many of the less accessible primary sources cited in this article, such as Selbit's *Magician's Handbook* and Robert-Houdin's *Memoirs* are archived online at the website of The Learned Pig Project. While this is a members-only site, membership is free, and the site can be joined at http://www.thelearnedpig.com.pa/home.html. Because of the ease of access which the site provides, references in endnotes and bibliography are, where possible, given to the pages of these online editions.

1. Horace Goldin, *It's Fun to be Fooled* (London, 1937), archived online at http://www.thelearnedpig.com.pa/magos/books/goldin/09.html. Accessed 4 January 2010.
2. Gary R. Brown, 'Sawing a Woman in Half', *Invention and Technology Magazine*, 9 (1994), archived online at http://www.americanheritage.com/articles/magazine/it/1994/3/1994_3_34.shtml. Accessed 4 January 2010.
3. Jean Eugène Robert-Houdin, *Memoirs of Robert-Houdin, Ambassador, Author, and Conjuror*, trans. Lascelles Wraxall (London, 1859), archived online at http://www.thelearnedpig.com.pa/magos/books/memrh/001.html. Accessed 4 January 2010.
4. Percy Tibbles ('Selbit'), *The Magician's Handbook. A Complete Encyclopedia of the Magic Art for Professional and Amateur Entertainers* (London, 1904), archived online at http://www.thelearnedpig.com.pa/magos/books/selbit1/082.html. Accessed 4 January 2010.
5. Selbit, *Handbook*, http://www.thelearnedpig.com.pa/magos/books/selbit1/082.html.
6. Selbit, *Handbook*, http://www.thelearnedpig.com.pa/magos/books/selbit1/083.html.
7. Selbit, *Handbook*, http://www.thelearnedpig.com.pa/magos/books/selbit1/080.html.
8. *Ibid.*
9. Jim Steinmeyer, *Hiding the Elephant: How Magicians Invented the Impossible* (London, 2004), pp. 292–3.
10. *Ibid.*, p. 277.
11. Walter B. Gibson, *The Original Houdini Scrapbook* (New York, London and Sydney, 1976), p. 39. See also Michael Mangan, *Performing Dark Arts: A Cultural History of Conjuring* (Bristol, 2007), pp. 156–7.
12. Steinmeyer, *Hiding the Elephant*, p. 292.
13. An excellent digitised collection of these is available online at the website of The Learned Pig Project, http://www.thelearnedpig.com.pa/home.html (see above). They include reprints of J.H. Burroughs's programmes of magicians from 1864 to 1893, Max Holden's programmes of famous magicians, and Ellis Stanyon's explanatory programmes from *Magic Magazine* 1900–14 and 1917–20.
14. Will Goldston (comp. and ed.), *Stage Illusions* (London, 1912), archived online at http://www.thelearnedpig.com.pa/magos/books/stageill/017.html. Accessed 4 January 2010.
15. Apart from an unsuccessful 1908 visit to London, the Grand-Guignol did not make it across the channel until 1920, when it opened at the Little Theatre in London. Even then, the English version of the genre, which lasted for only two theatrical seasons, was actually much less sensational than its Paris counterpart, relying largely on poisonings and strangling rather than the more gruesome and visceral deaths favoured by French audiences. Despite its comparative blandness, the Little Theatre's Grand-Guignol programme was subject to constant problems with censorship from the office of the Lord Chamberlain, pressure from which finally ensured its closure. See Richard J. Hand and Michael Wilson, *Grand-Guignol: The French Theatre of Horror* (Exeter, 2002), p. 20.
16. See, for example, Adrienne Auslander Munich, *Andromeda's Chains: Gender and Interpretation in Victorian Literature and Art* (New York, 1989).
17. Roland Barthes, *Mythologies*, trans. and ed. Annette Lavers (London, 1972), quoted in John Storey, *Cultural Theory and Popular Culture: A Reader* (Harlow, 1998), p. 117.

18. Laura Mulvey, 'Visual Pleasure and Narrative Cinema', *Screen*, 16 (1975), pp. 6–18.

19. John Hill and Pamela Church Gibson, *The Oxford Guide to Film Studies* (Oxford, 1998), p. 119.

20. See, for example, Susan Bennett, *Theatre Audiences: A Theory of Production and Reception* (London, 1990).

21. Mulvey, 'Visual Pleasure', p. 17.

22. Steve Neale, 'Masculinity as Spectacle', *Screen*, 24 (1983), pp. 2–16; Gaylyn Studlar, *In the Realm of Pleasure: von Sternberg, Dietrich and the Masochistic Aesthetic* (Urbana, IL, 1988); Richard Dyer, 'Don't Look Now: The Male Pin-up', *Screen*, 23 (1982), pp. 61–73.

23. Eugene Burger and Robert E. Neale, *Magic and Meaning* (Seattle, WA, 1995), pp. 96–8.

24. Mulvey, 'Visual Pleasure', p. 17.

25. Dennis Regling, 'Women in Magic', in *BellaOnline: The Voice of Women*, http://www.bellaonline.com/articles/art36816.asp. Accessed 7 September 2009.

26. John F. Kasson, *Houdini, Tarzan, and the Perfect Man: The White Male Body and the Challenge of Modernity in America* (New York, 2001), p. 79.

27. Cutter, played by Michael Caine, speaks the lines as an introductory voice-over to *The Prestige* (2006).

28. Linda Williams, 'When the Woman Looks', in Barry Keith Grant (ed.) *Dread of Difference: Gender and the Horror Film* (Austin, TX, 1996), pp. 32–3.

29. Mulvey, 'Visual Pleasure', p. 14.

30. *The Chambers Dictionary* (Edinburgh, 1993), *s.v.*

31. Ernst Jentsch, 'On the Psychology of the Uncanny (1906)', trans. Roy Sellars, http://www.cpmg.org.br/artigos/on_the_psychology_of_the_uncanny.pdf, p. 8. Accessed 4 January 2010.

32. Marina Warner, *Phantasmagoria: Spirit Visions, Metaphors and Media into the Twenty-First Century* (Oxford, 2006) pp. 53–4.

33. Sigmund Freud, 'The Uncanny', in James Strachey (ed.), *The Standard Edition of the Complete Psychological Works of Sigmund Freud*, vol. 17 (London, 1955), p. 244.

34. Freud, 'The Uncanny', p. 244

35. For example, Robin Wood, 'The Return of the Repressed', *Film Comment*, 14 (1978), pp. 25–32; Linda Badley, *Film, Horror and the Body Fantastic* (Westport, CT, 1995).

36. As with, for example, the Penguin edition of Freud's collected works.

37. Sigmund Freud, 'The Future of an Illusion' in Albert Dickson (ed.) *The Penguin Freud Library 12: Civilization, Society and Religion* (London, 1985), p. 227.

38. Sigmund Freud, 'Lecture 35. The question of a *Weltanschauung*', in James Strachey and Angela Richards (eds) *The Penguin Freud Library 2: New Introductory Lectures on Psychoanalysis* (London, 1973), pp. 195, 211.

39. These include *Totem and Taboo* (1913), *The Future of an Illusion* (1927), *Civilization and its Discontents* (1930) and *Moses and Monotheism* (1938).

40. British viewers would have been familiar with a similarly inoffensive version a few years later in the shape of David Nixon's comedy conjuring routine 'The Zig-Zag Girl'.

41. See Burger and Neale, *Magic and Meaning*, pp. 90–93.

42. Sue-Anne Webster, *Sue-Anne Webster Magician*, http://www.sueannewebster.com/452.html. Accessed 4 January 2001.

43. See, for example, the performances of Drake's 'Saw' and 'Raising hell/Wrathchild' archived at http://www.youtube.com/watch?v=gGr7RWc-lpw and http://www.youtube.com/watch?v=x4N9yWE4GBk&feature=related.

11

Visions of Xs: experiencing La Fura dels Baus's XXX and Ron Athey's Solar Anus

Roberta Mock

The Xs to which I refer in the title of this essay are intended to conjure a web of associations clustering around eroticism, death and visual theatricality: excess, of course; but also negation, annihilation, crossing out; the indication of a specific location – X marks the spot – a location that is always liminal; the sign of the sacrificial cross; the laceration of subject and object, of performers and spectators, of the artform itself; a point of convergence; pornography. I am trying here to see and feel back to a near-historical moment – during the first half of 2003 – when I was among many who were struggling to rethink the ways in which we articulate, position and critique our *experience* of contemporary theatrical performance events. It started with a coincidence: my attendance, within a fortnight, of La Fura dels Baus's production of *XXX* at the Riverside Studios in London[1] and Ron Athey's *Solar Anus* at a lap-dancing club in Birmingham. These performances had much in common despite their very different styles: that is, the apparently different ways they positioned the audience, used space, constructed textual narrative and signalled metaphoric intention.

XXX could most easily be classified as a play, drama, theatre; *Solar Anus* as a solo performance, live art, risk art, body art, or (using Richard Schechner's terminology) an actual. Both, however, centred on the embodiment of taboo through the dislocated mechanisms of fantasy, identification, illusion, allusion, body and act. They were not only 'about' eroticism and death; they were performances that theatricalised eroticism and death, that were about the theatricalisation of eroticism and death, as well as the way these three terms are inherently and essentially inter-related. In returning to them now it is possible to identify a period during which certain aesthetic concerns emerged and crystallised. Adrian Heathfield, at that time, described the manifestation of these concerns in live art as 'excessive performance':

> This broad tendency of contemporary performance towards immediacy, not just present in those practices based on physical limits, endurance or pain, enables artists to make works whose live force is excessive. The aesthetic powers and cultural consequences of such moves are often reduced by their popular miscomprehension within a generic notion of 'shock tactics', which supposes a fixation on and superficial taste for the very moment of a spectator's 'trauma'.[2]

In reflecting upon immediacy, shock tactics and miscomprehension in this chapter, I will attempt to the resist the temptation to read these performances retrospectively – that is, to draw heavily on ideas that have emerged since the mid 'noughties' or my experiences of performance since first seeing them (and, in particular, of *Solar Anus* as part of *The Monster in the Night of the Labyrinth* at the Hayward Gallery, London, in 2007).[3] Rather, I wish to concentrate on how and why the coincidental proximity of *XXX* and *Solar Anus* triggered for me a network of associations that connected Georges Bataille, the Marquis de Sade and Antonin Artaud. The dialogue that ensued, traced in this essay, explores the ways in which the theatricalisation of transgressive sexualities which approach and allude to death are able to challenge cultural expectations of theatrical disciplinarity through the performance of excess.

First performed by Ron Athey in 1998, *Solar Anus* was presented as part of Fierce, an annual festival which, as its publicity states, 'frolick[s] where others fear to tread' and provides platforms where 'watching and being watched is a recurrent theme'. These would serve as appropriate straplines for La Fura dels Baus's *XXX* as well. Tickets for both performances were restricted to those over eighteen years of age. This perhaps should come as no surprise since both were based on, and/or devised and adapted from, the writings of two closely connected French political pornographer–philosophers. *Solar Anus*, described by Dominic Johnson as 'an esoteric tour de force of unseemly erotics, half-mad splendor, and offbeat gravitas', was a response to an essay of the same name by Georges Bataille.[4] It occurred midway through a 24-hour 'durational/experiential arts event' entitled 'Visions of Excess' at the Demon lap-dancing club, curated by Athey himself with drag queen Vaginal Davis. The Demon Club was mapped into several areas each hosting booths, platforms, installations, screenings and performances designed to be experienced either collectively or as an exchange between artist and individual spectator–collaborator. These areas, mostly named after Bataille's writings, included The Acephalica Lounge, L'Histoire de L'Oeil Lounge, the Absence of Myth Annex and the outdoor Courtyard where *Solar Anus* was performed.

XXX was inspired by the Marquis de Sade's 1795 novel *Philosophy in the Bedroom*, which many consider his most lucid and coherent political statement. Despite its re-contextualisation from late eighteenth to early twenty-first century, and the omission of small (but significant) details, La Fura re-presents Sade's vision with remarkable accuracy and faithfulness. Very briefly stated, the narrative concerns the sexual (and therefore political and philosophical) initiation of an eighteen-year-old virgin, Eugénie (who was fifteen in Sade's original), by a team of incestuous brother and sister porn-industry veterans and their über-libertine accomplice, Dolmancé. This education culminates in the willing girl raping her repressive mother with a strap-on and then crudely stitching her vagina together. Sade's original story augmented this final scene rather more horrifically: Following penetration by her daughter, Eugénie's mother is raped vaginally and anally by a syphilitic valet and then sewn up so none of the poison can escape. We also discover that it is Eugénie's father who has sanctioned and arranged the education of his daughter and licensed the treatment of his wife who would inevitably come to fetch her. In one of the production's more balanced reviews, the *Financial Times* noted that Sade's novel 'delves into areas of sexuality that we still find uncomfortable to talk about, let alone see enacted on stage'.[5]

Sade's libertines (both male *and* female) conflate sexual and political power. As Angela Carter proposes in her classic study, *The Sadeian Woman*, from the inverted axiom 'I fuck therefore I am'

[Sade] constructs a diabolical lyricism of fuckery, since the acting-out of a total sexuality in a repressive society turns all eroticism into violence, makes of sexuality itself a permanent negation. Fucking, says Sade, is the basis of all human relationships but the activity parodies all human relations because of the nature of the society that creates and maintains those relationships.

Sade's protagonists 'fuck the world and fucking, for them, is the enforcement of annihilation'.[6] La Fura's publicity stated that they attempted to make 'no moral judgement' on the story's narrative. Alex Ollé, XXX's co-director, recognised that most commentators on Sade's work find at least one system of morality inherently at work in his texts, stating in an interview before the production came to Britain: 'Sade takes you to a point where you are forced to reject him. Actually, I think he is a bit moralistic.'[7]

Presumably, the omissions I outlined in the final scene (that is, syphilitic inoculation, the treatment of wives as chattel, the implications of incestuous paedophilic abuse, and so on) represent the point at which La Fura rejected Sade. It would perhaps have been clearer to say that La Fura were making no moral judgement on the Sadean universe they felt able to recreate under the circumstances, refusing to indicate to audience members precisely how they should react to what they were experiencing. The questioning of morality was left to the individual; its tolerable limits (that is, the definitions of taboos and the identification of where and how transgression takes place) were not located by the company on our behalf. Perhaps even more accurately, La Fura publicly situated their audiences in the same space, with the same dilemma, as Sade's private readers, just as Ron Athey places his audiences for *Solar Anus* in the position of Georges Bataille's private readers.

It was Bataille's generation that resurrected and rehabilitated Sade, that held a public séance and first made him perform on their behalf, both as justification for and illuminating contrast to their own concerns and beliefs. Many who were Bataille's friends, colleagues, collaborators, detractors and sparring partners – such as Maurice Heine, Pierre Klossowski, André Breton, Jean Paulhan, Maurice Blanchot and Simone de Beauvoir – published ground-breaking studies of Sade's life and work. Bataille wrote the preface for the 1950 edition of *Justine*. But, more than any of his contemporaries, Bataille has been identified with Sade – occasionally simplistically identified *as* a reincarnated Sade – owing to his methodologies, subject matter, obsessions (with waste products, for example), his materialist atheism and the correlative relationship he proposed between eroticism and death. Each produced both 'clandestine' and 'signed' writings. Each was accused of either advocating fascism or providing highly sophisticated critiques of its dangers and repugnance.

I have no intention of embarking here on a detailed comparison of Bataille and Sade. For two reasons, however, it is worth outlining some of the main points raised by others elaborating their divergence. The first is to indicate that there are no simple syllogisms available for those who wish to draw conclusions about the interplay between violent sexuality and death. The second is that, to illustrate this point, the 'messages' and experiences conveyed by *Solar Anus* and *XXX* broadly correspond to those found in Bataille and Sade respectively. According to Athey, reading Bataille helped him to make sense of, and then inspired, his performance work:

> Some of Bataille's major premises as the 'excremental philosopher' and his accusations (such as his critique of conservative Surrealists in their name-dropping of de Sade), resonated deeply in me. He elevated filth to sacred status, Incestuous Mother, Perverted Priests, while completely destroying familial, cultural and societal myths … His essay 'Solar Anus' triggered and fit my view of the magic tricks inherent in the anus.[8]

Michael Richardson points out that, like Sade, Bataille 'believed writing should be thrown down as a challenge to the reader; it should be a deliberate provocation, and not serve a one-to-one relation in which the reader assimilates a message from the author'.[9] I think it is reasonable, here, to substitute 'spectator' for 'reader' and 'performance-maker' for 'author' in relation to the performances inspired by their writings. For both Athey and La Fura, if their work is intended to challenge and provoke, it is also intended as a gift to their audiences.

Famously, Bataille wrote that 'eroticism is the assenting to life even in death', which, as Richardson notes, would be unthinkable to Sade, for whom 'sex served to annul death'. For Bataille, sex is the 'intermediary between birth and death, and in the sexual encounter we experience the chasm at the edge of existence'.[10] At this point we strive to extend beyond our limits, to reach the impossible. Our identities merge with our partners; we are lacerated, and we collapse into a state of undifferentiated being, what Bataille calls the continuity of existence. The Sadean encounter avoids such contamination by keeping the sexual subject and sexualised object separate, as this connection with an other weakens our assertion of sovereignty as isolated beings. Bataille noted that 'Sade makes his heroes uniquely self-centred; the partners are denied any rights at all: this is the key to his system. If eroticism leads to harmony between the partners its essential principle of violence and death is invalidated.'[11] Bataille's notion of sovereignty and freedom, on the other hand, necessarily includes engagement and communication as a social being. For him, sexual communion between participants results in an eruption of violence; it is not the pre-requisite for a rupture that leads to violence.

Bataille's biographer, Michel Surya, expresses these ideas in the economic terms Bataille himself used:

Bataille, unlike Sade, is not a libertine, but debauched, which distinguishes them profoundly. The eroticism Bataille puts in play soils, spoils and wrecks. By projection, it shares common cause with an obsessional representation of death. It wrecks memory, self-indulgence, vows, the possibility of beauty, of salvation, fidelity, education, morality, women, God ... it's all the same. The libertine adds while the debauched man takes away. The first lives in an economy of accumulation: of pleasure, of possession ... the second in a spending economy, one of loss, waste and ruin.[12]

For Bataille, a debauched sexuality – that is, one simultaneously excremental and sacred – was at the heart of mystical experience. In a question and answer session at Club Maintenant in 1948 he stated that 'in sadism we begin by suppressing the object, while in mysticism it is necessary to suppress the subject'.[13] Bataille's essay 'The Use Value of D.A.F. de Sade' is among his early writings, and was completed at the end of the three-year period from 1927 to 1930 which began with the writing of 'The Solar Anus'. Both are published in the first section of Allan Stoekl's collection of Bataille's work entitled *Visions of Excess*, which also contains a short 1929 essay entitled 'Formless'. According to Yve-Alain Bois, the *informe* (or formless) 'has only an operational existence: it is a performative, like obscene words, the violence of which derives less from semantics than from the very *act* of their delivery'.[14]

Both La Fura and Athey chose to devise their pieces from texts that were performative but not blueprints for performance (that is, scripts or playtexts). As in Bois's explanation of the formless, I am referring to performativity in the Austinian sense of 'doing things with words'. Sade's *Philosophy in the Bedroom* was written in the form of a philosophical dialogue, not to be enacted but read. Sade, of course, considered himself a dramatist and at least one of his plays was professionally produced during his lifetime. However, as his twentieth-century translators Austryn Wainhouse and Richard Seaver note:

> It is an understatement to maintain that, were his seventeen plays all that history had bequeathed us of his writings, Sade would hardly have a claim to immortality. The force, and indeed the essential worth, of Sade's works varies directly in proportion to their clandestine nature. The more open and public they are, the more conventional they become. The dramatic works, being most public, suffer most from conventionality and from what appears to be Sade's inherent timidity when faced with the dramatic form.[15]

Unlike Sade, Bataille did not leave us with any performance scripts, although apparently he wrote at least one which was later lost: it was a film script, never made, about a Marseille soap manufacturer who likes to pretend to be the Marquis de Sade and engages in the practices described in *One Hundred and Twenty Days of Sodom* and *Philosophy in the Bedroom*. Not unlike La Fura, Bataille believed that this film would be 'commercial'.[16] *XXX* and *Solar Anus* each attempt to transpose and translate the essence of both form and content to a visual embodied medium. In the process they destroy the separation of these two terms, inscribing the operation of the formless, to which I will return later in this chapter. In the case of Athey's work, it is already mirroring the instability of Bataille's polemic in 'The Solar Anus', in which Bataille's copula/copulation dyad, according to Allan Stoekl, leads to 'obscene, parodic, burlesque, and ever-inverted significations'.[17]

Solar Anus and *XXX* are linked not only through their source materials, themes and specific philosophers[18] but also their tension or elision or collapse of performative 'form' and 'content'. Although I experienced both in Britain, they were conceived, created and performed by artists who are neither French nor British: La Fura dels Baus is a Catalan company that was founded in 1979; Ron Athey is an American writer and performer who, from the early 1990s to the mid 2000s, toured productions such as *Martyrs and Saints*, *Four Scenes in a Harsh Life*, and the autobiographical *Joyce* to the UK with his company. According to Athey, by 'using casts that take pride in being marginalized, not only s/m queers but [those] having hardcore appearances', he tried 'to create a pageant of erotic torture and penance'.[19] Regardless of whether it took place in gallery settings, traditional theatre spaces or club environments, the heart of his performances always revolved around, in his own words, the bringing of 'overdone gothic religious tableaux to life using medical based S&M techniques'. *Solar Anus* continued this tradition. When I saw it for the first time, however, it was fairly atypical for UK audiences who were engaged with Athey's body of work, not only because it was a solo performance but also because it dispensed with rich scenographic environments which often included projection and other uses of technology. Athey has said that he thought that *Solar Anus* was a clean departure for him from 'story telling'.[20]

What is important to note is that in 2003 it was as inappropriate to consider Athey *only* as a solo live artist as it was to classify La Fura as a traditional 'theatre' company.[21] La Fura originally brought together artists from different disciplines (sculpture, mechanics, dance, music and so on) in order to create radical industrial street theatre. Their 1983 production *Accions*, best described as site-specific performative installation, made the company's agenda concrete: audience members, stimulated viscerally by sensory bombardment, were to act as co-participants in the creation of a performance text. They described it as 'a game without rules, a drink thrown in your face ... a brutal stream of hammer blows, a sound execution, a chain of unlimited situations'.[22] Since then, the company has created large-scale spectacle, digital theatre, internet-based projects, corporate events and opera. *XXX* was only La Fura's third text-based production in twenty-five years, and one of relatively few staged in traditional theatre buildings.

By describing their past work, I am neither simply attempting to contextualise the productions I attended in May 2003 nor arguing that one cannot fully appreciate specific performances without access to the background noise of intertextual knowledge. Rather, I wish to draw attention to the use of inappropriately limiting frameworks when attempting to situate, and thereby make meaning with, productions that transcend the boundaries of genre and disciplinarity. In the case of *XXX*, I am not primarily referring to the furore which played itself out on the front pages of the tabloid press: 'Art? This is Nothing More than Porn' (*Daily Mail*, 24 April 2003); 'Sex on Stage Storm: Raunchiest Show Ever Hits UK' (*Daily Star*, 24 April 2003). Frankly, for me, this is how the popular press *should* be reacting to intentionally provocative experimental theatre and, in general, it refrained from too much xenophobic rabble-rousing. Quoting interviews with those members of the opening night audience who somehow missed the warning that 'this production contains extreme and explicit sexual themes and images throughout', these articles could barely conceal their disappointment that *XXX* was operating well within the law. The live sex may have *appeared* real but appearances are deceiving. Every tabloid quoted the same interview with Carlos Padrissa, its co-director: 'This is not pornography. It is art. The sex in *XXX* is not real but virtual. It is all theatre. It looks like real sex and the actors are often naked but it is just touching and kissing, there is no penetration. The man who comes out of the audience is a plant and what you see is really made of silicone. But our aim is to make it look as if it were real.'[23]

Figure 11.1. Ron Athey in *Solar Anus*. (Image: Cyril Kuhn)

Interesting, then, that a few weeks later, not a peep was heard about *Solar Anus*: a man naked except for stockings and high heels exposes his tattooed anus to us and pulls a string of pearls out of his rectum; he engages in *real* auto-penetration with a shoe-mounted dildo just inches away from the audience's faces (should they so desire, as there is no formal seating), and then pierces his face with hooks in such a way as to create a 'lift' of wide-eyed surprise (Figure 11.1). The lack of fuss could have been due to a number of reasons: that the performance took place in a lap-dancing club – although the events performed there were as much a parody (of the corporate pornography of lap-dancing) as were La Fura's actions within the *XXX* setting of a porn movie studio; or that it was publicised with much less ferocity than *XXX* – it was actually quite difficult to find out about it if you lived outside Birmingham. Or perhaps Britain's mass media had already been convinced that performances such as these are marginal but legitimate 'art' activities, defined as such by 'experts'. In 1998, Athey was featured, along with Franko B, Fakir Musafar and Orlan, on a South Bank programme about body art, introduced by Melvyn Bragg on the very populist ITV, which presented his work within an established tradition of religious art imagery.

A few weeks before experiencing *XXX* and *Solar Anus* I attended the *Live Culture* programme at the Tate Modern in London, a four-day event including performances and a symposium which celebrated and contextualised live art practice. In their programme preface, the curators of *Live Culture*, Lois Keidan, Daniel Brine and Adrian Heathfield, outlined the significance of contemporary live art practices and also provided frameworks by which to analyse them. These include the way they have

> spread out of the gallery into other spaces and disciplines; their disruption of cultural borders and traditions; their engagement with risk and extremity; their correlation with the technological culture of immediacy; their impact on political activism and social intervention; and their role in the expression of new identities.[24]

Ron Athey's work is clearly located in this 'fluid landscape' where, as Keidan and Brine state, '[i]n the simultaneity, interactivity and convergence of our media saturated culture, Live Art invests in questions of immediacy, reality and hybridity: creating spaces to explore the experience of things, ambiguities of meaning and the responsibilities of agency.'[25] Athey contributed to the symposium discussion and here I first saw a film of *Solar Anus*.

It is important to remember, however, that the protection of expert academic and critical opinion can be a fragile safety barrier when moral fundamentalists get their knickers in a twist and the popular press smells blood (both figuratively and literally). In 1994 Athey was at the centre of what amounted to a censorship campaign following a performance of *Four Scenes in a Harsh Life* at the Walker Art Gallery in Minneapolis.[26] This production included a 'human printing press scene' in which Athey ritualistically cut patterns into the back of another performer, creating impressions of the drawn blood on towels and then flying the imprinted towels like little flags above and near the audience. The problem? Athey was HIV positive and so, it was erroneously presumed, was his co-performer Darryl Carlton (aka Divinity Fudge). Death and sexuality were deemed to be in too close a proximity to the audience. This was considered a political act, and an obscene act – therefore not an artistic one. The performance served as an example as to why National Endowment for the Arts (NEA) funding should be cut, not just to the 'undeserving' like Athey, but across the board. The irony is that Athey never received NEA funding; the Walker Art Gallery received about $150 toward producing Athey's art. It was the gallery, therefore, that was threatened virtually with closure through lack of funding should they continue to present work like Athey's.

Experience has shown us (for instance, in the case of the *Romans in Britain* trial) that the tabloid media often plays a crucial role in the demonisation of certain performances. Ironically, however, in tossing the bait to the supposedly slathering masses (who chose not to take it), the tabloid journalists who had not seen *XXX* seemed to understand and express its significance far more astutely than the broadsheet critics who had. According to Wendy Steiner,

[p]ornography and pornographic art are important because they mark the bounds between thought and deed, and like every such liminal zone they are fraught with fear – fear that fantasies will come true, will invade the world of public action – and the opposite fear, that there

will be no such crossover, that the pleasure and energy and justice of this zone will have no realization outside it.[27]

This is a debate with which the 'serious' critics failed, or perhaps refused, to engage and yet seemed to suggest if one paid close attention to the sublimated leakings of their collective text. *XXX* was described as both too simulated and too stimulating (Figure 11.2); it was boring and yet there was too much going on; it was too distanced and yet the audience was too forcefully involved; it was repetitive and yet contained a string of remarkable – or gratuitous – images and visual effects; it was both tired and exuberant, witty and witless, reactionary and too naively literal.[28] Over and over again, the critics referred to what they personally *experienced* and *felt* but this, somehow, was not considered *enough*. I had never seen reviews in which the critics pushed themselves so far to the front of the writing – and their seemingly unintentional exposure, perhaps, is why they needed to protect themselves by ultimately rejecting *XXX*. In discussing this production the critic was forced to open up, to publicly admit his or her fantasies and limitations.

Figure 11.2. Sonia Segura and Teresa Vallejo in La Fura dels Baus's production of *XXX*, Riverside Studios, London (2003). (Photo: Tristram Kenton)

The critical responses to *XXX* uncannily mirrored those generated by Sade's writing itself – which the vast majority of reviewers had clearly never read (but alluded to as if they had). The startling visual image which opened the production was considered spectacular but either empty or confusing: the Madame, exercising her pelvic floor muscles with a light pen, scrawled the words 'A better world is possible' on a tablet that was simultaneously projected on a giant screen. Admittedly, this is an extremely truncated version of the fifth section of *Philosophy in the Bedroom* entitled 'Yet another effort, Frenchman, if you would become Republicans' (which was detached from the novel and published as a patriotic pamphlet during the Revolution of 1848). But those who know Sade's life and work also know that he, like Bataille later, loved revolution for the revolt itself, not because he believed in utopian realisation. They might also have recognised that La Fura's dramaturgy – based on excess, accumulation and saying (and showing) everything – mimicked the formalities of Sade's writing.

My point here is not that audiences *should* know this but that the specific political point expressed by La Fura, through their stagecraft, textuality and visual imagery, was interpreted based on the critic's assumption rather than signposts erected by the company. What was *really* being critiqued was not the company's supposed message but its performance strategy, and in particular the way this reflected precisely that which disturbs many in Sade's work. As Marcel Hénaff has noted:

> [The] repletion of excess brings about a change in the nature of knowledge: no longer a simple knowledge of objects, but instead an experience of sexual pleasure that transforms the 'normal' body into a libertine body. What is discovered in and through excess is not simply added to other kinds of knowledge. Instead, it radically overturns them by exposing the repressed elements of their operation: violence and desire.[29]

What, for me, was being expressed in the reviews of *XXX* was that La Fura was not making what the critics could then 'know' as 'theatre' and that they therefore did not have the vocabulary to discuss it. Unlike in live art, the artistry in theatre seems here only to be recognised in the depth, as opposed to the transparency, of the illusion; in the clarity and explicitness of interpretative opportunity; in the Cartesian duality of mind and body. This is perhaps summed up best by Michael Billington's review in *The Guardian*, first objecting to La Fura's 'unquestioning acceptance of Sade's dubious philosophy' and then blaming the company for not providing us with 'the genuine dialectic' of Weiss's *Marat/Sade*.[30]

And it was while reflecting on this review that I stumbled across another set of coincidences, this time revolving around Antonin Artaud. Just as Billington banished *XXX* from the garden of theatre by evoking Brook's Theatre of Cruelty season, I once discovered that not all Artaudians wished to share their patron saint with Ron Athey. In 1996, during the closing panel discussion of a three-day event at the ICA in London entitled 'Incarcerated with Artaud & Genet', I was met with stunned silence – followed by outright hostility – when I suggested that risk artists like Athey (since I did not know the term 'live art' then) may be the closest contemporary embodiment of Artaud's theories of cruelty. No, I was told, Artaud's cruelty was symbolic, metaphoric. No amount of persuading, before I was unceremoniously ignored and shut up, could convince the assembled group that Athey's art worked on these interpretive performance levels as well. Here again, I now believe, what I was being told was that Athey's work (even that which played with critical distance, representational strategies, spoken text and large casts) was not 'theatre', mainly because the index and referent were seemingly too close to recognise distinctions.

Both Athey and La Fura evoke the spectre of Artaud in discussing their own work. At one point, Athey wrote that the only way he could articulate why he chose to make disturbing images was by referring to Artaud's essay on theatre and the plague: the theatre, like the plague, 'releases conflicts, disengages powers, liberates possibilities, and if these possibilities and these powers are dark, it is the fault not of the plague nor of the theatre, but of life'.[31] Similarly, it was Artaud's vision of the need to return to ritual, to engage the audience in the possibility of danger and risk, that formed the keystones of the 'Furero' language.[32] There are other lessons to be learned from Artaud, however. In the quotation that follows, Artaud is writing about his production of *Les Cenci* in 1935; his words could equally apply to La Fura's intentions in *XXX*:

My heroes … place themselves in the domain of cruelty and must be judged outside good and bad. They are incestuous, sacrilegious persons, adulterers, rebels, insurgents, blasphemers. And this cruelty in which the entire work is bathed … is not a purely corporal cruelty but a moral one. It goes to the limits of instinct and forces the actor to plunge in up to the roots of his being so completely that he leaves the stage exhausted. Cruelty also acts against the spectator, and it must not permit him to leave the theatre intact, but he also must be exhausted, involved, transformed perhaps! Also I have sought, by all available means, to place the audience in the middle of the action.[33]

Unfortunately, it seems the audience did not really rise to Artaud's challenge. According to Raymonde Latour's report in *Paris-Midi* following the premiere, *Les Cenci*'s 'audacity' was occasionally 'lost for a pleasing image'. He concluded that 'I do not know what the reviews will be like, but what struck me most during intermissions was the absence of animated discussions. One can either love or detest this unusual play, but one should not remain indifferent to the courage and audacity of the effort.'[34] Nearly seventy years later, following performances of *XXX*, the Riverside Studios bar *was* full of animated discussions. This, however, was not valued by the broadsheet critics, who also felt that the production's audacity was either problematic and/or diminished by its spectacular visual aesthetics.

Pilar Orti, who interpreted between Spanish-speaking performers and English spectators during the audience participation sections of *XXX*, suggested in *Total Theatre Magazine* that perhaps the production could be better understood as live art rather than traditional theatre.[35] There is certainly some benefit to this strategy: the production's scenography, its vocabulary of visual imagery based on actuality – such as Eugénie's whipping by Dolmancé from his flying metal sex machine, her immersion in a water tank as she communicates through an internet chat room, and group sex on a trapeze – were perhaps better appreciated by live art audiences used to reading bodily extremity, immediacy and technological innovation as creative languages in themselves (as opposed to those acting in the service of another language). Unfortunately, attempting to re-categorise a performance within a different genre in which it equally does not quite fit simply doubles the problem.

Similarly, Ron Athey recognises that there are distinctions to be made between what he does and 'theatre', and yet he is resistant to labelling himself as a live artist. He has preferred to describe his work as 'performance', stating that 'an action is both the act performed, and representational of something with a bigger meaning. For instance, a surgical arrow inserted in the flesh is the act of piercing. It is also the act of representing the martyrdom of St. Sebastian.'[36] In an important early analysis, John Edward McGrath draws together semiotic and phenomenological understandings of Athey's work:

> [I]n putting everything on the surface – death, religion, sex, all displayed, all intricately played with on the skin – his work indicates a life practice which does not use spatial metaphors of the deep, the hidden, the terrible to hold at a distance our most profound experiences … Perhaps, like Athey, we can take the imagery of religion, posited as the consolation of, and therefore justification for, death and find in its surfaces – its shapes, not its meanings – the vectors of a pleasure which is supposed to disappear in death.[37]

Solar Anus, like *XXX*, cannot be read as either 'theatre' or 'live art'; it needs to be read as both or perhaps neither. To be more specific, performances like these need to be read experientially in terms of the slippage between our understanding of the two terms. This means that audience members, like the performance-makers, must allow themselves to fall into the gaps created where actuality and illusion can never quite meet – the spaces Bataille might call 'the impossible' where we are both free and powerless.

It is for this reason that I return to his concept of the formless as an attempt to describe a process or an alteration that replaces semantic registers with an interpretive grid.[38] Admittedly, Bataille's own short essay on the formless is in many ways less than helpful in establishing a methodology. His definition subverts the very act of definition, by stressing the function of a word rather than its meaning: 'Thus *formless* is not only an adjective having a given meaning, but a term that serves to bring things down in the world, generally requiring that each thing have its form.'[39] Like most of his writing, it is witty, contradictory, provocative and ultimately implodes on itself, annihilating its ideas in the process. In this sense then, Bataille's writing on the formless is what it describes.

Yve-Alain Bois and Rosalind E. Krauss summarise and distil Bataille's pre-Second World War writings, such as 'The Solar Anus' and his essay on Sade, in their understanding of the formless. They describe it as a process of declassification that operates through various processes of deviance – that is, the generation of waste and monstrosity through the making of the ideal.[40] These processes are all found at work in *XXX* and *Solar Anus*, productions which both begin with the image of excreting anus: Athey expels pearls; the giant projected ass of *XXX* spurts a blob of runny shit, the image followed immediately by the vaginal poetry suggesting the possibility of a better world. Using Bataille's vocabulary, the process of displacement from the face downward, or rather horizontally, is not 'conducted in the services of an obscene *thing*' but 'as a defiance of the top that, in its very ridiculousness becomes attractive, attractive *because* repellent, high because lower than low'.[41]

Figure 11.3. Ron Athey in *Solar Anus*. (Image: Cyril Kuhn)

Bataille insisted that aesthetic value lay in immediacy, that to reach the purest form of ecstasy we must elude concern for the next moment and equally all those that follow after.[42] *Solar Anus* and *XXX* both entropically remove objects and actions away from productive activity in the 'interest of the instant itself'.[43] Simultaneously, however, they seem to destabilise time. Central to *Solar Anus* was Athey's tattooed anus (Figure 11.3), the tattooing of which was fundamental to the moment of performance and performed in the service of the performance and yet took place at least six years earlier. The instant of tattooing is collapsed into the instant of ritual we later experienced. Similarly, La Fura created the illusion that the non-penetrative sexual actions we were watching live on stage were actually the scenes of penetration we were simultaneously watching on the screen behind. However, this penetration *did* take place, although in a different time, in the service of the production, in the service of the moment.

It may seem unusual to apply Bataille's theories to an activity he seemed to choose not to write about. In fact, I have only found one mention of theatrical performance in his writing, but it is a revealing one: Bataille claims to have 'got to know Antonin Artaud *to some extent*'.[44] They were certainly not close friends, although they obviously moved in similar circles. Artaud frightened Bataille but also made him feel strangely sympathetic; both challenged Surrealist orthodoxy and were therefore summarily dismissed by André Breton. Bataille recalls attending a lecture by Artaud at the Sorbonne and listening in a state of 'half-somnolence' until he became aware that Artaud 'had suddenly risen':

> Before an auditorium packed with the bourgeoisie …, he grasped his stomach and let out the most inhuman sound that has ever come from a man's throat: it created the sort of disquiet that would have been felt if a dear friend had suddenly become delirious. It was awful (perhaps the more so for being only *acted out*).[45]

It is no coincidence that the performances which I feel can best be illuminated by being read against Bataille are also those that are indebted to Artaud.

Bataille's 'use value' (to mime his own application of Sade) for those considering live performance events lies in his theorisation of two forms of communication: human sacrifice and poetry. Although he (thankfully) notes their very different levels of modern social acceptability, he also sees in them a close correlation:

> [B]oth a sacrifice and a poem withhold life from the sphere of activity; both *bestow sight* on what, within the object, has the power to excite desire or horror. The general result of sacrifice is death ... poetry is no less directed toward the same aim as sacrifice: it seeks as far as possible to render palpable, and as intensely as possible, the content of the present moment.[46]

Using Bataille, we can thus experience certain types of performance events as a form of embodied sacrificial poetry that approaches and alludes to death. There are distinct references to sacrifice (and also Bataille's parodying of Christianity which he sees as a force for denying human spirituality in its refusal to admit ecstatic ritual as well as its belief in a sovereign Godhead) in both *XXX*, which featured a symbolic crucifixion generated through projection, and *Solar Anus*, with its allusion to Christ's crown of thorns. In his essay 'The Solar Anus', the paradoxical 'luminous violence' of Bataille's sacrificial vision of sexuality is clear in his use of metaphors.

The '*solar annulus*' for Bataille's narrating voice is 'the intact anus of her body of eighteen years to which nothing sufficiently blinding can be compared except the sun, even though the *anus* is the *night*'. Although the intentions are superficially reminiscent of those for Sade's virgin Eugénie, it is 'Bataille' – 'the filthy parody of the torrid and blinding sun' – who is sacrificed through the sexual encounter: 'I want to have my throat slashed while violating the girl to whom I will have been able to say: you are the night'.[47] The object of desire and the performing subject collapse into a state of continuous being. For Bataille, 'inner experience' transcends the flesh and is 'revealed in the death of the sacrificial victim. Underlying eroticism is the feeling of something bursting, of the violence accompanying an explosion.'[48]

In order to enact the sacrificial, performance must exceed the semiotic and move into ritual transcendence for both performer and audience. Ron Athey does more than *act out* the continuous being of Bataille's narrator and the girl he violates;[49] he is present in such a way as to position his audience simultaneously as potentially both or either. My experience of 'reading' Solar Anus as a film and decoding its imagery profoundly differed from my experiencing Solar Anus as an event. The live performance was overwhelmingly moving and affective. At midnight in the Demon Club courtyard, time stood still. It seemed like I watched Athey for a fraction of a second and also for eternity. The images burned. I felt firmly grounded and as if I was about to collapse. He performed on behalf of himself, on my behalf, on behalf of everyone present. In his account of Solar Anus, Pat Califia described the moment Athey began to extract the long double-strand of pearls from his asshole as an act of communication and gifting:

> This act was somehow touching and romantic, the trick of a Victorian whore, Athey offering us something that came from a deep and intimate place inside himself. A treasure produced at no slight risk to himself. He was also, on a metaphorical level, making a roomful of people watch him shit. As a spectator, what should I choose to focus on, the beauty revealed here or the foul use that was being made of my time and attention? Deep in this dilemma, I fell into a state of silent wonder.[50]

Athey considers the role of his audience as one of 'bearing witness'. This act of witnessing, in me, provokes what Bataille calls 'inner experience'.

I have to admit that XXX did not incite the same response in me. The attempt to involve the audience was too deliberate; I was forced to consider myself too much; I did too much thinking. Perhaps debauchery is more engrossing than libertinism (which is essentially always about somebody else's desire or pain). Or perhaps, not unrelated, La Fura's strategies of simulation and voyeurism work against spectatorial transcendence. Nevertheless, I believe XXX was a performance that derives from the same impulse as Solar Anus, a genuine attempt to communicate experientially. The performers, the directors and the dramaturgs made themselves vulnerable and performed on our behalf. And, like Athey, they did so through a form of nearly unpalatable beauty, evoking both horror and desire. Susan Sontag has suggested that the pornographic imagination may access a truth 'about sensibility, about sex, about individual personality, about despair, about limits' that 'can be shared when it projects itself into art ... That discourse one might call the poetry of transgression is also knowledge. He who transgresses not only breaks a rule. He goes somewhere that the others are not; and he knows something the others don't know.'[51]

Experiencing *XXX* and *Solar Anus* so close to each other enabled me to articulate why we need to develop new frameworks with which to discuss theatrical performances that exceed disciplinarity, primarily through the collapsing distinction of form and content. This is especially the case for visceral performances (not just by La Fura dels Baus and Ron Athey, but also by companies such as Sočìetas Raffaello Sanzio) that revolve around a transgressive engagement with death and sexuality, resulting in the rupture of generic structure. As Simon Shepherd and Mick Wallis have noted, '[t]he experiential provides the conditions for signification; in trying to write about what is ungraspable phenomenology needs signification.'[52] The collision in collective environments of fantasy and inner experience, by definition private and personal, and outer or public experience challenges vocabularies of reception. Concepts such as formlessness, by focusing on declassification and deviance, may help us to articulate the ways theatres of cruelty, excess, accumulation, sacrifice, pornographic imagination and doubling are able to operate as channels of communication between the bodies of spectators and performers.[53]

Notes

1. La Fura dels Baus, *XXX* at Riverside Studios (London), 17 May 2003. Dramatised by Mercedes Abad, Alex Ollé, Carlos Padrissa and Valentina Carrasco; directed by Alex Ollé and Carlos Padrissa; performed by Teresa Vallejo (Madame), Pau Gómez (Giovanni), Sonia Segura (Eugénie) and Petro Gutiérrez (Dolmancé).
2. Adrian Heathfield, 'Alive' in Adrian Heathfield (ed.), *Live: Art and Performance* (London, 2004), p. 9.
3. This event was curated by Lee Adams and Ron Athey and produced by the Hayward Gallery in conjunction with their exhibition 'Undercover Surrealism: Picasso, Miró, Masson and the Vision of Georges Bataille', 11 May–30 July 2006. Video documentation is available as *The Monster in the Night of the Labyrinth: Contemporary Live Art Reflections on the Dark Vision of Georges Bataille* (2007) on DVD-PAL from www.thisisunbound.co.uk.
4. Dominic Johnson, 'It Only Hurts Because It's True: Recent Live Art and Performance in the UK', *Western European Stages*, 19(1) (2007), p. 10.
5. Peter Aspden, Review of *XXX*, *Financial Times* (25 April 2003). Reprinted in *Theatre Record*, 23(9) (2003).
6. Angela Carter, *The Sadeian Woman: An Exercise in Cultural History* (London, 1979), p. 26.
7. Giles Tremlett, 'More Sex Please, We're Spanish', *The Guardian* (5 June 2002), http://www.guardian.co.uk/culture/2002/jun/05/artsfeatures.culturaltrips.
8. Dominic Johnson, 'Perverse Martyrologies: An Interview with Ron Athey', *Contemporary Theatre Review*, 18(4) (2008), p. 506.
9. Michael Richardson, 'Introduction', in Georges Bataille, *The Absence of Myth: Writings on Surrealism*, trans. Michael Richardson (London and New York, 1994), p. 16.
10. *Ibid.*
11. Georges Bataille, *Erotism: Death and Sensuality*, trans. Mary Dalwood (San Francisco, 1986), p. 167.
12. Michel Surya, *Georges Bataille: An Intellectual Biography*, trans. Krzysztof Fijalkowski and Michael Richardson (London and New York, 2002), p. 137.
13. Bataille, *The Absence of Myth*, p. 90.
14. Yve-Alain Bois, 'The Use Value of Formless', in Yve-Alain Bois and Rosalind E. Krauss, *Formless: A User's Guide* (New York, 1997), p. 18.
15. Austryn Wainhouse and Richard Seaver, 'Introduction to Part Four', in the Marquis de Sade, *One Hundred and Twenty Days of Sodom* (London, 1966/1989), p. 682.
16. Surya, *Georges Bataille*, p. 349.
17. Allan Stoekl, 'Introduction', in Georges Bataille, *Visions of Excess: Selected Writings: 1927–1939*, ed. and intro. Allan Stoekl, trans. Allan Stoekl with Carl R. Lovitt and Donald M. Leslie Jr. (Minneapolis, MN, 1985), p. xiv.
18. Athey also refers frequently to the Italian film director Pier Paulo Pasolini as an influence and has used Pasolini's controversial *Salò o le 120 giornate di Sodoma* (1975), based on Sade's *One Hundred and Twenty Days of Sodom*, as source material when leading workshops. In 2002, Athey and Vaginal Davis co-curated an 18-hour performance art homage to Pasolini in Los Angeles, much like the Vision of Excess events that they have curated internationally in tribute to Bataille.
19. Quoted in RoseLee Goldberg, *Performance: Live Art Since 1960* (New York, 1998), p. 119.
20. Wayne Thexton, email interview with Ron Athey forwarded to the author, 3 June 2003.

21. Since then, Athey has made a number of solo pieces, including a series of *Incorruptible Flesh* durational performances and a series of *Self Obliteration* actions, since 2008. In 2004–2005 he collaborated with Juliana Snapper to make and tour *Judas Cradle*, a two-hander that brought together extended vocal techniques, opera, video and archaic torture devices.

22. Quoted in Mercè Saumell, 'Performance Groups in Contemporary Spanish Theatre', trans. Jill Pythian and Maria M. Delgado, *Contemporary Theatre Review*, 7(4) (1998): *Spanish Theatre 1920–1995: Strategies in Protest and Imagination*, Pt. 3, p. 19.

23. Quoted in John Bynorth, 'Sex On Stage Shock,' *Daily Star* (24 April 2003), p. 25. The headline on the continuing page of this article, quoted here, is different from the one that appears on the front page of the paper ('Sex On Stage Storm: Raunchiest Show Ever Hits UK').

24. Lois Keidan, Daniel Brine and Adrian Heathfield, *Live Culture* programme, ed. Adrian Heathfield (London, 2003), p. 1.

25. *Ibid.*, p. 4.

26. See William Grimes, 'For Endowment, One Performer Means Trouble,' *New York Times* (7 July 1994), http://www.nytimes.com/1994/07/07/arts/for-endowment-one-performer-means-trouble.html?pagewanted=1; Kateri Butler, 'Ron Athey', *Los Angeles Times Magazine* (28 January 2007), http://articles.latimes.com/2007/jan/28/magazine/tm-athey04?pg=4. Both accessed 19 August 2009.

27. Wendy Steiner, *The Scandal of Pleasure* (Chicago, IL, 1995), p. 38.

28. For a collation of critical reviews of *XXX* at the Riverside Studios, see *Theatre Record*, 23(9) (23 April–6 May 2003), pp. 541–5.

29. Marcel Hénaff, *Sade: The Invention of the Libertine Body*, trans. Xavier Callahan (Minneapolis, MN, 1999), p. 72.

30. Michael Billington, Review of *XXX*, *The Guardian* (25 April 2003). Reprinted in *Theatre Record*, 23(9) (2003).

31. Artaud quoted by Ron Athey, 'Some thoughts on the politics of the body and the problematics of documentation', in Manuel Vason, Lois Keidan and Ron Athey, *Exposures* (London, 2002), no pagination.

32. Saumell, 'Performance Groups in Contemporary Spanish Theatre', p. 19. See also Antonio Sánchez, 'La Fura dels Baus and the Legacy of Antonin Artaud', *Contemporary Theatre Review*, 16(4) (2006), pp. 406–18.

33. Quoted in Roger Blin, Antonin Artaud, *et al.*, 'Artaud's *Les Cenci*', trans. Charles Marowitz, in Rebecca Schneider and Gabrielle Cody (eds), *Re:direction. A Theoretical and Practical Guide* (London, 2002), pp. 135–6.

34. *Ibid.*, pp. 136–7.

35. Pilar Orti, 'X-rated', *Total Theatre Magazine*, 15(2) (2003), p. 23.

36. Wayne Thexton, email interview with Ron Athey.

37. John Edward McGrath, 'Trusting in Rubber: Performing Boundaries during the AIDS Epidemic', *TDR*, 35(2) (1995), pp. 36–7.

38. Bois, 'The Use Value of Formless', p. 18.

39. Georges Bataille, *Visions of Excess: Selected Writings, 1927–1939*, ed. Allan Stoekl, trans. Allan Stoekl with Carl R. Lovitt and Donald M. Leslie Jr (Minneapolis, MN, 1985), p. 31. Emphasis in original.

40. Rosalind E. Krauss, 'The Destiny of the Informe', in Bois and Krauss, *Formless*, p. 252.

41. *Ibid.*, pp. 248–9.

42. Bataille, *The Absence of Myth*, p. 91.

43. *Ibid.*, p. 148.

44. *Ibid.*, p. 42. Emphasis in original.

45. *Ibid.*, p. 43. Emphasis in original.
46. *Ibid.*, p. 149. Emphasis in original.
47. Bataille, *Visions of Excess*, p. 9. Emphasis in original.
48. Bataille, *Erotism*, p. 93.
49. The actions and imagery of *Solar Anus* were also inspired by the autoerotic photographs of the artist Pierre Molinier (1900–76). Dressed up in stockings, corsets and heels, Molinier used accessories such as silk dildos attached to his ankles for his performances of self-penetration to camera. Echoes of Molinier's montages of dislocated body parts are also evident in the artwork for La Fura's *XXX* website.
50. Pat Califia, 'In Praise of Assholes', *Out* (May 1999), p. 44.
51. Susan Sontag, 'The Pornographic Imagination', in Georges Bataille, *Story of the Eye by Lord Auch*, trans. Joachim Neugroschal (London, 1982), p. 116.
52. Simon Shepherd and Mick Wallis, *Drama/Theatre/Performance* (Abingdon and New York, 2004), p. 239.
53. Thanks are due to Carl Lavery, Cariad Astles, Jenny Graham and Karoline Gritzner, each of whom generously offered their expertise at various stages in the writing of this chapter. Any misreadings of the ideas they shared are entirely my own. Much of the material in this chapter also appears in Roberta Mock, 'La Fura dels Baus's *XXX*: Deviant Textualities and the Formless', in Susan Broadhurst and Josephine Machon (eds), *Sensualities/Textualities and Technologies: Writings of the Body in 21st-Century Performance* (London and New York, 2010), which focuses on La Fura's challenge to understandings of authenticity through technological simulation.

12

La petite mort: *erotic encounters in* One to One *performance*

Rachel Zerihan

It was dark.

There was a chair that I sat in and I seem to remember having my arms fixed to its. I was blindfolded. More excited than nervous, more eager than fearful and more awake than I'd been in ages, my sense of expectation was immense. I'd been asked to select which kind of tale I would be told. This might have been signified by an object, a word or a more revealing description – I don't remember now.

I'd chosen quite intuitively and sat expectantly desiring the narrative, awaiting my courtesan's tale. I don't recollect words, though it's likely there were some. Instead, the embodied gestures carried the vocabulary of the/our story with apparent ease and a command of (inter)corporeal relations.

There was touch, and no touch. I felt fingers on my fingers, hands on mine and at one point a palm pressing into me. My shoulders were pushed down and pulled in, my body moved.

A feather.

On my neck.

It tickled.

The weight of her body sunk into my thighs, straddling me. Lips. Opened. Soft. Something slipped inside. Sweet. Hot. Something shared. I recall feeling her glide away from me.

I was untied and slowly stood upright. I walked a few steps away from the chair and opened the door to see the queue of people next in line. The red blood vessels in my face burst to expose the intimacy of my erotic encounter, which, even if I'd wanted to, I couldn't hide.[1]

Western performance in particular has played host to a proliferation of One to One works since 2003. Incorporating reflection and analysis from recent One to One performances I have encountered, this examination will draw out psychoanalytical and erotic frameworks that I will use to interrogate the current lure of this unique theatrical form. Considering critical co-ordinates emerging from both fields of analysis, my writing investigates the solo-audience experience as satisfying a desire blurred through therapeutic/sexual/ethical assemblages of affect. Foregrounding the intimacy of the relational exchange in a One to One performance, the presence and nature of (feminist) *jouissance* will be proposed as an overflowing outcome affiliated to the experience of *la petite mort* (the little death).

In order to introduce and contextualise One to One practices, I proffer two threads of analysis emerging from two lineages of One to One performance. Such lines of enquiry can be considered conceptual lenses through which to discuss the selected works under examination. Firstly I propose the One to One interaction as epitomising what performance theorist Peggy Phelan terms 'the psychic stage' and I question the therapeutic quality of recent One to One encounters I was privileged to experience. After unpacking my understanding and experience of the nature of intercourse as a critical quality of such works, I then go on to elaborate on my (provocative) proposal regarding *jouissance* and *la petite mort* as I assess the erotic, sexual and transformative qualities of performances of this kind. The relation between these two viewpoints is intriguing and emerges unforced – it is not the purpose of this analysis to tie the strands together in a neat bow, rather to consider one side by side with the other for their meeting points and collisions.[2] Immersing itself in a selection of One to One encounters, this short study seeks to unpack distinguishing features, methodologies and strategies of different sorts of transformative experiences being offered to and taken by an increasing number of contemporary audiences.

Diverse conditions of One to One experiences are considered alongside each other, primarily in order to uncover their shared concern with creating responsive encounters that address issues of embodiment, impulse, viscerality, immersion, perception and transgression. The impulse behind the insistence of *écriture féminine* for women to 'write with the body' applies also to a scholarly approach that, as I understand it, requires that one responds to and with the body. My analytical approach therefore complements the aesthetics from which the performances under discussion emerge via a focus on the centrality of the body in performance. Building upon the group of methodologies that transgress the Cartesian mind/body split in performance, these One to One artworks can be considered to address both cognitive and visceral impulses through their construction of an exclusive interface sealed by sensed interaction. It is this familiarity, security and closeness that ensures the artists under discussion are able to use conceptual counterpoints to directly trouble assumptions of truth, fixed meanings and distance between 'viewer' and 'artwork' in favour of making works that thrive on risk, instinct, shared dialogue and cohesive production of meaning, while also having the potential to expose their 'other' to a uniquely personal transformation. Combining tenets of performance, live and body art, the fluid aesthetics that the artists profiled work across focuses my writing on demonstrating (their) corporeal manifestations of the body as signifier and transmitter of energy, as performing the subject and as embroiled in the vast array of body politics to which spectators are invited to bear witness.[3]

Nicole Blackman's *The Courtesan Tales* was one of the first One to One, or Audience of One, performances I experienced. It was 2003 and I'd travelled to Birmingham for the first UK 'Visions of Excess' – a through-the-night collection of Bataille-inspired performances co-curated by Ron Athey and Vaginal Davis. Live and performance artists, burlesque strippers, porn stars and international actors came together to perform various pieces in a seedy strip club as part of Fierce Festival's annual programme of Live Art. Several One to Ones were on offer, including a work by Kira O'Reilly entitled *My Mother* which was an altogether different yet similarly moving interaction involving an extremely tender opportunity to share more than words.[4]

Blackman's description of *The Courtesan Tales* as 'tales of the senses' is symptomatic of this overriding feature that exists between performer and spectator in One to One performance – in short, the heightened affective nature and felt intensity of such a close(d), intimate experience.[5]

By design, these bespoke inter-experiences are made for an audience of one, so it is hardly surprising that the practitioners who have made One to One performances engage with issues of proximity that play on the interface in the shared space between one and other. Concentrating on exploring the connections between eroticism and death in the live art works under discussion, my writing focuses on reading the interfaces between performer and spectator in these staged – yet authentically felt – encounters. Identifiable qualities of this intimate environment might include transformation, connectivity, risk, trust, confession, responsibility, therapeutics and many more beside. This chapter forms a study into the response and affect of the intimate opportunities that are created by adopting these qualities as vehicles of visceral potency, means of mapping milieu and signs of sensing psycho-social structures.

Visceral, sensual and experiential responses are drawn out in order to shape acute analysis across visual art, performance and live art disciplines. The One to One performance pieces I examine here are Angela Bartram's *Tonguing* (2006), Jiva Parthipan's *LICK* (2007), Davis Freeman's *Reflection* (2004) and Adrian Howells's *Foot Washing for the Sole* (2009). This diverse array of performance pieces has been chosen to unpack not only the erotic and psychoanalytic qualities of One to One works but also to illustrate the various cultural, sociological, psychological and ethical lines of enquiry that are heightened in such an encounter and, indeed, the very different kinds of environments designed to host such experiences. Attempting to articulate the inter-experiences of One to One performances requires that I not only take on an embodied gesture of response but also that I disclose self-reflexive analysis stemming from the very personal encounters I had with the artists. The telling of these experiences also points towards a transient, fleeting, decaying, deathly state, similar to what Phelan calls 'performative writing' in *Mourning Sex: Performing Public Memories*:

> Performative writing enacts the death of the 'we' that we think we are before we begin to write. A statement of allegiance to the radicality of unknowing who we are becoming, this writing pushes against the ideology of knowledge as a progressive movement forever approaching a completed end-point.[6]

These passages of (my) descriptions invite you to imagine yourself in my place, to stimulate your senses to foreground the experience I am sharing. Notwithstanding the fact that performance analysis is always subjective, it is important to stress that the explicitly individual responses that follow are mine alone.

Intimate experiences

To intimate is to communicate with the sparest of signs and gestures, and at its root intimacy has the quality of eloquence and brevity. But intimacy also involves an aspiration for a narrative about something shared, a story about both oneself and others that will turn out a particular way.[7]

My experiences of each of the One to One works I will discuss have differed enormously, yet all have affected my felt sense of intimacy. Interpreted as existing at various points on what Dominic Johnson has called 'a continuum of intimacy'[8] or with each one playing out what Karen Finley might term a 'different kind of intimacy',[9] these performative liaisons have felt personal, regardless of the practitioner's attitude towards the stream of singular visitors they perform to/for/with.

This article responds to selected One to One works as inter-experiences, sliding between psychoanalytic theory and social phenomenology under the influence of R.D. Laing: 'Social phenomenology is the science of my own and of others' experience … That is, with inter-experience. It is concerned with your behaviour and my behaviour as I experience it.'[10] Underpinning my critical voice is a desire to share with the viewer/reader a binocular vision of the works under discussion. Bert States uses the term 'binocular vision' to define the extended post-structuralist reading that enables a study of both semiotics and affect through which signifying sign-systems are read and interpreted together with ephemeral and phenomenological analysis.[11] Mobilising analysis through the use of binocular vision enables me to critically convey the experiential, non-mimetic contemporary performance works under investigation.

One to One

One to One performance foregrounds subjective narratives that define – and seek to redefine – questions of identity, belief-structures and strategies of behaviour and response. Refused the inherent anonymity that traditionally structures mass spectatorship, in One to One an 'other' is lifted out of the passive role of audience member and repositioned into an activated state of witnessing or collaborating, or is even subtly energised into 'acting' as a voyeur. This 'gift' of explicit responsibility is frequently infiltrated by an ambiguous invitation, between offer and bane that brings the other into an obscure place of opportunity. Formally, such interaction could be considered as an extended elevation of the spectator's participatory role recognised in other forms of performance, including cabaret, interactive theatre, forum theatre and psychodrama. The special quality of the One to One performance format lies in its ability to cultivate a particularly intense relationship which has the potential not only to evoke emotions, illicit enquiry and sensually seduce an intimate exchange but also to embody critical signs and functions of transient – and sometimes lasting – transmission. Jennifer Fisher introduces her examination of *Technologies of Intuition* with an explicitly affect-led methodology investigating 'an enhanced understanding of art involving an expanded sensorium, a vocabulary of corporeal intensities, and a continuum of experience open to the flash of insight'.[12] My analysis of eroticism and therapeutics in One to One performance examines a desire to focus attention on the receptive, exposed (and paradoxically) closed relationship between one and other.

Heightened response-ability and intensified perceptual awareness personalise the complex layers of semiology embedded in the politics of the One to One performance event, stripping bare and simultaneously problematising the relation between one and other. Scheduling 'alone-time' with the performer carries with it the implication that the performance will be your own – an exclusive encounter moulded by intimacy. Like the (felt) difference between a briefest encounter and a one-night stand, the temptation to imagine the presence of intimacy when face to face with another – spanning time, sharing space, blending breath, sensing touch – can (sometimes quite deceptively) reinstate intimacy's presence and re-empower its affect. Who carries the intimacy, where it resides, who sustains it and who or what has the ability to destroy it are all subliminal questions that flutter at the core of this chapter's analysis into the lure of One to One performance. The intertwined notions of self-giving and self-losing in intimate environments are mapped onto the economies of exchange in this formal encounter. Negotiating this relationship involves adopting strategies of overcoming or accepting risk and succumbing to multifarious displays and encounters that might be considered as psychologically or physically challenging, together with the (shared) creation and maintenance of an environment of trust.

The significant increase in One to One performance works raises some interesting questions in terms of our demand for, and artists' use of, this format in contemporary performance, body and live art. Interrogated by emerging artists and tested by established artists, this radical play on form is gradually being recognised as an exciting and important development in the ever-changing practice of contemporary performance. Over the last few years, live and performance art festivals as well as independent commissions have become much more willing to platform One to One performance pieces. The queue to book One to Ones at performance festivals, such as the annual National Review of Live Art, is undoubtedly getting longer with each passing year. In May 2006 Nottingham Trent University's Sensitive Skin season showed works by fifteen artists, seven of which used a One to One format. Celebrated performance outfit Duckie have been offering a themed collection of One to Ones over the last decade or so in their annual alternative to a night of Pride under the banner of 'Gay Shame'.[13] The trend to make it One to One – a kind of compulsive monogamy with the other – has seemingly been nurtured especially by British and European artists since the turn of the millennium. Unearthing a variety of environments that stage intensities of togetherness, this chapter is interested in foregrounding psychoanalytic or healing and erotic frameworks of interpretation while articulating potential states of inter-corporeality and re-embodiment that emerge from intimate encounters of 'proximal' or 'presence-led' One to One pieces under examination.

The 'psychic stage'[14]

I have recently argued that the emergence of One to One as a form of performance – an ostensibly packaged, consumer-led 'performance-for-one' – appears, paradoxically, to have originated via the art form that most disparaged the idea of art as product, defining itself as vociferously 'anti-art-as-commodity', namely performance art.[15] In April 1971, at a time of feverish cultural experimentation in explicitly testing physical endurance through performed acts that extended perceived corporeal limitations, American artist Chris Burden made a performance work entitled *Five Day*

Locker Piece. Gina Pane, Marina Abramovic, Vito Acconci and the Viennese Aktionists were among Burden's visceral-led body artist contemporaries. C. Carr observes that, as one of Burden's earliest recorded performances, the act produced unexpected responses, most notably for the artist himself:

> he just expected to curl up and endure for five consecutive days. But to his surprise, people he didn't even know came unbidden to sit in front of the locker, to tell him their problems and the stories of their lives.[16]

Confining himself, without food or drink, to a locker two by two by three feet for five days, Burden established an environment that his audience read as encouraging their communication with him in a secure and outwardly intimate space. In his study of 'immersive art', Oliver Grau articulates the radical shift in the performer/spectator dynamics of post-Happenings. This shift

> encouraged the trend toward dissolving the fixed spatial and temporal limits of the work, dislocating the central position of the author, and enhancing the work through harnessing the imagination of the participating spectators.[17]

Re-imagining and in effect redefining Burden's performed role as that of priest or healer, judge or lover, spectator psychology and behaviour became instrumental and affective as the spectators' secret intimacies (fantasies and fears) were projected onto him, recasting him as confidant. The audience's act of (re)claiming the space of performance and re-appropriating Burden's role to suit their own needs can be seen as evocatively pursuing the performer/ spectator, analyst/analysand politics of therapeutics that shadow this confessional scene. Since, as Lauren Berlant has argued, 'therapy saturates the scene of intimacy',[18] the roles of analyst and analysand float and settle onto each player, denoting what Peggy Phelan terms the 'psychic stage'.[19]

In One to One performance, formal consumerist anxieties become laced with our therapy culture's promise of a talking cure. Nowhere has my experience of a therapeutic encounter in performance been received and sensed more fully than in a One to One I felt privileged to have with Davis Freeman from Random Scream in late 2004 called *Reflection*. My intense response to this encounter was a feeling, I was told by the performance

Figure 12.1. Davis Freeman, *Reflection* (Image courtesy of artist)

assistant, that was echoed by many. The company had been invited to perform as guests of Forced Entertainment's twenty-year anniversary celebrations that took place at Riverside Studios, London. Called to have my photograph taken a short while before my performance 'slot', a sense that my own part in the piece would be on show began to emerge. A short wait in the vestibule ended when a bulb turned from red to green and I entered the darkened space. Soft lighting on an armchair and a free-standing lamp guided me to take a seat. Settling into my surroundings, I found myself facing an identical chair and lamp at the other end of the dark studio space; the mirror image of 'my' set, the only part missing in the reflection was 'me'. From the opposite corner of the room, a man gingerly appeared. His movements were slow and considered, tenderising the fact that he was wearing the photograph of my face.

For five minutes, Freeman's acutely sensitive movements and gently reassuring gestures moved himself/myself closer towards myself/other. His seemingly intuitive episodes of *tableau vivant* were led by a gliding momentum that demonstrated his conviction and self-assurance. Freeman's mastery in adopting my form (face) felt liberating and secure rather than jarred and intimidating. At one moment he slid to the floor and positioned himself/myself into a playful yet provocatively seductive pose, his hands stretching over and down his body and an odd sensation of being the object of my own desire stimulated my senses and dilated my pupils in desire and confusion in equal parts. That my gaze at this moment was filled with the reflection of myself enabled a tender desire and will for reconnection with my-self. As Freeman's movements gradually brought him closer to my place, his sensitivity in representing my own being/body grew and emanated with each gesture and step closer. His trained dancer's total control of his/my body resensitised my feelings toward it/myself. Standing tall above me, Freeman took my hand and placed it on his thumping heart. This brief moment of touch was charged with an inexplicable sensory electrification as, looking down at me, Freeman gestured towards solace, peace and an overwhelming expression of love. I felt re-embodied.

Dis-played and freed from my own thoughts of cognitive self, my time of 'reflection' had allowed the fixity of Cartesian duality to be released and with it the ever-present sense of my own responsibility. Freeman (fitting name) had, it appeared to me, invited his other to relinquish responsibility so that an intimate immersion (of myself?) might take place. In allowing me to indulge in facing my-self as other, Freeman had enabled a reconnection to begin that had, setting aside Lacan's Mirror Stage, never happened before. Responding to his immensely gentle and simplistic movements and gestures, an extremely safe environment played host to the most intimate and liberating performance experience I have ever encountered. My sense of being (me) felt liberated and simultaneously stimulated through his non-threatening adoption of my (corporeal) self. The opportunity to re-embody one's own corporeal sense of self is a rare invitation that provides with it the possibility of re-establishing our awareness of our mind/body, self/other relationship. Freeman's gift of a form of corporeal catharsis provided the opportunity for an intimate self-sharing and self-discovering that, I believe, is unique to and lies at the core of the lure of interaction in One to One performance.

Furthering the therapeutic potential of a One to One performance is a strategy that performance artist Adrian Howells has consciously and deliberately explored since he began making One to Ones in around 2000. In the summer of 2009 the Live Art Development Agency commissioned me to write a guide for their specialist Study Room on One to One performance. I took this opportunity to invite a selection of seventeen international practitioners who make or have made One to One works to respond to four central questions about their work. What follows is Howells's response to a question I posed about what led him to begin making One to One works by drawing on his previous acting experience:

> I remember thinking that if the art of 'acting' is to try and achieve intimacy or connection with each individual in an audience, as though you're performing just for them, even when you're clearly performing to a large collective, then why not just have a more conducive set up and actually just perform a piece for one person at a time? ... I was craving a more authentic and nourishing experience of exchange with another human being and one-to-one performance was able to facilitate this. My whole *raison d'être* is what can I do to make this a really special, memorable and qualitative experience just for one person and how can I realise this. My motivation is often how can I best create experiences that are, above all, mutually nourishing and nurturing for both myself and the audience-participant, and how can I simultaneously exploit the potential for two people to be very intimately responsive to each other.

Although I had worked with Howells while he was carrying out his research project – on ideas of risk and intimacy within a One to One confessional context in contrasting sites – for his AHRC Creative Fellowship at Glasgow University, my first encounter with his practice was at Battersea Arts Centre for a piece I shared with him in Spring 2009 called *Foot Washing for the Sole*. Howells's approach to investigating One to One works through the notion of confession develops the idea of a healing encounter into one that privileges the intertwined gesture of self-giving and response-ability.

Non-verbal displays of connectivity, closeness and ritual revelation fre-quently decorate the gift of experiencing One to Ones, set in environments ripe for disclosure of personal testimonies. The gesture of confession – to disclose, admit, tell, spill – is shot through with cathartic overtones, forming a central tenet of the kinds of responsive One to One performances I am describing here. In the description of my inter-experience of Howells's piece that follows, the idea of acute or heightened presence appeared to come to the foreground – in critical reflexiveness and in the practice of being there, in the space, with Howells himself. This notion reminded me of R.D. Laing's understanding of healing, which rests on the provision of three

212

basic conditions or stances: presence, invoking the actual, and vivifying resistance. Presence refers to Laing's capacity to hold and illuminate that which is palpably (immediately, affectively, kinesthetically and profoundly) relevant within his clients and between himself and his clients. Invoking the actual refers to Laing's capacity to assist his clients into that which is palpably relevant (or charged) as a conduit to their liberation. Finally, vivifying resistance pertains to Laing's capacity to assist his clients to overcome the blocks to that which is palpably relevant.[20]

What surprised me about Howells's piece was his sensitive yet astute command of the framed space and time and the sense of heightened presence he bestowed that led me to reflect upon his (relatively) long history of making One to One works. Howells's role evoked an affinity and a relationship with the form that was organic and fluid rather than imposed and formulaic. Not only was the pace effortlessly monitored and honed but the rhythm, score and composition of our time together was impeccably measured while free to breathe a life of its own. Howells's gentle command of our interaction was strong and comforting while being tender and responsive.

Marking our shared time, Howells bookended our encounter with the invitation to breathe together. We breathed seven breaths in and out at the start of the piece and a few breaths at the end to close our meeting. This loose frame is just one illustration of the subtle yet firm structure of the performance piece, bound by moments of shared embodiment that Howells had created for me, his 'other'.

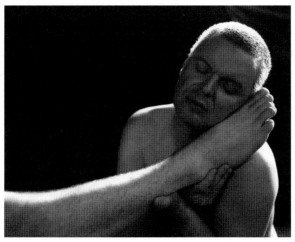

Figure 12.2. Adrian Howells, *Foot Washing for the Sole* (Photo: Hamish Barton)

During the course of our time together, Howells washed, massaged and kissed my feet. The ritual was fuelled by social, political and anthropological reflections revealed by Howells's narrative detail and inquisitive probing for me to share too. His role as facilitator of this inter-experience intensified, personalised and energised the sequence of performed gestures to leave me feeling thoroughly refreshed and imbued with that aforementioned sense of calm I already disclosed. Sat on a chair with Howells's face at my raised feet I felt like I could not hide. Howells's body became the roots where I was standing, feeding into me something new and unusual. As he traced the contours of my feet with his apothecary-oiled hands I felt as if the landscape of where I place myself, the ground on which I stand, was momentarily shifted, causing me to gently re-evaluate my position. The sound of the wind outside the window layered the meditative environment that evoked the gentle sense of communion I felt we shared.

Making contact to demonstrate the efficacy of doing so, Howells addressed this truism on a number of levels, played out through his performed interaction with me. Incorporating his memories of performing the piece in Tel Aviv and Nazareth, Howells told without preaching of the different encounters he'd had in both places and said that he hoped some of the people who had attended his performances would pass the gesture of touch, of healing, on to another. Howell stripped the act, a ritual originating from biblical writings, down to proffer an urgent, focused will for contact and peace and it was this message that I continue to have at the forefront of my mind.

I walked away from my encounter with Adrian Howells feeling completely at peace. My body felt like it was still absorbing the physical effect of what we had just shared and my mind – or was it my soul? – felt washed over, stimulated and soothed by Howells's gentle provocation that urged a reconsideration of the gift of touch and the sense of healing we can easily give to another, yet seldom care to. The entire experience felt shaped by Howells's generous insistence for me to take a moment, let down my guard and be open to the interaction he presented me with.

Jouissance and *la petite mort* in intercourse discourse

The politics of One to One performance frequently becomes riddled with another set of questions that intensify the act in which both parties take part, as the form becomes either separate from – or, more frequently, intertangled with – the nature of the content. One and an-other come to stage to mark out the tugging, tangling and tenderising of the politics of power, making up a live autopsy of the inter-relationship between performer and spectator. The meeting between two parties is not always predicated on a playful approach to creating mini-unions, as Howells inferred above. In conversation with Franko B for the Study Room Guide I was commissioned to write, he described how a culture of encounter, as he saw it, in fetish clubs, inspired him to consider isolating his audience. Proposing an alternative to my theory that Burden's might have constituted the first One to One performance, Franko told me:

> When I started to work on my One to One which was in 1997, nobody was doing One to One. When I say nobody [I mean] nobody in performance or theatre. Nobody as far as I know it, if you look at it in terms of the artistry of performance ... nobody in the 80s or 90s were doing One to Ones in England, never mind Europe.[21]

His first UK One to One was *Aktion 398*, performed in South London Gallery in 1999. The piece entailed the solo audience member entering the space to find Franko B naked, painted white and wearing a plastic collar.[22] The time spent together was the interaction. In my interview with Franko he talked candidly about his infuriation with practitioners who appropriate the One to One format as an 'easy' way to make performance.[23] He stressed:

> I think to do One to One [performance], to me it's most like you are having sex with somebody, although sex doesn't happen, you have an intimacy – **a serious intimacy**. It's not purely about confession or therapy but as well about the fact that anything could happen – somebody could touch your wound – you could fuck somebody or actually the sex – what is the sex? The sex is the moment of fear, a moment of abandonment, a moment of danger – I just think – 'Go to a fetish club and learn how to be in a dark space with people you can see in the face. Learn how to be with strangers, real strangers.'[24]

This passionate call returns me to my encounter with Blackman that I evoked at the start of this essay. 'You have this kind of range of things in which, in a way, some kind of intercourse happens. Not as we understand it but that's what it is. That is totally what it is.'[25] Franko's suggestion of an intercourse existing between performer and spectator to fuse a union that can be exciting, seductive, entrancing at best, and banal, straight and obvious at worst, is a state that I am familiar with and in some way emerges from the presence-led state that I have reached in illustrating the interface of One to One performance.

Returning to the crux of my assertion that such intercourse contains, or rather spills, moments of *jouissance* needs clarifying and expounding upon at this critical stage of writing. A revisiting of the Lacanian definition of the concept of *jouissance* – as a pre-symbolic stage in which there are no distinctions between self and other – is useful in reading the wider form of One to One performance, as this notion can be seen to exist intrinsically through the performances' adoption of intimate interfaces. In *Reflection* and *Foot Washing for the Sole*, touch and non-touch, language and non-language, and narrative and non-narrative could be argued to demonstrate the practitioners' desire to examine, on an immediate, sensory, kinaesthetic level, the line between self and other, using reflective strategies to mirror an exposure of this relationship back to their audience.

Taking into account yet wishing to move on from both the Lacanian definition and Barthesian understanding of the 'text of *jouissance*', it is important to situate the place from which I am writing as a female – and feminist – writer. In these terms I am interested, rather, in the concept of *jouissance* as evoking experiential occurrences of affective, visceral states of dialogue between one embodied being and another. In her significant text *Volatile Bodies: Toward a Corporeal Feminism*, Elizabeth Grosz critiques Mary Douglas's position in her seminal 1966 work *Purity and Danger* for

... positing the body in a synecdochial relation to the fluids it contains. But [Grosz continues] hydraulic models, models of absorption, of incorporation, are all culturally validated representations that may make sense in our culture but are by no means inevitable. They all share the characteristic of establishing male sexuality and corporeality as the singular form, which is inadequate in establishing a symmetrical female sexuality and body morphology. The 'precious stuff' circulating in sexual relations is not the movement of desire, the exchange of pleasures, but the transmission of seminal fluids, oozing through the male body into its resting place, the female body.[26]

Mobilising the concept of *jouissance* through a feminist understanding of the term enables me to redesignate the 'precious stuff' that Grosz underscores the loss of back into the category of preciousness. In the One to One performance works that figure in this writing, therefore, 'the movement of desire, the exchange of pleasures' are re-cognised and re-established as primary qualities of *jouissance* bound into and sensed through the artistic processes, aesthetic manifestations and spectator reception of these contemporary performance artworks.

The place and potential occurrence of *la petite mort* extends this notion of *jouissance* to its cathartic conclusion. My use of the term, French for 'the little death' and a well-known metaphor for orgasm, in relationship to One to One performance not only is sexual and/or erotic but also, vitally, brings the possibility of referencing a deathly framework made up of ideas and states including mortality, risk, sacrifice and finitude, qualities rich in contemporary One to One practice. These facets could be argued as bringing the One to One encounter into the social, cultural arena by encouraging human, ethical and political questions of selfhood and society.

Angela Bartram's piece *Tonguing* jarred voyeurism with transfixed awe to leave me hot, red and rosy-cheeked. The tongue is the strongest muscle

Figure 12.3. Angela Bartram, *Tonguing* (Photo: Antonio Juarez, Centro de Documentacion, Ex Teresa Arte Actual)

in the human body. Having seen Bartram lick walls at the National Review of Live Art in 2005 I was aware of her appetite for experimenting with all things tongue. The sexual intimacy of One to One performance was here drawn out in Bartram's demonstration of her impressive tonguing ability.

A model tongue protruded at head-height to Bartram from one wall of the little basement room. Slowly extending the full length of her tongue, Bartram touched tongues with the model other. She licked a little as she probed and prodded with the force of her tongue. She turned. Facing the opposite wall, the licked-down remnants (I discovered later) of another model of the artist's tongue, this time made of candy, were fixed at a similar height. For four minutes Bartram teased, tickled, licked, lapped, slurped, bit and nibbled her own sugar tongue. She looked at me once as she placed her hand suggestively – and forcibly – onto the wall's body. I expect this is where my soft blush first appeared. Bartram walked up to me and offered me a rock-sweet with the words 'Suck Me' running through it. Senses stimulated and eyes dilated, my gaze had misted and mesmerised into a fixed stupor. My critical eye stunned, I took a sweet and popped it into my dry mouth, attempting a different kind of muscle work-out.

Between one and another, Bartram's *Tonguing* was literally designed to infect and affect a movement of desire, an exchange of pleasures. Originally this piece was not a One to One but a form Bartram adopted as part of her performance process. She writes that she was interested in

> how this piece would function through one-to-one: my intimacy with the object brought up close and personal to a solitary individual engaged with it. It also allowed me to explore how the sexual overtures (sucking, suckling) would occupy the space between me and one other person and if it was possible to make them swell and envelope us in the performance space, which was very small. Essentially I thought it would bind us together in an intimate, or at least recognition of an intimate exchange during the performance and the piece was modified to facilitate that.[27]

Jiva Parthipan's One to One performance *LICK* was made for 'Revisions of Excess' (2007) and performed in the same lap-dancing club as the original 'Visions of Excess' that platformed Blackman's seductive piece. Parthipan says:

Here I wanted to revisit the parameters of physical intimacy without emotional entanglement. I was interested in touch as a sensation. The one two [*sic*] one performance seemed to be the most obvious choice for this form since that was the nature of the engagement of a sex worker. The content dictated the form. I slightly dislocated it for the performance without actually referring to the same sex nature and wanted to purely test the limits of touch and eroticism within a controlled environment.[28]

The interactions that Bartram and Parthipan offer their audiences cross all kinds of safe distances that spectators would normally expect. Here, instead, questions of object and subject come to the foreground to trigger questions about the nature of art and contracts and transactions. An erotic interaction is invited, but one steeped in the knowledge that, as mentioned earlier, audiences become a factory line of expectant consumers as opposed to specially invited guests.

At an invited symposium that Adrian Howells organised to close his fellowship, he brought together around thirty practitioners, writers,

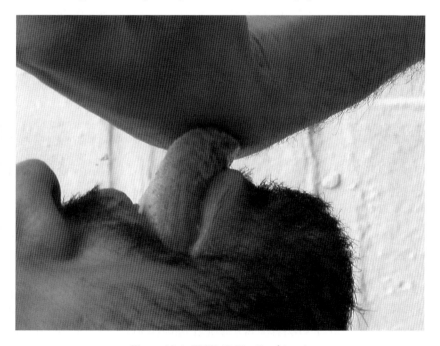

Figure 12.4. *LICK* (© Jiva Parthipan)

academics and interested parties under the heading of 'I Confess...' to examine works that invite an intimate exchange. We experienced some wonderfully inspiring One to Ones and discussed various qualities of these increasingly popular artworks. A host of areas was pawed over, including embodiment, presence, consent and responsibility, but the most interesting discussion for me came at the end of our two-day meeting when Dominic Johnson put forward an idea about economies of exchange that had been partially evoked and mused over in smaller discussions but not quite articulated in full. Johnson provoked the idea that some One to One performances could be considered in relation to sexual giving in terms of sex work. He went on to describe a semblance in the contract in sex work and One to Ones because the 'worker' in both contexts gives but only gives so much as to produce the appearance of investment in the contract/relation – to give too much would be inefficient considering the centrality of repetition in sex work (and, indeed, One to Ones). This suggestion, evoked in part through several performers at the event performing a desire to please, was reacted to with some difficulty, further analysis and copious debate. Johnson's thinking exemplified the issue of the contract of consent between the two parties of a One to One while raising, specifically, the notion of sexual relations in current discourse on One to One performance works. Johnson's assertion stirred my thoughts about eroticism and *jouissance* in One to One works and, beside this study's concerns, evidences the scope and potential for further analysis into intercourse discourse of One to One performance.

Plus One

My passion for engaging (with) performance works frequently favours the unsettling and provocative experience of the moment of corporeal and psychological interaction with an-other. Intrinsic to the attraction of One to One performance works is the opportunity of immersing oneself in a truly subjective experience. Whether this entails a form of psychological release through the offer of a confessional, a visceral journey into the tangled space of incorporation and in-between-ness that Freeman's and Howells's sensitive interactions offered me, or Blackman's, Bartram's and Parthipan's invitations to respond, to be titillated, touched, turned on – the outcomes of such intimate motions in One to One of (self) giving offer an improved sense of clarity, understanding and awareness of our-selves and 'others'.

Connections such as these begin with another's corporeal display of the possibility of intimacy as visceral closeness and phenomenological responsiveness, and mark the encounter between this other and our own mind's agenda. In this analysis I have taken the opportunity of drawing on therapeutic and erotic lines of enquiry to stage my proposition that *jouissance* figures poignantly in the intimate interface between One and Other of a One to One performance experience. The essence of my attraction to this nearness is framed by non-verbal communication that gestures to the human experience of intimacy and intuition as interaction similar to what Vivian Sobshack describes as 'the carnal, fleshy, objective foundations of subjective consciousness as it engages and is transformed by and in the world'.[29] In the performance works I have discussed, embodied corporeality and proximal closeness braid to form an affective force that is simultaneously ordinary yet highly charged. This sense, action and state not only define a meeting between one and other; they also contain important strategies for continuing to interrogate the politics of the gaze in performance. Bodily presence in these scenarios can be visualised as pressing into individual cultural/social/political narratives, coming through our skins and opening us up to dialogue. Fuelling my refusal to allow the corporeal body to become obsolete in contemporary performance works, the force of this human encounter reverberates around the valuable experience of contact. Multi-media technology's increasing use of cyberspace in performance is one significant method of performance-making that enjoys the absence of the body and is symptomatic of a wider trend in contemporary performance. For me, immediate, sensory, responsive relations are tested and re-evaluated through the body's instinctive physiological impulses and sensory reflexes together with our mind's cognitive and reflexive consciousness. The impact of a One to One does not necessarily need to be as forceful or affective as the cases discussed in this chapter. Rather, the potential of this form to enable a shared desire to connect, engage and discover an 'other' elucidates a critical opportunity offered through the ephemeral liveness of live art: its aptitude for delivering relational experiences.

Notes

1. I made no notes at the time, so the performance description is a series of recollected fragments of memory alone.

2. I borrow these terms from Ang Bartram, who used them in the title of a paper on her practice at the live and digital-art programme event *Intimacy: Across Visceral and Digital Performance* (2007). See www.goldsmiths.ac.uk/intimacy (accessed 11 March 2010) for details.

3. See Amelia Jones, *Body Art: Performing the Subject* (Minneapolis, MN, 1998).

4. An article exploring my experience of *My Mother* and another of O'Reilly's works, *Untitled Action: NRLA, The Arches, Glasgow*, has recently been published in *Theatre Research International*, 35(1) (2010) under the title 'Revisiting Catharsis in Contemporary Live Art Practice: Kira O'Reilly's Evocative Skin Works'.

5. http://www.fiercetv.co.uk/index.php?controller=event&mm_action=view&id=141. Accessed 20 October 2009.

6. Peggy Phelan, *Mourning Sex: Performing Public Memories* (London and New York, 1997), p. 17.

7. Lauren Berlant, *Intimacy* (Chicago, IL, 2000), p. 1.

8. Dominic Johnson proposed the notion of a 'continuum of intimacy' at *Intimacy: Across Visceral and Digital Performance*. In an unpublished paper from the *Intimacy* symposium, Johnson suggests 'In common parlance, to be "overly intimate" with another's body implies abuse, and clearly positions this relation within the (traditionally utopian) domain of intimacy. If the abusive encounter constitutes an upper limit of intimacy – another's touch that takes more than it gives – its opposite extreme is the experience of the touch to which one returns too little, where intimacy with another – sexual or otherwise – is closer to solitude or abandonment. Intimacy is therefore seemingly bounded by danger, risk and other troubling eventualities, such that too little or too much intimacy augurs of a dereliction.' Johnson pursues this thesis through performance, posing a 'continuum of intimacy' that includes both abandonment and abuse.

9. I borrow this title from New York performance art activist Karen Finley's publication *A Different Kind of Intimacy* (New York, 2000). The publication contains performance texts and candid reflections on Finley's extensive experience of making uncompromising performance works.

10. R.D. Laing, *The Divided Self: An Existential Study in Sanity and Madness* (Harmondsworth, 1960), p. 16. Emphasis in original.

11. Stanton B. Garner, *Bodied Spaces: Phenomenology and Performance in Contemporary Drama* (Ithaca, NY, 1995), p. 13.

12. Jennifer Fisher (ed.), *Technologies of Intuition* (Ontario, Canada, 2006), p. 27.

13. I have reported on the last two of these hilarious nights for *Dance Theatre Journal*. See 'Gay Shame 2008: Duckie Gets Macho', *Dance Theatre Journal*, 23(2) (2009), pp. 20–26, and, forthcoming, 'Gay Shame 2009: Gay Shame Goes Girly', *Dance Theatre Journal*.

14. Phelan, *Mourning Sex*, p. 59.

15. For a detailed discussion of my assertions that *Locker Piece* could be considered the first (albeit accidental) One to One performance, see 'Intimate Inter-actions: Returning to the Body in One to One Performance', *Body, Space, Technology Journal*, 6(1) (2006).

16. C. Carr, *On Edge: Performance at the End of the Twentieth Century* (London and New York, 1994), p. 18.

17. Oliver Grau, *Virtual Art: From Illusion to Immersion*, trans. Gloria Custance (Cambridge, MA, 2003), p. 205.

18. Lauren Berlant, 'Intimacy: A Special Issue', *Critical Inquiry*, 24 (1998), p. 281.
19. See particularly Phelan, *Mourning Sex*.
20. Kirk J. Schneider, 'R.D. Laing's Existential–Humanistic Practice: What Was He Actually Doing?', *The Psychoanalytic Review*, 87(4) (2000), p. 597.
21. Franko B in 'Explicating Intercourse: Excerpts from a Dialogue on One to One Performance with Franko B', in Rachel Zerihan and Oreet Ashery, Franko B, Ang Bartram, Jess Dobkin, Davis Freeman/Random Scream, Adrian Howells, Dominic Johnson, Eirini Kartsaki, Leena Kela, Berni Louise, Susana Mendes Silva, Kira O'Reilly, Jiva Parthipan, Michael Pinchbeck, Sam Rose, Samantha Sweeting and Martina Von Holn, *Live Art Development Agency Study Room Guide on One to One Performance* (2009), http://www.thisisliveart.co.uk/resources/Study_Room/guides/Rachel_Zerihan. html, p. 10.
22. For a first-hand account of this piece, see Emma Safe, 'Come Into My Parlour', in *The Guardian* (25 May 2002), http://www.guardian.co.uk/artanddesign/2002/may/25/artsfeatures.books1. Accessed 12 November 2009.
23. Franko B in 'Explicating Intercourse', p. 11.
24. *Ibid.*
25. *Ibid.*, p. 12.
26. Elizabeth Grosz, *Volatile Bodies: Toward a Corporeal Feminism* (Bloomington and Indianapolis, IN, 1994), p. 196.
27. Ang Bartram in Zerihan *et al.*, *Live Art Development Agency Study Room Guide on One to One Performance* (2009), http://www.thisisliveart.co.uk/resources/Study_Room/guides/Rachel_Zerihan.html, p. 20.
28. Jiva Parthipan in *Ibid.*, p. 59.
29. Vivian Sobchack, *Carnal Thoughts: Embodiment and Moving Image Culture* (Berkeley, CA, Los Angeles, CA, and London, 2004), p. 2.

13

Saint Nick: a parallax view of Nick Cave

David Pattie

I don't know what you're all about, but I like the way you handle yourself on stage.[1]

Cave and his shadows

On stage in Paris in 2001, Nick Cave, appropriately, is bathed in red light: during the opening song ('Do You Love Me', from the album *Let Love In*), he comes to the front of the stage and delivers the lyrics directly to the front row of the audience, his finger jabbing at the faces in the crowd. He wears an immaculate suit and a crisp white shirt. His hair is long, but carefully and simply cut: he is clean-shaven and manicured – in contrast to the rest of the Bad Seeds, whose stage suits are rather more idiosyncratic (Blixa Bargeld wears a black suit, waistcoat and shirt), if not downright shabby (Warren Ellis looks as though he slept in the suit he is wearing). The red wash that covers the stage seems a fitting accompaniment to the song: 'Do You Love Me' is, as the name suggests, about love – but it is about a love tinged with the disturbingly erotic and the apocalyptic. Under these lights, Cave and the band are the epitome of a peculiarly American Gothic: the hellfire preacher and his reprobate crew, cutting a violently erotic swathe through the bible belt, a carnival mixture of religious probity, overt respectability, twisted sex, pain and death.

That Cave should apparently present himself and his band as the musical incarnations of William Faulkner or Flannery O'Connor should come as no surprise to his fanbase. Cave's fascination with the darker and rather more *outré* aspects of US culture has been public knowledge since the days of The Birthday Party, the band that first brought him a measure

of notoriety in the early 1980s. In an *NME* article, Cave and Rowland
Howard (the Birthday Party's guitarist) listed their 'consumer faves':

> the touchstone list included [Flannery O'Connor's] *Wiseblood*, Johnny
> Cash, Evel Knievel, Robert Mitchum in *Night of the Hunter*, Caroline
> Jones (a.k.a. Morticia from *The Addams Family*), Lee Hazlewood, and
> Raymond Chandler ...²

The first song that Cave recorded with the Bad Seeds ('Saint Huck', on the
band's first album) told of the sordid death of Mark Twain's archetypal
American free spirit, Huck Finn, in a modern, corrupt and venal America.
Cave's first novel, *And the Ass Saw the Angel* (1989), describes the murderous career of Euchrid Eucrow, a mute psychotic who comes to believe that
he is God's avenging angel; his exploits are set in a version of the American
South which easily outdoes anything in Cormac McCarthy. One of his
most famous songs, 'Tupelo', conflates God, Satan and Elvis Presley;
another, 'The Mercy Seat', is a hallucinatory imagining of a convict's last
few hours on Death Row.

All performers in popular music, as they build up a performance history
in front of an audience, find that certain readings predominate; and it is fair
to say that, in Cave's case, the influence of his early work still determines the
way his performances are read. However, even though at first glance Cave
would seem to be easily understandable, he has generated a surprisingly
varied number of analyses; and his image shifts from something fixed and
certain to something evanescent and almost impossible to determine. It
could be said that, in the performance described above, we have a visible
symbol of the sheer difficulty of determining the relationship between
Cave and his material. Two lights have been deliberately placed at ground
level, angling slightly upward so that two shadows are cast on the walls
on either side of the venue. Given that Cave's default position is on the lip
of the stage, these shadows feature heavily in the performance; they loom
over the audience, recalling nothing so much as the famously animated
shadow of the vampire in Murnau's *Nosferatu*. The two shadows are, it
seems, an integral part of the *mise-en-scène* of the performance and of the
persona that Cave projects – and not just for this tour (they are used again
in 2004, for example).

It is worthwhile reflecting on these shadows: they take a moment that usually signifies the authentic investment of the performer in the ideology of popular music performance, and they stylise and abstract the performance choices which generally serve to demonstrate that investment. Although in one respect they might be easily read (these are the shadows that would necessarily accompany all the darkness, all the death, that forms the world of the songs), they might also, perhaps, recall a rather more ambiguous use of the shadow motif in Cave's lyrics; in particular, the lines from 'Black Crow King' ('I just made a simple gesture / They jumped up and nailed it to my shadow'[3] – a line which suggests strongly that everything the song's protagonist does will be misread and misapplied. These shadows are fixed, and shifting: they suggest ambiguity, while at the same time strongly indicating (if only through association) one particular, overdetermined meaning. In performance, they simultaneously re-enforce and amplify the choices made by Cave the performer; they also serve as a distraction, drawing our attention away from the stage. Whatever meanings accrue to Nick Cave the pop-cultural icon, whatever links there are between him and the songs that he sings, emerge from the complex dance between Cave and his various shadows.

Interpreting Cave

> The older a person gets the more different things are in his mind – sex and death. In that order.[4]

Anyone whose engagement with Cave's work is more than merely casual might wonder at the above quote: sex and death seem to have been pretty much constant features of Cave's imaginative world since The Boys Next Door. This is not to say that sex and death feature in the same way throughout a career which now stretches back over thirty years. In his work with the Bad Seeds, for example, the high-water mark of Southern Gothic comes in the albums of the 1980s, from From Her to Eternity to Tender Prey – very roughly covering the period during which Cave was writing his first novel. Since this period, Cave's writing for a while lost some of its eschatological fury; he began to draw inspiration from the New, rather than the Old, Testament; and in the latter half of the 90s, with The Boatman's

Call, he seemed, in Emma McEvoy's dismissive phrase, to have 'entered the world of ego-psychology'.[5] Since then, the albums *Abattoir Blues/The Lyre of Orpheus* and *Dig!!! Lazarus, Dig!!!*, as well as the *Grinderman* side-project, seem to have shaken Cave loose from conventional balladry and back toward more apocalyptic subject matter.

However, when Cave is interviewed, or when non-academic articles are written about his work, the image that emerges is strongly influenced by the more notorious parts of the singer's past (his long-standing heroin addiction, the streak of apparent self-destructiveness which he manifested during the 1980s). For example, Gary Mulholland, interviewing Cave in the wake of the release of *Murder Ballads*, begins his *Time Out* piece with a parodic roll-call of Caveian clichés:

> When I mentioned to various voyeurs of my acquaintance that I was interviewing singer, novelist and leading purveyor of darkly humorous musical stories concerning death, sex, God, hellfire, and death Nick Cave, and that I had been invited to his flat, they all insisted I check out his bathroom. I knew what they wanted: walls covered in crucifixes; details of grisly murders on customized toilet paper; a bath painted black and decorated with various rivers to which numerous beautiful and treacherous women had been taken to die.[6]

This is a trope picked up by Thomas Bartlett, whose 2004 article is called 'The Resurrection of Nick Cave', and Simon Hattenstone, whose 2008 interview (entitled, with a fair degree of inevitability, 'Old Nick') contains the following: 'There is something terse and scary about Cave – which is not surprising, considering he's spent so long modelling himself as a modern-day Beelzebub. ...'[7]

Similarly, one of the earliest academic analyses of Cave, in Simon Reynolds and Joy Press's *The Sex Revolts: Gender, Rebellion and Rock and Roll* (1994), was as unambiguous as any magazine article or interview. The book none-too-subtly elided Cave and the protagonists in his work: their lust and their violence came directly from a streak of romantic misogyny in Cave himself. More generally, however, academics assume that there is some distance between Cave and his various protagonists. Susan Broadhurst argues that Cave is a liminal performer, operating in an indeterminate space marked out by irony, fragmentation and the inversion or suppression of conventional hierarchies. For Broadhurst, Cave qualifies as a liminal performer because the passion and violence of his work are always tempered by a 'partial commitment to duplicity'.[8] Bannister lumps Cave in with a category of popular musician that he terms 'the sadistic intellectual'; a type of artist whose approach to even the most extreme material is primarily aesthetic – with acts of bloody, sexualised violence treated, on record and in performance, with a detached irony.[9] Emma McEvoy (2007) notes that the ironic approach that Cave takes to much of the material on his earlier albums is part of an inherently Gothic worldview. Interestingly, unlike Bannister, she does not see the use of irony as a device which keeps Cave separate from the world that he describes (at least, in the early days; McEvoy is less impressed by Cave's later work, from *The Boatman's Call* onwards). The investment that Cave makes, according to McEvoy, even in the most violent material, is not offered up to the audience as detached parody; there is something hyperbolic about certain songs, but in performance they are delivered with as much passion as the rest of the material, as though they are vessels through which Cave might attain transcendence.

For the contributors to the recent collection of essays, *Cultural Seeds: Essays on the Work of Nick Cave* (2007), the idea of Cave as a fragmented, contradictory artist is pretty much a given. This splitting manifests itself in an apparently overt investment in the tropes of Romanticism, which Cave follows to and past the point of absurdity;[10] the gendered ambiguity of Cave's body, in early performances with The Birthday Party;[11] and, most overtly, in his religious faith. As Lyn McCredden points out, for Cave:

[The] world of abjection and violence, of elusive erotic possibilities, of loved and degraded flesh ... bodes forth the sacred. Dreaming of another place of mercy and justice beyond the fleshed word sometimes leads Cave to separate the sacred and the profane. However, his complex poetic theology also reaches for a vision of sacred and profane, flesh and spirit, as already everywhere in this world.[12]

In other essays, Chris Bilton teases out the inherent contradictions in Cave's attitude to celebrity and Angela Jones unearths contradictions in

228

the apparently stripped-down rock of *Grinderman* – an album which, as she notes, starts with Cave's fulsome declaration of a return to first principles:

> [*Grinderman*] appears to strip away the trappings of fame and stardom, to take the audience behind the scenes, and to expose a glimpse of the 'real me' behind the rock star. And yet, all that is revealed, in the end, is a performance; it is the gesture itself – the gesture of stripping down – which is held up for the audience's listening pleasure.[13]

It is tempting to conclude that writing about Cave is either monolithic (the same concerns, returned to time and time again) or kaleidoscopic (presenting an image of Cave which is shifting and unfixed). The academic commentators, with the exception of Reynolds and Press, see the relation between Cave and his work as ambiguous. And yet Cave does not have a public image that is as fragmented as the academic discussions suggest. It is rather fixed – the template established early in his career has undergone some variations, but these variations have largely been determined by changes in the public perception of his life. Also, in performance, the fragmentation, the irony and the parody that academics discern in his performances is enacted by a man whose image has stayed more or less fixed since the early 1980s. We have, it seems, two contradictory views (broadly typed as the academic and the popular) of Cave's work; there is a consensus that his territory is clearly staked out, but Cave's position in that territory shifts depending on the viewpoint of the observer.

Cave is perfectly aware that the relation between his life and his work is necessarily ambiguous, as he put it in a 2008 interview:

> Songs can become excruciatingly personal so you can't help writing in a guarded way ... So lyric writing is obscuring the truth, writing in a way that doesn't reveal all that much about yourself ...[14]

In other words, he is distanced from his songs, but the exact distance is hard to define. In performance, this distance raises an interesting question. The idea of authentic communication as a key feature of the ideology of rock music has been comprehensively critiqued by a number of authors,[15] and the role of the live event as a moment of authentic communication has also been examined, although not with the same comprehensiveness or acuity.[16] As I have argued elsewhere, the idea that the gig itself confirms that the performer is both capable of performing the music, and is capable of performing the music as though it means as much to them as it does to the most dedicated fan, rests on a paradoxical reading of the event, where the term 'performance' is both positive and negative. It is positive because the performer must put on a good show – that is, engage in a style of performance appropriate to the genre and to the performance history established by the performer and others who work in the same style. It is negative because the term performance connotes something premeditated, something which prevents the performer from investing him or herself fully in the moment of performance, and therefore something which is performatively empty.

In Cave's performances, though, something more overtly paradoxical seems to be taking place. Cave, as I note above, thrives on close contact with the audience: even when there is a substantial forestage area he will tend to occupy the strip right at the stage's edge. However, there is undeniably something theatrical about his songs and the vocal and performative styles he adopts: something as stylised as the silhouettes projected on the walls of the venue. Cave is not a naturally tuneful singer (although, as his career develops, he does learn to bring his tuning under control); nor is he a particularly good actor (his performance in *Ghosts ... of the Civil Dead* notwithstanding). He is, however, an adept vocal performer, very skilled at blending speech and singing in a manner which animates his lyrics (note, for example, the way the voice becomes increasingly uncertain as the narrative of 'Dig!!! Lazarus Dig!!!' unfolds; the very subtle, but revealing, harshness in 'Song of Joy' from *Murder Ballads* – a vocal delivery which, on its own, implicates the singer in the murder of his wife and children). We therefore have a performative paradox: the vocalist who seems to struggle with his demons in front of our eyes also performs in character. Unlike other rock performers (Bowie as Ziggy Stardust; the composite hobo-poet crafted by Tom Waits; Eminem's trinity of personae – Eminem/Marshall Mathers/Slim Shady) Cave does not tease the audience by blurring the relation between character, performer and song. However, for all the directness, and for all the angst and energy that Cave has always been able to summon, it is never entirely clear whose struggles we witness. On stage, the apparently singular Cave is surrounded by shadows: the shadows of his own performance history, certainly, but also the shadows of the characters he creates.

In his monumental work *The Parallax View*, Slavoj Žižek deals with a problem that bedevils the process of interpretation: the co-presence of irreconcilable readings of subjects, objects, events and ideas. Characteristically, he approaches this question through Hegel; not the Hegel of transcendental idealism, but an inverted Hegel (similar to Žižek's inverted Freud) who is the theorist of unresolvable, dialectically opposed antinomies. To describe this in operation, Žižek invokes the idea of the parallax.

> The standard definition of parallax is: the apparent displacement of an object (the shift of its position against a background), caused by a change in observational position that provides a new line of sight. The philosophical twist to be added, of course, is that the observed difference is not simply 'subjective', due to the fact that the same object which exists 'out there' is seen from two different stances, or points of view. It is rather that, as Hegel would have it, subject and object are inherently 'mediated', so that an 'epistemological' shift in the subject's point of view always reflects an 'ontological' shift in the subject itself.[17]

It is not, in other words, that meanings accrue around the central core of a subject; on the contrary, a subject exists because of the contradictory readings that it opens up. As Žižek puts it, 'Parallax means that the bracketing itself produces its object …';[18] and the process of bracketing an object does not reflect or distort an essential, unchanging self. Rather, the self exists at the point at which it is defined, or at the point at which it defines itself.

> [W]hen I say 'I' – when I designate 'myself' as 'I' – this very act of signifying something adds to the 'real flesh and blood entity' (inclusive of the content of its mental states, desires, attitudes) thus designated, and the subject is that X which is added to the designated content by means of the act of its self-referential designation. It is therefore

231

misleading to say that the unity of the I is 'a mere fiction' beneath which there is the multitude of inconsistent mental processes: the point is that this fiction gives rise to 'effects in the Real,' that is to say, it acts as a necessary presupposition to a series of 'real' acts.[19]

Adrian Johnson notes that this analysis incorporates the inverted Hegelianism described above alongside the Lacanian framework that informs much of Žižek's writing, and a line of argument derived from current scientific thinking about the relation between mind and body.[20] Žižek argues that recent discoveries about the nature of thought (discoveries which would place the perception of having thought at the centre of the self's conception of the self) imply that the philosophical conception of identity needs to change, and change radically: this change in our perception of the direction of thought (from electrical impulse to conscious cognition, rather than the other way around) means that 'there is no "true substance" to the Self beneath its self-appearance ... the Self "is" its own appearance to itself.'[21]

In performance, and especially in the type of performances given by musicians like Cave, the application of a parallax view which sees the self as composed of incommensurate images and narratives could be very useful. It would take us away from the rather simplistic argument put forward by Auslander that performers in certain forms of popular music shift between personae as actors move from role to role;[22] a Žižekian perception of the same process would suggest that what is happening is rather the subject's ceaseless movement through a series of performative selves, each one the result of a refocusing of the self's appearance to itself (and of the self's appearance to others). There is ample evidence from the interviews that Cave has given over the years that he recognises this. In 1994 he noted:

I'm actually becoming more and more concerned about writing about myself and writing a far more personal kind of lyrics, but still very often putting it into a narrative form as if I'm telling some kind of story. I often times use characters to tell these kinds of stories instead of an I, I, I kind of story, but it shouldn't be assumed that these things aren't a part of my life.[23]

This quote makes an interesting companion-piece to the quote given above, in which Cave is wary about the possibility of direct self-revelation. The two statements, however, are not mutually exclusive: rather, they can be thought of as two acts of self-referential designation, one asserting a distance between Cave and the characters he creates, one asserting proximity (which is itself difficult to determine; the characters reflect Cave, but in a way which cannot be easily defined). As a description of the dance between Cave and his various shadow-selves, both quotes can exist as part of a parallax view of the relation between the artist and his work.

Saint Nick: parallax performances

Before the Bad Seeds launch into a performance of 'Saint Huck' (on *God is in the House*), an enthusiastic fan shouts, 'Saint Nick'. As an illustration of what could be described as an unwittingly parallax view of Cave's relation to his material, his performance and his fans, this title is hard to better. It suggests, in one neat package, saints, the Devil, Cave himself, his songs and the adulation both he and his work attract. It is fitting, also, that the phrase was uttered during a live performance, because it is here, more than anywhere, that the multiple readings that Cave generates are given an apparently unified form.

'From Her to Eternity': Amsterdam 1991

Cave takes a step back to the middle of the stage; rocking back and forward on the balls of his feet, he speaks the song's first line unaccompanied. 'I wanna tell you about a girl'[24] is one of the most famous openings of any Bad Seeds track. On record it is almost thrown away; Cave mutters the words ten seconds after the jerky, one-note vamp that runs through the song has begun. On stage, in contrast, neither he, the band nor the audience are in any doubt of the song's iconic status. As soon as Cave speaks, the audience begin to cheer and whistle; the band crash in; and Cave bellows the line again, bent double by the force of his delivery, the microphone jammed tight against his mouth. Cave's reading of the song is impassioned, with clear peaks of total investment. He is buffeted by the music; he throws himself into the song, unleashing the large-scale gestures for those moments when the volume peaks (leaping into the air and slamming down on his knees on the third chorus), and making small, appropriate illustrative choices when delivering the lyrics (while singing, he mimes the track of tears down his cheek). In other words, Cave gives every sign of being the archetypal rock performer, completely overwhelmed by the music.

Except for two things. Firstly, Cave's clothing: it is very rare for a rock performer to wear a suit. Generally, it either signifies a genre (the immaculately coiffed soul/R&B artist, for example) or it is parodic and hyperbolic (two classic examples of this would be the oversized suit worn by Talking Heads' David Byrne, or Wayne Coyne of the Flaming Lips, whose white cotton suit usually ends up covered in stage blood). As noted above, Cave's suit is understated (certainly at this point in his career: we will, however, return to this point later); it does not exist in the same performative universe as either Cave's performance style or his general appearance (during this period, Cave was extremely thin; his hair was at its longest and worn swept back from his forehead). By the time that 'From Her to Eternity' is performed, Cave has worked up a sweat, and his jacket has been jettisoned. Most of the time, when clothing is removed by musicians in performance it is to demonstrate either sexual power or physical dynamism; in Cave's case, though, losing his jacket leaves him oddly private and vulnerable – he looks thinner, more unkempt and rather desperate.

This paradoxical weakness chimes with the content of the track: a tale of desire gone sour, in which the narrator is unhealthily fixated on an unseen woman. This scenario is pursued to the point of hyperbolic excess; so much so that it threatens to collapse into melodramatic absurdity. This possibility is glancingly referred to in the lyrics ('I know it sounds absurd ...').[25] In performance, however, this moment is foregrounded: the music quietens, as Cave sits awkwardly on the edge of the stage, his legs straddling the monitor speakers. The line is spoken: it is directed to the audience, and more specifically, to people in the front row. The line, in this context, is both part of the accepted performance of the song and a comment on the song's performance. Just for this moment, the possibility opens up that Cave understands how far the narrative of the song, and his over-wrought performance, can take him – and the delivery of the line stands at an ironic distance from the material. However, the irony is not so marked that it violates or disrupts the emotional investment that Cave brings to the rest of the performance. Rather, both these readings – passionate investment and ironic detachment – exist in unresolved tension.

'God is in the House': Paris 2001
Cave sits at the piano, picking out the song's introductory chords: as the band join in, he settles himself, smoothing his hair down. The music pauses for an instant and, slightly behind the beat, Cave starts to sing. 'God is in the House', from *No More Shall We Part*, deals with the practice of religious faith – an issue that has exercised Cave throughout his career. In 'The Secret Life of the Love Song' Cave makes an explicit link between his preferred material and his faith. Unsurprisingly, he does not see the path to God as smooth; rather, the expression of faith in his work is bound up with pain, desire and death:

> Though the Love Song comes in many guises ... they all address God, for it is the haunted presence of longing that the true Love Song inhabits. It is a howl in the void for love and for comfort, and it lives on the lips of the child crying for his mother. It is the song of the lover in need of their loved one, the raving of the lunatic supplicant petitioning his god. It is the cry of one chained to the earth and craving flight, a flight into inspiration and imagination and divinity.[26]

Given this definition, 'God is in the House' is an anti-love song. The narrator prides himself on the fact that his community has completely eschewed howling, raving or crying. He is at pains to establish that everything in his 'little town'[27] is calm and quiet: it is only by meticulously extracting all passion from life, by expunging the erotic, the violent and the disturbing, that a fitting setting can be created – one that will allow God fully to manifest himself. However, as the above quote suggests, this is the wrong way to go about it; and the song finishes with the narrator pleading, desperately, for a moment of incarnation which simply will not come.

One might expect that a performance of the song would stress its irony. This, though, is not what Cave does; the performance is entirely honest – or, rather, all of the performance codes he uses are ones that signify complete investment. As I note elsewhere, there is a characteristic moment which informs performances by singer-songwriters like Joni Mitchell; a moment where the singer closes their eyes, shuts off any connection with the audience or the other musicians, and seems to be communing with his or her muse. It signifies an absolute, unironic investment in the material; this, Cave seems to be saying, is something I mean, something I will not fake because I cannot. And yet this performance is played out in front of an audience that is fully aware of Cave's life and the rest of his work; they know that the character who sings this song is not the Cave revealed in most of his songs. In performance, we have the enactment of Will Self's comment that this song 'demonstrates Cave's ability to ironise, then re-ironise again, engendering a dizzying vortex as received values are sucked down the pointed plughole'.[28] For example, there is a moment near the song's end when Cave brings his voice down to a whisper: and on the final word of the line 'if we all hold hands and quietly shout / hallelujah ...'[29] his voice cracks, and his face registers effortful pain. From there, the song builds to its last cry ('God is in the house / oh, I wish he would come out ...'[30]); and the audience respond as though this were an authentic gospel song. This response, on cue as it were, is all of a piece with Cave's performance: if the content were less obviously ironic, we would have no compunction about accepting the performance and the response at face value. Self is right: the performance ironises and re-ironises the song, and the destruction of 'received values' that the song demonstrates is achieved in performance through the unironic replication of those very values.

'We Call Upon the Author': London 2008

At some point after the release of *Abattoir Blues/The Lyre of Orpheus*, Cave rediscovered noise. The piano-led ballads disappeared, and in the *Grinderman* project, and on *Dig!!! Lazarus, Dig!!!*, Cave and his fellow musicians produced music which harked back to the fragmented, atonal tracks on the band's earlier albums. Lyrically and melodically Cave's approach was noticeably less polished than it had been in previous albums; a neat fit between expressive lyrics and smooth melodies was replaced by a vocal style that alternated between conversation and harangue. On stage, Cave's image underwent a similar transformation: the most obvious sign was a large moustache, which grew down past Cave's mouth on both sides, making him look like a particularly disreputable riverboat gambler. This change was compounded by others; filmed in 2008 in London, Cave wore purple trousers and a striped shirt, half unbuttoned – a rather more louche version of the Cave the audience had come to know. This new Cave was, in effect, a variation on the old template: the trousers were still part of a suit, and the moustache harked back to the excessive hair of the 1980s. The subject matter of the songs was, similarly, not too far removed from the rest of Cave's work: God, sex and death still featured, although were less closely allied than on previous albums. The track 'We Call Upon the Author', for example, does not invoke God's will as the pretext for violent death; rather, it rails against a God who is perhaps ineffectual or downright malicious. However, this is not a disciplined diatribe: the imagery Cave employs is extreme ('Myxamatoid kids spraddle the streets',[31] for example), and his delivery is a determinedly unmelodic (and occasionally arrhythmic) rant. Twice, the flow of the rant is broken by the invocation 'Prolix!/Prolix!/ Nuthin' a pair of scissors can't fix!',[32] as though the narrator of the song is himself aware that there might be no end to the list, and that there is something Sisyphean in his attempt to itemise it.

In performance, most of the song is delivered via a familiar series of performance tropes: the direct address to the audience, the finger raised in admonition. However, the variation of Cave's basic stage costume complicates the image: the version of the suit he wears simply does not fit the conventional way that such a performance style might be read. The costume and the moustache help to tip Cave's performance from impassioned diatribe to bizarre black comedy; he looks like a lounge lizard aping a Pentecostal preacher. There are other contributing factors: the stylised pose that Cave adopts when he moves back from the audience to play the organ positioned centre stage – he plays with his body turned to the audience, his left arm raised, as though he is riding a surfboard. Warren Ellis, his hair and beard long and unkempt, acts as a performative foil for Cave; his gestures mirror the singer's, except that Ellis, strangely, is crouched on his haunches over a range of effects pedals, playing them as though they were themselves an instrument. When the band provides backing vocals, Ellis joins in: but the microphone is tilted at an awkward angle, and to sing into it Ellis has to bend backward like a limbo dancer. Most strikingly, on the line quoted above ('Prolix! / Prolix! / …'), Cave does a parodic bump and grind as the music moves from a straightforward four by four beat to something altogether funkier; these moves irresistibly suggest an older man's desperate attempt at cool. To borrow from the world of Cave's fiction for a moment, it is as though Bunny Munro, the sexually predatory salesman anti-hero of *The Death of Bunny Munro*, had wandered by mistake into the territory occupied by the characters in *And the Ass Saw the Angel*; and he simply cannot react to this new territory with the seriousness it seems to deserve.

Conclusion: shadowing Cave

As Žižek notes, Lacan in his seminar on the ethics of psychoanalysis:

> claims that 'the sovereign Good is das Ding' [This] identification of the highest Good with the evil Thing can be properly understood only as involving a parallax shift; the very thing which, viewed from a proper distance, looks like the supreme Good changes into repulsive Evil the moment we come too near it ... [There] is no substantial difference between the God of love and the God of excessive, arbitrary cruelty ...[33]

An interesting notion, when placed alongside the supposed development of Cave's theology described above: the journey from a vengeful God to a loving God is not as great, perhaps, as it might at first appear. After all, even in the tenderest of Cave's love songs (for example, 'Are You The One That I've Been Waiting For' from *The Boatman's Call*) we are never far from the threat of destruction. However, this is not the only opposition in play in Cave's performances: in practice, the parallax view of God as loving and destructive (and, in fact, the intermingling of love, violence and death in Cave's work as a whole) plays against another opposition – this time between investment and distance. It is as though, in performance, Cave holds himself at the point where (to adopt the terminology Lacan uses) the God of love and the God of violence and death are both equally present; when, in Zizek's gloss, 'it is one and the same God who appears in a different light only due to a parallax shift of our perspective'.[34]

Lyrically, in each one of these performances, Cave worries around familiar themes: God, sex, violence and death jostle for position in each one of the songs (in 'From Her to Eternity' and 'We Call Upon the Author', they are insistently present: in 'God is in the House' they are present in absence – all the more apparent in the narrator's passionate desire to expunge their effects). In performance, in each instance, there are clear signs that Cave is invested in the material; there is passion enough here to satisfy the most die-hard fan. However, in each performance there are also clear signs of distance between Cave and his material; the nod to absurdity in 'From Her …', the passionate reading of a position that Cave does not espouse in 'God …', the nod toward comedy in 'We Call …', all cut against a simple reading that would conflate Cave and his work. In effect, when Cave performs his work, he never does so as a single, simple character: in each performance the songs are animated through a series of incommensurate performance choices, running in series and in parallel. To return to the opening image, it is as though Cave and his shadows shift position during performance, so that we are never sure which is authentic performance and which the stylised, abstracted, consciously performative choice. It is, in Žižek's terms, an exercise in parallax performance: and, as such, the relation between Cave and the excesses in his material remains a troubling one. We are never allowed an easy resolution that will either condemn Cave as a violent misogynist, whose apocalyptic fantasies are clearly manifest in his work, or on the other hand would safely contain the charge contained by the material in an all-embracing distanced irony. What we have, in Žižek's phrase, is a succession of real acts; each one built on the multiple self that Cave's performances explore. These real acts – those moments in performance where Cave incarnates the fury or the passion in his songs, or seems to – remain problematic, remain live, because they are never allowed to settle to a single, unifying reading.

Notes

1. *The Road to Who Knows Where*, Dir: Uli M. Schueppel, Mute Films/German Film Academy/Schueppel-films 1990
2. Simon Reynolds, *Rip It Up and Start Again* (London, 2005), p. 430.
3. Nick Cave, *The Complete Lyrics 1978–2007* (London, 2007), p. 109.
4. 'The Daily Grind', *HARP magazine* (May 2007).
5. Emma McEvoy, '"Now, who will be the witness/When you're all too healed to see?" The Sad Demise of Nick Cave', in *Gothic Studies*, 9(1) (2007), p. 87.
6. Gary Mulholland, 'If Looks Could Kill…', *Time Out* (1996)
7. Simon Hattenstone, 'Old Nick', *The Guardian*, 23 February 2008.
8. Susan Broadhurst, *Liminal Acts: A Critical Overview of Contemporary Performance and Theory* (London, 1999), p. 156.
9. Matthew Bannister, *White Boys White Noise: Masculinities and 1980s Indie Guitar Rock* (Aldershot, 2006).
10. Karen Welbery, 'Nick Cave and the Australian Language of Laughter', in Karen Welbery and Tanya Dalziell (eds), *Cultural Seeds: Essays on the Work of Nick Cave* (Aldershot, 2007).
11. Laknath Jayasinghe, 'Nick Cave, Dance Performance and the Production and Consumption of Masculinity', in Welbery and Dalziell, *Cultural Seeds*.
12. Lyn McCredden, 'Fleshed Sacred: The Carnal Theologies of Nick Cave', in Welbery and Dalziell, *Cultural Seeds*, p. 184.
13. Angela Jones, 'Grinderman: All Stripped Down', in Welbery and Dalziell, *Cultural Seeds*, p. 135.
14. Interview, *Mojo* (April 2008).
15. See Philip Auslander, *Liveness: Performance in a Mediatized Culture* (London, 1999); Simon Frith, *Performing Rites* (Oxford, 1998); Theodore Gracyk, *I Wanna Be Me: Rock Music and the Politics of Identity* (Philadelphia, 2001); Keir Keighley, 'Reconstructing Rock', in Simon Frith, Will Straw and John Street (eds), *The Cambridge Companion to Pop and Rock* (Cambridge, 2001); Allan Moore, 'Authenticity as Authentication', *Popular Music*, 21(2) (2002).
16. See Philip Auslander, 'Performance Analysis and Popular Music' in *Contemporary Theatre Review*, 4(1) (2004); Daniel Cavicchi, *Tramps Like Us: Music and Meaning among Springsteen Fans* (Oxford, 1998); Susan Fast, *In the Houses of the Holy: Led Zeppelin and the Power of Rock Music* (Oxford, 2001); Iain Inglis, *Performance and Popular Music* (Aldershot, 2007); Deena Weinstein, *Heavy Metal: The Music and its Culture* (New York, 2000).
17. Slavoj Žižek, *The Parallax View* (Cambridge, MA, 2006), p. 17.
18. *Ibid.*, p. 56.
19. *Ibid.*, pp. 244–5.
20. Adrian Johnson, 'Slavoj Žižek's Hegelian Reformation: Giving a Hearing to the Parallax View', *Diacritics*, 37(1) (2007).
21. Žižek, *The Parallax View*, p. 217.
22. Auslander, 'Performance Analysis and Popular Music'.
23. Interview, *Hypno Magazine* (December 1994)
24. Cave, *Complete Lyrics*, p. 84.
25. *Ibid.*
26. *Ibid.*, p. 7.
27. *Ibid.*, p. 324.
28. *Ibid.*, p. xii.
29. *Ibid.*, p. 325.

30. *Ibid.*, p. 325.
31. Nick Cave, 'We Call Upon the Author', *Dig!!! Lazarus, Dig!!!* (Mute Records, 2008).
32. *Ibid.*
33. Žižek, *The Parallax View*, p. 187.
34. *Ibid.*, p. 187.

14

Afterword: The corpse and its sexuality

Howard Barker

To resolve one paradox by substituting another: while the corpse by virtue of being insensate cannot be said to possess a sexuality any more than an intelligence or a personality, it might nevertheless be said to have the potential for acquiring a sexual character, and one not narrowly confined to the immutable fact of its gender, gender being a precondition of sexuality and not the confirmation of it.

In the living body the origin of the sexual character is only to a limited extent *sui generis*. Equally, it is the creation of those others who, encountering it in the public sphere, express by the quality of their regard the power of its fascination. Just so in the creation of character on stage, what is spoken of an individual is no less significant than what is spoken by it. It is therefore reasonable to say of the living body that its sexuality is simultaneously inherent and ascribed, and that these oscillate with one another, both to the enhancement and the detriment of the character itself.

By contrast, the sexual character of the corpse exists only in so far as it is beheld. No mutual stare, tentative or shameless, resolute or faltering from modesty, connects subject and object in this impenetrable cold. Reciprocation is abolished. If there is desire, it is a desire condemned or stimulated by the singular direction of its flow. To this extent the sexual character of the corpse partakes of the sculptural, and like sculpture is essentially a provocation to collective memory, conscious or unconscious sensuality and cultural pride.

The erotic status of the corpse lies precisely in the absence of those transactions which condition sexuality in mutually lived life, a thing perfectly understood but never articulated in the multitude of necrophiliac narratives extending from antiquity to the nineteenth century. The exquisite vacancy of the corpse is in utter contrast to the infinitely active plenitude of the living body with its cultural inhibitions and susceptibility to opinion. It is supremely acquiescent, if never strictly speaking, collaborative. Its bloodless character seems to indicate a fatigue, even a contempt, for the frantic interrogations of the social world, with its tedious vocabularies of seduction. This profoundly erotic absence is celebrated in the genre of the death-painting of the nineteenth century, and is the critical sub-text of the Dracula narrative, where the victims (or inamorata) of the vampire are essentially dead by virtue of being asleep (i.e. with neither will nor personality) and rapidly rendered bloodless by the act. It is not coincidence that the ecstasy of the living face in the climax of sexual love so uncannily reproduces the utter repose that follows the agony of death. In both moments, the burden of culture, the quarrel of souls, is abolished, and facial collapse is the evidence of a profound relief.

The aesthetic necrophilia of nineteenth-century painting finds its apotheosis in the subject of the anatomy class, a theme vying in popularity with the battlefield and distinguished by some of the same hierarchic categories (the great commander/the great surgeon, the massed ranks of soldiers/the packed theatre of anatomy, the killed/the cadaver). The sacrificial body is posed naked on a table, and the table intuitively evokes the bed (there are also sheets, and the white sheet, like the bridal gown, possesses its own ambiguities). Onto the as-yet unviolated corpse (conventionally female) the collective gaze of the students (conventionally male) is drawn with that ferocity or detached connoisseurship redolent of an aroused sexuality. For their delectation the surgeon flourishes the scalpel with which he will conduct operations as the general in the field wields maps or staffs. The cadaver of the female, formerly inviolable, formerly independent and, while provocative, untouchable in the public sphere, is now the property (and since he may dispose her limbs, the sexual property) of him who now assumes the right to intrude into her flesh (bloodless flesh, since the anatomical subject is never fresh but kept sufficiently long to eliminate the potential shock of bleeding) by that surgical technique known now as then as invasive. In the anatomy class the sexual character of the corpse is revealed as nowhere else as a provocative surface. What permeates her stillness is the prospect of infinite permission, something strangely akin to the absolute permission granted only through the intimacy of the greatest loves ... a permission subject to revocation in the living, and decay in the dead.

The corpse's inventory of absences (reluctance, discrimination, susceptibility to the *faux-pas*) renders it infinitely susceptible to imaginative inscription. The conventional representation of love makes Cupid blind, but his sightlessness not only originates in the wilful abolition of the shortcomings of the loved one (preferring not to know) but admits that in desire we ascribe (knowing only what we intend to know). The desirable is she upon whom we might impose a cherished fore-knowledge of the adorable – in effect, an erotic prejudice, and to this extent she may be said to have existed as opinion long before she materialised, a template of cultural and psychological origin. In lived love this ascription is necessarily tentative, both welcomed as gift and repudiated as charge, a fluctuating process calibrated by desire and refined by charm. In *Judith: A Parting from the Body* (The Wrestling School, 1995) charm is brutally extinguished by political expediency, but the murdered Holofernes becomes the lover precisely at the moment of his death. Headless he is the epitome of absence, in this case an absence of cultural and political hostility. Judith's passion for her enemy might have prevented the assassination for which she was the agent, but she is sufficiently disciplined to suffocate desire in the interests of the state. Only a violent nostalgia compels her to attempt an intimacy with a man denied to her in life but now rendered innocuous (and necessarily impotent) by death. A peculiar hygiene therefore attaches to the necrophiliac act.

The sexual character ascribed to the corpse, in its abolition of that volatility so ecstatically demanded by a living love, anticipates that condition to which all passion aspires in its apotheosis, the cease of argument, a stop to words. The act of love remains – for all the hypothesising of a neurotic culture as to its conditions and its cause – an act, experienced by some as wordless, by others through a rhetoric of abuse or adoration, but in either case brought to that condition of extremity inextricably associated with fatality, the *cry* ...

The end of all passionate encounters is the truce, a suspension of conflict not only inside the erotic partnership but extending its benign pause to the unceasing friction of the material world. This exquisite hiatus the corpse in its testamental stillness eloquently describes. In its imitation of post-coital repose – the relaxed jaw, the half-closed eyes dismissive of the active world – the cadaver represents the most disconcerting visual experience known to man, provoking us to flee its presence in a savage longing to affirm whatever remains to us of lived existence but, in a supreme paradox, simultaneously inviting us to enjoy this affirmation in its most vital form: where else but in the sexual, thereby returning us over and over again to the haunting spectacle of its extirpation …

Bibliography

Ades, Dawn and Baker, Simon, *Undercover Surrealism: Georges Bataille and Documents* (London, 2006)

Adorno, Theodor W., *Minima Moralia: Reflections from Damaged Life*, trans. E.F.N. Jephcott (London, 1978)

Aspden, Peter, Review of *XXX*, *Financial Times* (25 April 2003). Reprinted in *Theatre Record*, 23(9) (2003)

Assmann, Jan, *Die Zauberflöte. Oper und Mysterium* (Munich, 2005)

Athey, Ron, 'Some Thoughts on the Politics of the Body and the Problematics of Documentation', in Manuel Vason, Lois Keidan and Ron Athey, *Exposures* (London, 2002)

Auslander, Philip, *Liveness: Performance in a Mediatized Culture* (London, 1999)

Auslander, Philip, 'Performance Analysis and Popular Music', in *Contemporary Theatre Review*, 4(1) (2004)

Badley, Linda, *Film, Horror and the Body Fantastic* (Westport, CT, 1995)

Bakhtin, Mikhail, *Rabelais and His World*, trans. Hélène Iswolsky (Bloomington, IN, 1984)

Bannister, Matthew, *White Boys White Noise: Masculinities and 1980s Indie Guitar Rock* (Aldershot, 2006)

Barker, Howard, *Arguments for a Theatre*, 3rd edn (Manchester, 1997)

Barker, Howard, *Collected Plays Vol. 1* (London, 1990)

Barker, Howard, *Collected Plays Vol. 5* (London, 2001)

Barker, Howard, *Death, The One and the Art of Theatre* (London, 2005)

Barker, Howard, *The Fence in its Thousandth Year* (London, 2005)

Barker, Howard, *Gertrude – The Cry* (London, 2002)

Barker, Howard, *Plays: One* (London, 2006)

Barker, Howard, *Plays: Two* (London, 2006)

Barker, Howard (with Thomas Middleton), *Women Beware Women* (London, 1989)

Barker, Howard, 'The Ethics of Relevance and the Triumph of the Literal', in Margarete Rubik and Elke Mettinger-Schartmann (eds), *(Dis) Continuities: Trends and Traditions in Contemporary Theatre and Drama in English* (Trier, 2002)

Barker, Howard, 'Introduction' to *Seven Lears* (London, 1990)

Barker, Howard, Programme Notes, *Gertrude – The Cry* (The Wrestling School, London, 2002)

Barker, Howard and Houth, Eduardo, *A Style and Its Origins* (London, 2007)

Barthes, Roland, *Mythologies*, trans. and ed. Annette Lavers (London, 1972)

Bataille, Georges, *The Absence of Myth: Writings on Surrealism*, trans. Michael Richardson (London and New York, 1994)

Bataille, Georges, *Erotism: Death and Sensuality*, trans. Mary Dalwood (San Francisco, 1986)

Bataille, Georges, *Visions of Excess: Selected Writings, 1927–1939*, ed. Allan Stoekl, trans. Allan Stoekl with Carl R. Lovitt and Donald M. Leslie Jr (Minneapolis, MN, 1985)

Baudrillard, Jean, *Seduction*, trans. Brian Singer (New York, 1990)

Baudrillard, Jean, *Symbolic Exchange and Death*, trans. Iain Hamilton Grant (London, 1993)

Beckett, Samuel, *The Complete Dramatic Works* (London, 1986)

Bellonci, Maria, *Lucrezia Borgia* (London, 2000)

Benjamin, Walter, *The Arcades Project* (Cambridge, MA, 1999)

Benn, Maurice B., *The Drama of Revolt: A Critical Study of Georg Büchner* (Cambridge, 1976)

Bennett, Susan, *Theatre Audiences: A Theory of Production and Reception* (London, 1990)

Berlant, Lauren, *Intimacy* (Chicago, IL, 2000)

Berlant, Lauren, 'Intimacy: A Special Issue', *Critical Inquiry*, 24 (1998)

Billington, Michael, Review of *XXX*, *The Guardian* (25 April 2003). Reprinted in *Theatre Record*, 23(9) (2003)

Blin, Roger, Artaud, Antonin, *et al.*, 'Artaud's *Les Cenci*', trans. Charles Marowitz, in Rebecca Schneider and Gabrielle Cody (eds), *Re:direction. A Theoretical and Practical Guide* (London, 2002)

Bogart, Anne, *A Director Prepares* (London, 2001)

Bohm, David, *On Creativity* (London, 2002)

Bois, Yve-Alain, 'The Use Value of Formless', in Yve-Alain Bois and Rosalind E. Krauss, *Formless: A User's Guide* (New York, 1997)

Borchmeyer, Dieter, *Das Theater Richard Wagners* (Stuttgart, 1982)

Borchmeyer, Dieter, *Mozart oder die Entdeckung der Liebe* (Frankfurt am Main, 2005)

Borchmeyer, Dieter, '"El maestro vol cussi, e basta"! Verdi und die Struktur des Opernlibrettos', in Udo Bermbach (ed.), *Verdi-Theater* (Stuttgart, 1997)

Brassai, Robert, *The Secret Paris of the 30s* (London, 1976)

Brecht, Bertolt, *Collected Plays, Volume 1*, eds Ralph Manheim and John Willett (New York, 1971)

Brecht, Bertolt, *Collected Plays: Three*, ed. John Willett (London, 1997)

Broadhurst, Susan, *Liminal Acts: A Critical Overview of Contemporary Performance and Theory* (London, 1999)

Brodwin, Leonora Leet, *Elizabethan Love Tragedy 1587–1625* (London, 1972)

Brown, Gary R., 'Sawing a Woman in Half', *Invention and Technology Magazine*, 9 (1994), http://www.americanheritage.com/articles/magazine/it/1994/3/1994_3_34.shtml

Büchner, Georg, *Complete Plays, Lenz and Other Writings*, trans. John Reddick (London, 1993)

Büchner, Georg, 'Danton's Death', in *Complete Plays, Lenz and Other Writings*, trans. John Reddick (London, 1993)

Buckley, Matthew S., *Tragedy Walks the Streets: The French Revolution in the Making of Modern Drama* (Baltimore, MD, 2006)

Burger, Eugene and Neale, Robert E., *Magic and Meaning* (Seattle, WA, 1995)

Butler, Kateri, 'Ron Athey', *Los Angeles Times Magazine* (28 January 2007), http://articles.latimes.com/2007/jan/28/magazine/tm-athey04?pg=4

Bynorth, John, 'Sex On Stage Storm: Raunchiest Show Ever Hits UK', *Daily Star* (24 April 2003)

Califia, Pat, 'In Praise of Assholes', *Out* (May 1999)

Canetti, Elias, *Crowds and Power* (Harmondsworth, 1973)

Carr, C., *On Edge: Performance at the End of the Twentieth Century* (London and New York, 1994)

Carson, Anne, *Eros the Bittersweet* (Champaign, IL, 1998)

Carter, Angela, *The Sadeian Woman: An Exercise in Cultural History* (London, 1979)

Cave, Nick, *And the Ass Saw the Angel* (London, 1989)

Cave, Nick, *The Complete Lyrics 1978–2007* (London, 2007)

Cave, Nick, *The Death of Bunny Munro* (Edinburgh, 2009)

Cavicchi, Daniel, *Tramps Like Us: Music and Meaning among Springsteen Fans* (Oxford, 1998)

Daudet, Léon, *The Tragic Life of Victor Hugo* (London, 1939)

Doane, Janice and Hodge, Devon, *From Klein to Kristeva: Psychoanalytic Feminism and the Search for the 'Good Enough' Mother* (Ann Arbor, MI, 1993)

Dollimore, Jonathan, *Death, Desire and Loss in Western Culture* (New York, 2001)

Dollimore, Jonathan, *Radical Tragedy: Religion, Ideology and Power in the Drama of Shakespeare and his Contemporaries* (Brighton, 1984)

Donne, John, *The Complete English Poems*, ed. A.J. Smith (Harmondsworth, 1971)

Dufourmantelle, Anne, *Blind Date: Sex and Philosophy*, trans. Catherine Porter (Urbana and Chicago, IL, 2007)

Douglas, Mary, *Purity and Danger: An Analysis of the Concepts of Pollution and Taboo* (London, 1966)

Dyer, Richard, 'Don't Look Now: The Male Pin-up', *Screen*, 23 (1982)

Eagleton, Terry, *Sweet Violence: The Idea of the Tragic* (Oxford, 2003)

Edwards, Dic, *Casanova Undone* (London, 1992)

Edwards, Dic, *Utah Blue* (London, 2000)

Edwards, Dic, *Wittgenstein's Daughter* (London, 1998)

Eliot, T.S., *The Sacred Wood: Essays on Poetry and Criticism* (London, 1922)

Euripides, *Hippolytus* (London, 1980)

Ewen, Frederic, *Bertolt Brecht: His Life, His Art, His Times* (New York, 1967)

Fast, Susan, *In the Houses of the Holy: Led Zeppelin and the Power of Rock Music* (Oxford, 2001)

Finley, Karen, *A Different Kind of Intimacy* (New York, 2000)

Fisher, Jennifer (ed.), *Technologies of Intuition* (Ontario, Canada, 2006)

Freud, Sigmund, 'The Ego and the Id', in James Strachey (trans. and ed.), *The Standard Edition of the Complete Psychological Works of Sigmund Freud*, vol. 19 (London, 2001)

Freud, Sigmund, 'The Future of an Illusion', in Albert Dickson (ed.), *The Penguin Freud Library 12: Civilization, Society and Religion* (London, 1985)

Freud, Sigmund, 'Lecture 35. The Question of a *Weltanschauung*', in James Strachey and Angela Richards (eds), *The Penguin Freud Library 2: New Introductory Lectures on Psychoanalysis* (London, 1973)

Freud, Sigmund, 'Three Essays on the Theory of Sexuality', in James Strachey (trans. and ed.), *The Standard Edition of the Complete Psychological Works of Sigmund Freud*, vol. 7 (London, 1953)

Freud, Sigmund, 'The Uncanny', in James Strachey (trans. and ed.), *The Standard Edition of the Complete Psychological Works of Sigmund Freud*, vol. 17 (London, 1955)

Freud, Sigmund, 'Civilisation and its Discontents' [1930] in James Strachey (trans. and ed.), *The Standard Edition of the Complete Psychological Works*, vol. 21. (London: 1953–74)

Freud, Sigmund, 'The Future of an Illusion' [1927] in James Strachey and Albert Dickson (eds), *The Penguin Freud Library 12: Civilization, Society and Religion* (London, 1985)

Freud, Sigmund, 'Totem and Taboo' [1913] in James Strachey and Albert Dickson (eds), *The Penguin Freud Library 13: The Origins of Religion* (London, 1985)

Freud, Sigmund, 'Moses and Monotheism' [1939] in James Strachey and Albert Dickson (eds), *The Penguin Freud Library 13: The Origins of Religion* (London, 1985)

Frith, Simon, *Performing Rites* (Oxford, 1998)

Frost, Thomas, *The Lives of the Conjurors* (London, 1876)

Frye, Northrop, *Anatomy of Criticism: Four Essays* (New York, 1965)

Garner, Stanton B., *Bodied Spaces: Phenomenology and Performance in Contemporary Drama* (Ithaca, NY, 1995)

Gibson, Walter B., *The Original Houdini Scrapbook* (New York, London and Sydney, 1976)

Glebke, Michael, *Die Philosophie Georg Büchners* (Marburg, 1995)

Goethe, Johann Wolfgang, *Dichtung und Wahrheit*, ed. Klaus-Detlef Müller (Frankfurt am Main, 2007)

Goethes Werke, Hamburger Ausgabe, 10th edn, vol. 4 (Munich, 1981)

Goldberg, RoseLee, *Performance: Live Art Since 1960* (New York, 1998)

Goldin, Horace, *It's Fun to be Fooled* (London, 1937), http://www.thelearnedpig.com.pa/magos/books/goldin/09.html

Goldston, Will (comp. and ed.), *Stage Illusions* (London, 1912), http://www.thelearnedpig.com.pa/magos/books/stageill/017.html

Goltschnigg, Dietmar, *Georg Büchner und die Moderne: Texte, Analysen, Kommentar*, Band 3 (Berlin, 2004)

Gracyk, Theodore, *I Wanna Be Me: Rock Music and the Politics of Identity* (Philadelphia, 2001)

Grau, Oliver, *Virtual Art: From Illusion to Immersion*, trans. Gloria Custance (Cambridge, MA, 2003)

Grimes, William, 'For Endowment, One Performer Means Trouble', *New York Times* (7 July 1994), http://www.nytimes.com/1994/07/07/arts/for-endowment-one-performer-means-trouble.html?pagewanted=1

Gritzner, Karoline and Rabey, David Ian (eds), *Theatre of Catastrophe: New Essays on Howard Barker* (London, 2006)

Grosz, Elizabeth, 'The Time of Violence', in Scott Lash, Andrew Quick and Richard Roberts (eds), *Time and Value* (Oxford, 1998)

Grosz, Elizabeth, *Volatile Bodies: Toward a Corporeal Feminism* (Bloomington and Indianapolis, IN, 1994)

Grünbein, Durs, 'Den Körper zerbrechen (1995)', in Dietmar Goltschnigg, *Georg Büchner und die Moderne: Texte, Analysen, Kommentar*, Band 3 (Berlin, 2004)

Hand, Richard J. and Wilson, Michael, *Grand-Guignol: The French Theatre of Horror* (Exeter, 2002)

Harris, Duncan S., '"Again for Cydnus": The Dramaturgical Resolution of *Antony and Cleopatra*', *Studies in English Literature*, 17 (1977)

Hattenstone, Simon, 'Old Nick', *The Guardian*, 23 February 2008

Heathfield, Adrian, 'Alive', in Adrian Heathfield (ed.), *Live: Art and Performance* (London, 2004)

Hegarty, Paul, *Georges Bataille: Core Cultural Theorist* (London, 2000)

Hénaff, Marcel, *Sade: The Invention of the Libertine Body*, trans. Xavier Callahan (Minneapolis, MN, 1999)

Hill, John and Church Gibson, Pamela, *The Oxford Guide to Film Studies* (Oxford, 1998)

Hofmannsthal, Hugo von, *Gesammelte Werke*, ed. Bernd Schoeller (Frankfurt am Main, 1979)

Hooke, Alexander E., 'Silent Communities: Foucault and Lingis on the End of Philosophy', in Alexander E. Hooke and Wolfgang W. Fuchs (eds), *Encounters with Alphonso Lingis* (Lanham, MD, 2003)

Hooke, Alexander E. and Fuchs, Wolfgang W. (eds), *Encounters with Alphonso Lingis* (Lanham, MD, 2003)

Horkheimer, Max and Adorno, Theodor W., *Dialectic of Enlightenment*, trans. Edmund Jephcott (Stanford, CA, 2002)

Hugo, Victor, *Four Plays* (London, 2004)

Hugo, Victor, *Les Misérables* (Harmondsworth, 1982)

Iball, Helen, 'Dead Hands and Killer Heels', in Karoline Gritzner and David Ian Rabey (eds), *Theatre of Catastrophe: New Essays on Howard Barker* (London, 2006)

Inglis, Iain, *Performance and Popular Music* (Aldershot, 2007)

Jacobs, Jay S., *Wild Years: The Music and Myth of Tom Waits* (Toronto, Canada, 2000)

James, Henry, *The Scenic Art* (London, 1949)

Janik, Allan and Toulmin, Stephen, *Wittgenstein's Vienna* (New York, 1973)

Jayasinghe, Laknath, 'Nick Cave, Dance Performance and the Production and Consumption of Masculinity', in Karen Welbery and Tanya Dalziell (eds), *Cultural Seeds: Essays on the Work of Nick Cave* (Aldershot, 2007)

Jentsch, Ernst, 'On the Psychology of the Uncanny (1906)', trans. Roy Sellars, http://www.cpmg.org.br/artigos/on_the_psychology_of_the_uncanny.pdf

Johnson, Adrian, 'Slavoj Žižek's Hegelian Reformation: Giving a Hearing to the Parallax View', *Diacritics*, 37(1) (2007)

Johnson, Dominic, 'It Only Hurts Because It's True: Recent Live Art and Performance in the UK', *Western European Stages*, 19(1) (2007)

Johnson, Dominic, 'Perverse Martyrologies: An Interview with Ron Athey', *Contemporary Theatre Review*, 18(4) (2008)

Jones, Amelia, *Body Art: Performing the Subject* (Minneapolis, MN, 1998)

Jones, Angela, 'Grinderman: All Stripped Down', in Karen Welbery and Tanya Dalziell (eds), *Cultural Seeds: Essays on the Work of Nick Cave* (Aldershot, 2007)

Jones, Stephen, *Clive Barker's A–Z of Horror* (London, 1997)

Kahn, Coppélia, *Roman Shakespeare: Warriors, Wounds, and Women* (London and New York, 1997)

Kantor, Tadeusz, 'The Second *Insegnamento*', in *A Journey through Other Spaces: Essays and Manifestos, 1944–1990*, trans. Michal Kobialka (Berkeley, CA, 1993)

Kantor, Tadeusz, 'The Theatre of Death', in *A Journey through Other Spaces: Essays and Manifestos, 1944–1990*, trans. Michal Kobialka (Berkeley, CA, 1993)

Kasson, John F., *Houdini, Tarzan, and the Perfect Man: The White Male Body and the Challenge of Modernity in America* (New York, 2001)

Keidan, Lois, Brine, Daniel and Heathfield, Adrian, *Live Culture* Programme, ed. Adrian Heathfield (London, 2003)

Keighley, Keir, 'Reconstructing Rock', in Simon Frith, Will Straw and John Street (eds), *The Cambridge Companion to Pop and Rock* (Cambridge, 2001)

Kelleher, Joe, *Theatre and Politics* (Basingstoke, 2009)

Knight, George Wilson, *The Imperial Theme: Further Interpretations of Shakespeare's Tragedies including the Roman Plays*, 3rd edn (London, 1951)

Konold, Wulf, 'Der festgehaltene Augenblick. Zur Dramaturgie von Verdis Opern', in Udo Bermbach (ed.), *Verdi-Theater* (Stuttgart/Weimar, 1997)

Koppen, Erwin, *Dekadenter Wagnerismus. Studien zur europäischen Literatur des Fin de siècle* (Berlin/New York, 1973)

Kott, Jan, 'A Short Treatise on Eroticism', in Jan Kott, *The Memory of the Body: Essays on Theater and Death*, trans. Boleslaw Taborski (Evanston, IL, 1992)

Krauss, Rosalind E., 'The Destiny of the Informe', in Yve-Alain Bois and Rosalind E. Krauss, *Formless: A User's Guide* (New York, 1997)

La Fura dels Baus, *XXX* website (2003), http://www.furaxxx.com/xxx/english/menu/menu.htm

Laing, R.D., *The Divided Self: An Existential Study in Sanity and Madness* (Harmondsworth, 1960)

Lash, Scott, Quick, Andrew and Roberts, Richard (eds), *Time and Value* (Oxford, 1998)

Lenz, Jakob M.R., *Werke und Schriften*, Band 1 (Stuttgart, 1965–6)

Lenz, Jakob M.R., 'Anmerkungen übers Theater', in Jakob M.R. Lenz, *Werke und Schriften*, Band 1 (Stuttgart, 1965–6)

Lessings Werke, volume VI, ed. Georg Witkowski, (Leipzig/Wien [no year])

Lingis, Alphonso, *Abuses* (Berkeley, CA, 1994)

Lingis, Alphonso, *The Community of Those Who Have Nothing in Common* (Bloomington, IN, 1994)

Lingis, Alphonso, *Dangerous Emotions* (Berkeley, CA, 2000)

Lloyd, Jill, *Christian Schad and the Neue Sachlichkeit* (New York, 2003)

Lorde, Audre, *Sister Outsider: Essays and Speeches* (Freedom, CA, 1984)

Lorde, Audre, 'The Uses of the Erotic: The Erotic as Power', in Audre Lorde, *Sister Outsider: Essays and Speeches* (Freedom, CA, 1984)

Lukács, Georg, *German Realists in the Nineteenth Century*, trans. Jeremy Gaines and Paul Keast (London, 1993)

Lukács, Georg, 'The Real Georg Büchner and His Fascist Misrepresentation' (1937), in Georg Lukács, *German Realists in the Nineteenth Century*, trans. Jeremy Gaines and Paul Keast (London, 1993)

McCredden, Lyn, 'Fleshed Sacred: The Carnal Theologies of Nick Cave', in Karen Welbery and Tanya Dalziell (eds), *Cultural Seeds: Essays on the Work of Nick Cave* (Aldershot, 2007)

McEvoy, Emma, '"Now, who will be the witness/When you're all too healed to see?" The Sad Demise of Nick Cave', in *Gothic Studies*, 9(1) (2007)

McGrath, John Edward, 'Trusting in Rubber: Performing Boundaries during the AIDS Epidemic', *TDR*, 35(2) (1995)

Mahon, Alyce, *Surrealism and the Politics of Eros, 1938–1968* (London, 2005)

Mahon, Alyce, 'Staging Desire', in Jennifer Mundy (ed.) *Surrealism: Desire Unbound* (London, 2001)

Mangan, Michael, *Performing Dark Arts: A Cultural History of Conjuring* (Bristol, 2007)

Marcuse, Herbert, *Eros and Civilization: A Philosophical Inquiry into Freud* (Boston, MA, 1966)

Marsh, Derick R.C., *Passion Lends Them Power: A Study of Shakespeare's Love Tragedies* (Manchester, 1976)

Maurois, André, *Victor Hugo and His World* (London, 1966)

Michalski, Sergiusz, *New Objectivity* (New York, 1995)

Middleton, Thomas, *Women Beware Women*, in Bryan Loughrey and Neil Taylor (eds), *Five Plays* (London, 1988)

Mitchell, Peter (ed.), *The Nature and Culture of the Human Body*, *Trivium*, 37 (Lampeter, 2007)

Mock, Roberta, 'La Fura dels Baus's *XXX*: Deviant Textualities and the Formless', in Susan Broadhurst and Josephine Machon (eds), *Sensualities/Textualities and Technologies: Writings of the Body in 21st-Century Performance* (London and New York, 2010)

Moore, Allan, 'Authenticity as Authentication', *Popular Music*, 21(2) (2002)

Mulholland, Gary, 'If Looks Could Kill...', *Time Out* (1996)

Müller, Heiner, 'The Wounded Woyzeck', trans. Carl Weber, *Performing Arts Journal*, 10(3) (1987)

Mulvey, Laura, 'Visual Pleasure and Narrative Cinema', *Screen*, 16 (1975)

Munich, Adrienne Auslander, *Andromeda's Chains: Gender and Interpretation in Victorian Literature and Art* (New York, 1989)

Musil, Robert, *The Man Without Qualities*, trans. Sophie Wilkins (New York, 1995)

Neale, Steve, 'Masculinity as Spectacle', *Screen*, 24 (1983)

Néret, Gilles (ed.), *Erotica Universalis Volume II* (Cologne, 2000)

Nietzsche, Friedrich, *Kritische Studienausgabe*, vol. 8, eds Giorgio Colli and Mazzino Montinari (Munich, 1980)

Orti, Pilar, 'X-rated', *Total Theatre Magazine*, 15(2) (2003)

Pattie, David, *Rock Music and Performance* (London, 2007)

Paz, Octavio, *The Double Flame: Love and Eroticism*, trans. Helen Lane (London, 1995)

Phelan, Peggy, *Mourning Sex: Performing Public Memories* (London and New York, 1997)

Phelan, Peggy, 'Marina Abramović: Witnessing Shadows', *Theatre Journal*, 56 (2004)

Pierron, Agnès, *Le Grand Guignol: le théâtre des peurs de la belle époque* (Paris, 1995)

Pierron, Agnès, *Les Nuits-Blanches du Grand Guignol* (Paris, 2002)

Pinter, Harold, *Plays: Four* (London, 1993)

Pinter, Harold, *Plays: Three* (London, 1997)

Poe, Edgar Allen, *Tales of Mystery and Imagination* (London, 2003)

Prendergast, Christopher, *Paris and the Nineteenth Century* (Oxford, 1992)

Rabey, David Ian, *English Drama Since 1940* (Harlow, 2003)

Rabey, David Ian, *Howard Barker: Ecstasy and Death* (Basingstoke, 2009)

Rabey, David Ian, *Lovefuries* (Bristol, 2008)

Rabey, David Ian, *The Wye Plays* (Bristol, 2004)

Rabey, David Ian, 'The Theatrical in the Sexual, the Sexual in the Theatrical', *Essays in Theatre/Études Théâtrales*, 21(1 and 2) (2002/2003), published 2008

Rancière, Jacques, *The Politics of Aesthetics: The Revolution of the Sensible*, trans. Gabriel rockhill (London, 2004)

Rebellato, Dan, 'Sarah Kane: An Appreciation', *New Theatre Quarterly*, 15(3) (1999)

Reddick, John, *Georg Büchner: The Shattered Whole* (Oxford, 1994)

Regling, Dennis, 'Women in Magic', in *BellaOnline: The Voice of Women*, http://www.bellaonline.com/articles/art36816.asp

Reynolds, Simon, *Rip It Up and Start Again* (London, 2005)

Reynolds, Simon and Press, Joy, *The Sex Revolts: Gender, Rebellion and Rock and Roll* (London, 1994)

Richardson, Michael, 'Introduction', in Georges Bataille, *The Absence of Myth: Writings on Surrealism*, trans. Michael Richardson (London and New York, 1994)

Ridout, Nicholas, *Theatre and Ethics* (Basingstoke, 2009)

Robert-Houdin, Jean Eugène, *Memoirs of Robert-Houdin, Ambassador, Author, and Conjuror*, trans. Lascelles Wraxall (London, 1859), http://www.thelearnedpig.com.pa/magos/books/memrh/001.html

Rotenberg, Mark, *Forbidden Erotica: The Rotenberg Collection* (Cologne, 2000)

Rozett, Martha Tuck, 'The Comic Structures of Tragic Endings: The Suicide Scenes in *Romeo and Juliet* and *Antony and Cleopatra*', *Shakespeare Quarterly*, 36 (1985)

Rubik, Margarete and Mettinger-Schartmann, Elke (eds), *(Dis)Continuities: Trends and Traditions in Contemporary Theatre and Drama in English* (Trier, 2002)

Sade, Marquis de, *Justine, Philosophy in the Bedroom, and Other Writings*, trans. Richard Seaver and Austryn Wainhouse (New York, 1990)

Sade, Marquis de, *One Hundred and Twenty Days of Sodom* (London, 1966/1989)

Safe, Emma, 'Come Into My Parlour', in *The Guardian* (25 May 2002), http://www.guardian.co.uk/artanddesign/2002/may/25/artsfeatures.books1

Sánchez, Antonio, 'La Fura dels Baus and the Legacy of Antonin Artaud', *Contemporary Theatre Review*, 16(4) (2006)

Saumell, Mercè, 'La Fura dels Baus: Scenes for the Twenty-First Century', trans. Simon Breden, Maria M. Delgado and Lourdes Orozco, *Contemporary Theatre Review*, 17(3) (2007)

Saumell, Mercè, 'Performance Groups in Contemporary Spanish Theatre', trans. Jill Pythian and Maria M. Delgado, *Contemporary Theatre Review*, 7(4) (1998): *Spanish Theatre 1920–1995: Strategies in Protest and Imagination*, Pt. 3

Saunders, Graham, *About Kane: The Playwright and the Work* (London, 2009)

Schiller, Friedrich, *Sämtliche Werke*, vol. 1, ed. Albert Meier (Munich, 2004)

Schneider, Kirk J., 'R.D. Laing's Existential–Humanistic Practice: What Was He Actually Doing?' *The Psychoanalytic Review*, 87(4) (2000)

Schneider, Rebecca, *The Explicit Body in Performance* (London, 1997)

Schopenhauer, Arthur, *The World as Will and Representation*, trans. R.B. Haldane and J. Kemp (London, 1909)

Scot, Reginald, *The Discovery of Witchcraft, Proving the Common Opinions of Witches Contracting with Divels, Spirits, or Familiars ... to be but Imaginary, Erronious Conceptions and Novelties* (London, 1584)

Sellars, Roy, 'Translator's Preface', in Ernst Jentsch, 'On the Psychology of the Uncanny (1906)', http://www.cpmg.org.br/artigos/on_the_psychology_of_the_uncanny.pdf

Shakespeare, William, *The Complete Works*, eds Stanley Wells and Gary Taylor (Oxford, 1988)

Shakespeare, William, *The Tragedy of King Lear*, in Stanley Wells, Gary Taylor, John Jowett and William Montgomery (eds), *The Oxford Shakespeare: Tragedies* (Oxford, 1987)

Shepherd, Simon and Wallis, Mick, *Drama/Theatre/Performance* (Abingdon and New York, 2004)

Sigmoud, G., 'Impulsive Insanity – the French Vampire', *Journal of Psychological Medicine and Mental Pathology*, 2 (1849)

Simmons, J.L., 'The Comic Pattern and Vision in *Antony and Cleopatra*', *English Literary History*, 36 (1969)

Smith, Andy, '"I am not what I was": Adaptation and Transformation in the Theatre of Howard Barker and The Wrestling School', in Karoline Gritzner and David Ian Rabey (eds), *Theatre of Catastrophe: New Essays on Howard Barker* (London, 2006)

Sobchack, Vivian, *Carnal Thoughts: Embodiment and Moving Image Culture* (Berkeley, CA, Los Angeles, CA, and London, 2004)

Sontag, Susan, 'The Pornographic Imagination', in Georges Bataille, *Story of the Eye by Lord Auch*, trans. Joachim Neugroschal (London, 1982)

Steiner, Wendy, *The Scandal of Pleasure* (Chicago, IL, 1995)

Steinmeyer, Jim, *Hiding the Elephant: How Magicians Invented the Impossible* (London, 2004)

Sternberg, Josef von, *Der blaue Engel* [film], screenplay by Carl Zuckmayer *et al.*, based on the novel *Professor Unrat* by Heinrich Mann (1930)

Stoekl, Allan, 'Introduction', in Georges Bataille, *Visions of Excess: Selected Writings: 1927–1939*, ed. and intro. Allan Stoekl, trans. Allan Stoekl with Carl R. Lovitt and Donald M. Leslie Jr. (Minneapolis, MN, 1985)

Storey, John, *Cultural Theory and Popular Culture: A Reader* (Harlow, 1998)

Strauss, Richard / Hugo von Hofmannsthal, *Briefwechsel (Letters)*, *Gesamtausgabe* (Zürich, 1964)

Studlar, Gaylyn, *In the Realm of Pleasure: von Sternberg, Dietrich and the Masochistic Aesthetic* (Urbana, IL, 1988)

Surya, Michel, *Georges Bataille: An Intellectual Biography*, trans. Krzysztof Fijalkowski and Michael Richardson (London and New York, 2002)

Taylor, John Russell, 'British Dramatists. The New Arrivals', *Plays and Players*, 18 (1971)

Tennenhouse, Leonard, *Power on Display: The Politics of Shakespeare's Genres* (New York and London, 1986)

Tester, Keith, *The Flâneur* (London, 1994)

Tibbles, Percy ('Selbit'), *The Magician's Handbook. A Complete Encyclopedia of the Magic Art for Professional and Amateur*

Entertainers (London, 1904), http://www.thelearnedpig.com.pa/magos/books/selbit1/082.html

Traub, Valerie, *Desire and Anxiety: Circulations of Sexuality in Shakespearean Drama* (London and New York, 1992)

Tremlett, Giles, 'More Sex Please, We're Spanish', *The Guardian* (5 June 2002), http://www.guardian.co.uk/culture/2002/jun/05/artsfeatures.culturaltrips

Vincent, Barbara, 'Shakespeare's *Antony and Cleopatra* and the Rise of Comedy', *English Literary Renaissance*, 12 (1982)

Wagner, Richard, *Sämtliche Schriften und Dichtungen*, Volksausgabe, vol. 12 (Leipzig, 1911)

Wagner, Cosima, *Die Tagebücher. Volume I* (Munich, 1976)

Wagner, Cosima, *Die Tagebücher. Volume II* (Munich, 1977)

Wagner, Richard, *Gesammelte Schriften und Dichtungen (Complete works and poems)* (Leipzig, 1888)

Wainhouse, Austryn and Seaver, Richard, 'Introduction to Part Four', in the Marquis de Sade, *One Hundred and Twenty Days of Sodom* (London, 1966/1989)

Warner, Marina, *Phantasmagoria: Spirit Visions, Metaphors and Media into the Twenty-First Century* (Oxford, 2006)

Webster, Sue-Anne, *Sue-Anne Webster Magician*, http://www.sueannewebster.com/452.html

Weinstein, Deena, *Heavy Metal: The Music and Its Culture* (New York, 2000)

Weiss, Peter, *The Persecution and Assassination of Marat as Performed by the Inmates of the Asylum of Charenton under the Direction of the Marquis de Sade (Marat/Sade)*, trans. Geoffrey Skelton (London, 1965)

Welbery, Karen, 'Nick Cave and the Australian Language of Laughter', in Karen Welbery and Tanya Dalziell (eds), *Cultural Seeds: Essays on the Work of Nick Cave* (Aldershot, 2007)

Welbery, Karen and Dalziell, Tanya (eds), *Cultural Seeds: Essays on the Work of Nick Cave* (Aldershot, 2007)

Wilcher, Robert, '*Antony and Cleopatra* and Genre Criticism', in Nigel Wood (ed.), *Antony and Cleopatra*, Theory in Practice Series (Buckingham, 1996)

Williams, Linda, 'When the Woman Looks', in Barry Keith Grant (ed.), *Dread of Difference: Gender and the Horror Film* (Austin, TX, 1996)

Williams, Raymond, *Modern Tragedy* (London, 1966)

Wind, Edgar, *Heidnische Mysterien in der Renaissance* (Frankfurt am Main, 1981)

Wittgenstein, Ludwig, *Tractatus logico-philosophicus* (London, 1961)

Wood, Robin, 'The Return of the Repressed', *Film Comment*, 14 (1978)

Zerihan, Rachel, 'Gay Shame 2008: Duckie Gets Macho', *Dance Theatre Journal*, 23(2) (2009)

Zerihan, Rachel, 'Gay Shame 2009: Gay Shame Goes Girly', *Dance Theatre Journal* (forthcoming)

Zerihan, Rachel, 'Intimate Inter-actions: Returning to the Body in One to One Performance', *Body, Space, Technology Journal*, 6(1) (2006)

Zerihan, Rachel and Ashery, Oreet, Franko B, Bartram, Ang, Dobkin, Jess, Freeman, Davis/Random Scream, Howells, Adrian, Johnson, Dominic, Kartsaki, Eirini, Kela, Leena, Louise, Berni Mendes Silva, Susana, O'Reilly, Kira, Parthipan, Jiva, Pinchbeck, Michael, Rose, Sam, Sweeting, Samantha and Von Holn, Martina, *Live Art Development Agency Study Room Guide on One to One Performance* (2009), http://www.thisisliveart.co.uk/resources/Study_Room/guides/Rachel_Zerihan.html

Žižek, Slavoj, *The Parallax View* (Cambridge, MA, 2006)

Zournasi, Mary, 'Foreign Bodies: Interview with Alphonso Lingis, 1996', in Alexander E. Hooke and Wolfgang W. Fuchs (eds), *Encounters with Alphonso Lingis* (Lanham, MD, 2003)

Index

Abjection 136, 228

Adorno, Theodor W. 3, 97

Adultery 72, 74

Affect 10, 203, 205, 206, 207

Agit-prop 104

Aphrodite 1, 23, 25

Apollo 4, 14

Apuleius, Lucius 1

Aristophanes 6

Aristotle 4, 50, 123
  anti-Aristotelian 50
  Aristotelian 29, 36, 104, 124, 127, 152

Artaud, Antonin 179, 191–2, 195

Athey, Ron 178–98, 204

Auschwitz 106

Autonomy 8, 28, 61, 99

Bakhtin, Michael 36, 37

Barker, Howard 5, 129, 130, 135–7, 138, 144–59

Barthes, Roland 167, 216
  Barthes on myth 167

Bartram, Angela 217–18

Bataille, Georges 6, 7, 179, 180–4, 193–7, 204

Baudelaire, Charles 64, 110, 118, 119, 120

Baudrillard, Jean 3, 7, 127, 129

Beckett, Samuel 138

Beethoven, Ludwig van 92

Benjamin, Walter 64, 66, 68, 73

Benn, Maurice 48, 61

Benoît, Jean 9

Blanchot, Maurice 5, 6, 181

Body 7, 19, 21, 34, 54, 116, 119, 135, 151, 162, 190, 211, 214, 221, 242
  body art 178, 187, 204
  body politic 154, 204
  erotic body 105, 106
  explicit body 9
  female body 9, 55, 217
  human body 4, 60, 101, 132, 218
  sacrificial body 243
  sexual body 55

Bogart, Anne 125, 127

Bohm, David 111–12, 118–19, 120

Bond, Edward 132, 133, 144

Brassai, Robert 68, 73

Brecht, Bertolt 95–107, 149

Breton, André 9, 181, 195

Brothel 68, 73

Burden, Chris 208, 209, 215

Canetti, Elias 65

Capitalism 120
  capitalist 3, 100

Carson, Anne 1, 6

Carter, Angela 180

Casanova 109, 113–15, 120

Castration 170

    castration complex 172

Catastrophe 39, 100, 152

    'Theatre of Catastrophe' 148

Catharsis 4, 81, 124, 211

Cave, Nick 224–39

Christ 57, 92, 114

    Christian 81, 86

    Christianity 48, 53, 196, 91, 92, 196

Churchill, Caryl 152

Colette 77

Comedy 5, 36, 37, 38, 41, 103, 125, 237, 239

    romantic comedy 39

    tragicomedy 28, 43

Confession 5, 87, 90, 205, 212, 215

    confessional 209, 212, 220

Conjuror 160–2, 164–7, 169, 170–5

Corporeality 208, 216, 221

Corpse 20, 21, 30, 83, 242–5

    living corpse 109, 110, 112–14, 116, 118, 120

Cruelty 90, 151, 174, 191–2, 198, 238

Cupid 1, 244

Death 238, 243, 172, 175

    death drive 2, 3, 9, 151 *see also* Thanatos

    death kiss (*morte di bacio*) 84, 87, 90, 91

    theatre of death 5, 73

Delimitation experience 80, 84, 85, 91

    see also loss of self

Derrida, Jacques 128,

Desire 1, 8–10, 12, 28, 37–8, 46, 49, 88, 127, 129, 134, 135, 145, 147, 151–6, 170, 190, 196, 197, 211, 217, 242, 244

    bodily desire 54,

    erotic desire 6, 59, 156

    female desire 60, 95, 146, 148

    sexual desire 2, 23, 39, 42, 50, 55, 149

    transgressive desire 21

Destruction 2, 55, 58–61, 74, 103, 146, 152, 238

Determinism 47, 48, 51, 59, 106

Dietrich, Marlene 95

Dionysus 4, 80, 84, 91, 126

Divinity 87, 88, 235

Divinity Fudge 188

Dix, Otto 96, 101

Dollimore, Jonathan 6, 28, 29, 35

Donne, John 29, 31

Dracula 72, 243

Drake, Simon 175

Dufourmantelle, Anne 124, 126–9, 131, 133–5, 139

Dylan, Bob 126

Eagleton, Terry 48, 49, 153

écriture féminine 204

Ecstasy 4, 88, 106, 110, 132, 135, 148, 195, 243

    erotic ecstasy 151

    sexual ecstasy 150

Eiffel Tower 69

Eliot, T.S. 148

Enlightenment 50, 52, 96, 124, 145

Eros 10, 12, 19, 21, 39, 58, 61, 71, 80, 95, 160, 175

EROS (Exposition international du
surréalisme) 9
Eros and Psyche 1
eros funebre 85
Erotica 68, 69, 76, 96
Eroticism 5–10, 29, 47, 57, 64, 72, 77,
84, 102, 113, 118, 124, 126, 130,
144, 178, 183, 196, 205, 207
erotic encounter 203
Evil 92, 238
Excess 9, 22, 37, 131, 135, 167, 178,
190, 198
'Visions of Excess' 180, 204, 218
Existentialism 124
existentialist 15, 23
Expressionism 46, 96, 100–3
Expressionist drama 101

Fantasy 65, 170, 175, 178, 198
erotic fantasy 43
Gothic fantasy 67
Fatalism 47, 48, 52, 56
Feminist 9, 168, 203, 216, 217
anti-feminist 164
feminist film studies 168
post-feminist 174
Femme fatale 70, 71, 90
Film theory 167–8, 175
Fin de siècle 84, 90, 97
Flâneur 64
flânerie 77
Flesh 76, 105, 120, 134, 149, 193, 196,
228, 231, 243
'flesh and blood' 51, 53, 60, 61
formless 183–4, 193–4, 198
Franko B 187, 215

Freeman, Davis 205, 209–11, 220
Freud, Sigmund 3, 9, 61, 100, 124,
170–3, 231
Beyond the Pleasure Principle 2
'The Ego and the Id' 2
Civilisation and its Discontents 2
*Three Essays on the Theory of
Sexuality* 96
*New Introductory Lectures on
Psychoanalysis* 173
'The Uncanny' 171–2
Frye, Northrop 37, 42

Gaze 167, 175, 211, 218, 221, 243
gaze theory 168–70
male gaze 9
Gender 9, 162, 164, 169, 174, 242
Goethe, Johann Wolfgang 52, 83, 85,
86, 87, 91
Grand-Guignol 65, 73–7, 167
Grosz, Georg 96, 101
Grosz, Elizabeth 216, 217
Guillotine 59, 175

Hegel, Georg Wilhelm Friedrich 100,
231
Hegelian 48, 53, 56, 58
Hegelianism 47, 232
Heidegger, Martin 3
Heine, Heinrich 53
History play 32, 35, 36, 40, 41, 43
Hitler 95
HIV 188
Hofmannsthal, Hugo von 80, 81, 91
Homoerotic, homosexual 102
Horror 73, 74, 77, 135, 196, 197

Horror movie/film 65, 170, 172, 173, 175
Houdini, Harry 165, 166
Howells, Adrian 205, 211–15, 219, 220
Hugo, Victor 65, 67, 70–2, 77

Idealism 46, 47, 50, 56, 231
    Hegelian idealism 48, 53 see also Hegelian
Illusion 126, 169, 173, 175, 178, 190, 195
    sawing illusion 161–5, 170, 174
    theatrical illusion, stage illusion 103, 160
Imagination 4–5, 37, 39, 41, 105, 113, 125, 137, 209, 235
    erotic imagination 6
    pornographic imagination 197, 198
    sexual imagination 106
Incest 70
    incestuous 180, 181, 182, 192
Intimacy 129, 133, 206–7, 209, 212, 215, 221, 244
    sexual intimacy 49, 218

Jack the Ripper 98, 99
James, Henry 69, 70
Jentsch, Ernst 171–3
Johnson, Dominic 179, 206, 220
Jouissance 6, 8, 135, 203, 214, 216–17, 220

Kaiser, Georg 101
Kane, Sarah 132–4, 152, 157
Kant, Immanuel 48, 100
Kantor, Tadeusz ('theatre of death') 5

Kiss of death see death kiss
Klimt, Gustav 100
Kott, Jan 6
Kraus, Karl 98, 100

La petite mort 203, 214, 217
Lacan, Jacques 168, 170, 211, 216, 232, 238
    'mirror stage' 8, 211
La Fura dels Baus 178–98
Laing, R.D. 206, 212, 213
Lenz, Jokob Michael Reinhold 49, 50–1, 59
Lessing, Gotthold Ephraim 81, 144
Levinas, Emmanuel 123, 124
libertine 180, 183, 190
Libido 2, 168
Liebestod (Tristan and Isolde) 88, 120
Lingis, Alphonso 7, 124–5, 130–2, 134, 136, 137–9
Live art 9, 178, 179, 185, 187, 192, 193, 208, 221
Lorde, Audre 7
Loss 2, 7, 133, 163, 183
    loss of self 6, 55, 58, 86, 89
Love 1, 23, 28, 31, 49, 70, 80, 244
    Love Death see Liebestod
    Love in opera 80–93
    love song 235, 238
    broken love 60
    mad love 133
    romantic love 55
    sacrificial love 54
    sexual love 57, 88, 243
Lukács, Georg 46

Magic 21, 41, 90, 160–7
  magic trick 160, 162, 164, 182
Mann, Thomas 90
Marcuse, Herbert 3
Marlowe, Christopher 102
Marriage 16, 19, 20, 21, 25, 42, 83
Martyr 81, 193
Marxist 48, 100, 103, 104, 105
Masochistic 175
Materialism 53
  cultural materialist 28
  materialist 46, 48, 51, 55, 60, 182
Middleton, Thomas 144–8, 151, 153, 156
Mirbeau, Octave 76
Misogyny 105, 155, 165, 167, 174, 227
Modernism 97
  modernist 46, 59, 68
Morality 72, 96, 146, 181, 183
  morality play 80
Moulin Rouge 68
Mozart, Wolfgang Amadeus 80, 82, 92
Müller, Heiner 5, 46
Mulvey, Laura 168–70 *see also* gaze
  theory
Musafar, Fakir 187
Musil, Robert 97–8, 100, 102, 105
Myth 82, 84 *see also* Barthes on myth
  Greek mythology 1, 2
  Mythos 38
  Orpheus myth 82

Nancy, Jean-Luc 61
Necrophilia 67, 117, 144, 243, 244
Neurosis 173
Nietzsche, Friedrich 4, 88
Nihilism 54, 103

Obscene 59, 119, 183, 184, 188, 194
Oedipus 4, 12, 19
  Oedipal complex 173
Orgasm 29, 30, 31 217 *see also La
  petite mort*
Orgy 66, 71
Orlan 187

Pankhurst, Christabel and Sylvia 164
Parthipan, Jiva 205, 218–19, 220
Passion 4, 9, 31, 39, 49, 60, 70, 72, 76,
  136, 150, 244
Patočka, Jan 129
Patriarchy 47, 168, 169
Performance art 204, 208, 211, 217
Performative 9, 128, 183, 206, 230,
  232, 237, 239
  performative writing (Phelan) 205
  Performativity (Austin) 184
Phelan, Peggy 123, 124, 203, 205, 209
Phenomenology 193, 124, 198, 206
Pinter, Harold 136, 146, 150
Plato 4, 6, 86, 123, 126, 127
Pleasure 1, 6, 57, 65, 66, 99, 125, 145,
  154, 167–8, 170, 183, 189, 217
  pleasure principle 2, 3, 8 *see also*
  Freud, Sigmund
  sexual pleasure 73, 190
Plutarch 32
Poe, Edgar Allan 65
Politics 10, 35, 43, 55, 58, 61, 100, 103,
  123, 215, 221
  body politics 204
  gender politics 174
  revolutionary politics 9, 57, 104
Popular culture 105, 173, 175

Popular music 68, 225, 226, 228, 232
Pornography 66, 68, 74, 96, 178, 186, 187, 188
  pornographic imagination 197, 198
  also see Sontag, Susan
Prendergast, Christopher 65, 66, 67
Promiscuity 58
Prostitution 47, 55, 59, 67, 98, 99, 102
Proust, Marcel 66
Psychoanalysis, psychoanalytic theory 2, 168, 170, 173, 175, 206, 208, 238

Racine, Jean 21, 130
Rancière, Jacques 61
Reality principle 2, 3
Religion 28, 58, 84, 172, 173, 193
Renaissance 84, 86, 89, 96, 101, 112
Repression 3, 98, 146, 147
  'return of the repressed' 3, 172 *see also* Freud, Sigmund
Revolution 49, 54, 104, 113, 190
  French Revolution 48, 51, 52, 55, 56, 58, 67
  Russian Revolution 100
Risk 7, 8, 104, 137, 138, 187, 204, 212
  risk art 178, 191
Ritual 5, 13, 37, 66, 191, 195, 196, 214
Rock music 229
Romance 37, 125
Romanticism 47–8, 53, 61, 84, 89, 228

S&M, sadomasochistic 73, 76, 185
Sacred 7, 13, 18, 99, 182, 183, 228
Sacrifice 17, 31, 53, 66, 91, 92, 104, 133, 198
  human sacrifice 12, 13, 15, 196

sacrificial body 243
sacrificial love, sacrificial sexuality 54, 134, 196
Sade, Marquis de 6, 9, 56, 179, 180–4, 190–1, 194
  sadism 2, 74, 170, 183
  sadistic 76, 175, 228
Schad, Christian 96, 101
Schiele, Egon 100
Schiller, Friedrich 18, 48, 81, 83
Schoenberg, Arnold 96, 100
Schopenhauer, Arthur 4, 81, 84, 88–9, 100
Scopophilia 168, 170
Secret 5–6, 77, 85, 91, 93, 145, 153, 160, 163
  erotic secret 152
Seduction 7, 8, 57, 127, 129, 152, 243
Selbit (Percy Thomas Tibbles) 161–5, 167, 172–4
Seneca 21, 23
Sensuality 56, 57, 95–7, 101, 105, 242
Sex
  sex murder 97, 98, 106
  sex work 219, 220 *see also* Prostitution
Sexuality
  erotic sexuality 9, 57, 124, 126–9, 134, 135
  sexual act, sexual activity 5, 26, 55, 56, 59, 195
  sexual desire 2, 3, 10, 23, 39, 42, 55, 60, 149
  sexual encounter 29, 55, 66, 182, 196
  sexual instinct, sexual drive 2, 12 *see also* Eros, Libido

sexual relations 147, 216, 220
transgressive sexuality 59, 97, 99, 102, 105
violent sexuality 76, 182
Shakespeare, William 5, 28–43, 50, 130, 153, 157
  Antony and Cleopatra 28–43, 131
  Hamlet 30, 145, 147–8, 155–6
  Julius Caesar 32
  King Lear 145–6, 149
  Macbeth 5
  Othello 30
  Romeo and Juliet 31, 32, 83–4
Socialism 157
  Socialist 46, 48–9, 53, 56, 60, 105
Sontag, Susan 197 *also see* pornographic imagination
Sophocles 19, 20
Spinoza 117
Spirit 4, 34, 36, 47, 56, 81, 84, 225, 228
  spiritual 7, 48, 50, 58, 101
St. Sebastian 193
Strauss, Richard 84, 91
Sturm und Drang ('storm and stress') 47, 50, 52, 53
Sublime 8, 42, 171
Suffrage 164, 165
Suicide 21, 24, 28, 32, 39, 54, 55, 104
Surrealism 8, 9, 182, 195

Taboo 67, 70, 77, 139, 178, 181,
Thanatos 1–2, 4, 12, 19, 24–6, 71, 80–86, 90, 151, 162, 175
Therapeutic 203, 205, 207, 209, 211, 221
Tragedy 4–5, 32, 34, 36, 40, 48–9, 51, 59–60, 104, 130–1, 137, 152–3, 163

Attic Tragedy 12, 19
tragicomedy 28, 43
Transgression 4–7, 9, 57, 97, 105, 134, 136, 198, 204
  sexual transgression 25, 60, 149 *see also* transgressive sexuality
Trauma 2, 60, 128, 179

Uncanny, the 167, 170–3, 175
Unconscious, the 2, 9, 61, 99

Vaginal Davis (drag queen) 180, 204
vampire 67, 225, 243
  vampire movie 175
Venus 1, 80, 91,
Verdi, Giuseppe 80, 81, 83, 84
Victim 15, 16, 41, 47, 162, 165, 166, 175
  sacrificial victim 19, 196
Violence 4, 51–2, 59, 60, 66, 77, 105, 106, 132, 165, 180, 183, 190, 196, 238
  sexualised violence 76, 228
Voyeurism 66, 149, 170, 197, 207, 217, 227

Wagner, Richard 80, 84, 85, 120
  Tannhäuser 92
  Tristan and Isolde 81, 86, 87–90, 120
Waits, Tom 68
Weimar period 95, 96, 100, 101, 106
Williams, Raymond 48
Wittgenstein, Ludwig 100, 111, 112, 113

Žižek, Slavoj 61, 231–2, 238, 239